SPECTACULAR ROGUE: Gaston B. Means

SPECTACULAR ROGUE:
Gaston B. Means

by Edwin P. Hoyt

 THE **BOBBS-MERRILL** COMPANY, INC.
A SUBSIDIARY OF HOWARD W. SAMS & CO., INC.
Publishers • INDIANAPOLIS • NEW YORK

This book is dedicated to
Hiram C. Todd, former Special Assistant Attorney General of the United States, the first man to send Gaston Means to prison for his crimes. Without his assistance this book could never have become so complete a record of the wiliest scoundrel who ever lived in the United States.

SPECTACULAR ROGUE: Gaston B. Means

I

In an old cemetery on the side of a bleak hill in North Carolina lies the grave of the most spectacular rogue who ever lived in America. His name was Gaston Bullock Means.

Gaston Means was the symbol of American criminality and corruption in the gaudiest and most lawless era in the nation's history —the 1920's. He is still an enigma to many, and an unpleasant specter to J. Edgar Hoover's Federal Bureau of Investigation, for Means came close to wrecking that agency in the year he was employed there. Means did far more. He tried, and nearly succeeded in, turning a Congressional committee into a ribald circus; he made mockery of the justice of three states in celebrated cases that involved sudden death and forgery. He bilked, cozened, and blackmailed bootleggers and millionaires. Gaston Means served the German government as an agent in America during World War I. He successfully peddled assumed influence to larcenous souls for hundreds of thousands of dollars. He bedeviled two cabinet officers and helped destroy the career of one of them. He half-persuaded Americans that their President had been murdered; he tried to

9

make a game of Army Intelligence. He defrauded insurance companies, and tried to defraud an express company. By Means's own public boast, at middle age he had been accused of every crime known in America—and convicted of none.

Who was this arch-rogue who made sport of government and justice for so many years? The name—Gaston Bullock Means—is mellifluous and exotic, especially when spoken in the liquid accents of his native North Carolina, in the resonant voice Means trained so well. More than a name, Gaston Means was a presence to be remembered by all who encountered him. And he *was* remembered. A quarter of a century after his death, the name still evoked emotion in those who had known the man. Means's friends recalled his virtues, although they could not dismiss his gaudy sins; even his enemies remembered him as bitterly as ever.

Was Gaston Means an exacerbated example of American lawlessness—the robber baron born a generation too late, an incipient Jay Gould gone wrong?

Perhaps, but Means was more than that, and less. His successes occurred when the nation was careless and adolescent. When retribution came, Means was already a victim of change. The final downfall of Gaston Bullock Means was a result of his own excesses, but also, in its finality, it represented the coming of a renewed morality in American public life. Perhaps, in a way, Gaston Means helped bring about that renewal.

The beginnings of the Means story go far back in American history, for Means is an old name in the Carolinas. The family of Gaston Means was prominent in North Carolina before the American Revolution.

John Means, the first of the line, came to America from Europe in 1772, to join the Scotch-Irish settlers of the western section of what was to become North Carolina's Cabarrus County. By the 1740's the Scotch and Irish had moved into this land of red clay, coming in from the Cape Fear Valley to the slate hills that were bounded on the west by the Great Smoky Mountains. Some of the land was bog, some scrub brush, some covered with buffalo grass. Bison grazed in this eastern area of the North American continent then; Irish Buffalo Creek and Little Buffalo Creek were named for the shaggy creatures.

Where there were buffalo there were Indians—here Sioux of the Catawba tribe. The Catawbas ranged north and east into Virginia along The Great Trading Path, as far away from the Smokies as what is now Petersburg. In the beginning of the white man's stay there was plenty of other game in the area. Bear roamed the mountains and the foothills, deer ambled near creeks and down the Rocky River at the southern end of the region. Flocks of migrating passenger pigeons dotted the trees and blackened the skies.

Along The Great Trading Path, from the North, came another group of white settlers, Palatinate Germans from the Pennsylvania colony who wanted wider reaches of land than they could secure in the North. The Germans settled in the eastern region, the Scotch-Irish held steadfast to the Piedmont area of the west. The two groups were bound to clash, and they did clash. They were still clashing in 1792, when the North Carolina legislature considered pleas for creation of a new governmental unit from part of Mecklenburg County. The legislature was undecided, and its members were tied in the voting. The Speaker of the House, Stephen Cabarrus, cast the deciding vote in favor of the new county, and the county was named after him.

The Scots and Irishmen of the west and the Germans of the east could agree on nothing, it seemed, not even on a site for the county seat. After many weary arguments, they settled on a site midway between settlements. The sober heads among them agreed to call the new town Concord and to name its main street Union, in the hope that these gestures would put an end to bloody bickering.

So Concord, Cabarrus County, North Carolina, which was to be the birthplace of a violent man, was born in violence long before the name of Gaston Bullock Means had ever been devised.

11

Seven years after the county seat was established, gold was discovered in Cabarrus County by a twelve-year-old boy who was fishing in Meadow Creek on the county's eastern boundary. The boy, Conrad Reed, found a large yellow rock in the stream and took it home. His father used the odd rock for a doorstop for three years, before he finally sold it to a jeweler in Fayettesville for three dollars and a half.

Then came the North Carolina gold rush, bringing with it more violent men. John Reed organized a mining company (and it is said that he recovered $3,000 from the Fayettesville jeweler, too). Cabarrus County became famous in the nation for a time, since, between 1804 and 1810, North Carolina provided all the gold mined in the United States, and this county contributed most of it.

Fortunes in gold were earned overnight by a lucky few. The mining years left a mark and heritage behind them, although gold was not the region's only lure. The red clay grew fine cotton, and, in 1839, a group headed by General Paul Barringer built the first important cotton mill in the region. The search for gold was to move on westward but the cotton and the mills were to remain as mainstays of the Cabarrus County economy long after the end of slavery.

John Means's son, William, was born in the old country in 1769, but he grew up an American and settled on the land where his father brought him. William married Miss Isabella Work, the daughter of Robert Work of Iredell County, and settled down to raise a family. His son, William C. Means, was born in 1801, and distinguished himself by becoming a major general of militia before the Mexican War. He further enhanced his position by marrying into the Barringer family. This union brought the Means family into the finest society of the ante-bellum South. One Barringer had served long in Congress; one had been a member of the International Court of Claims, which met at Cairo to determine the liabilities of the Berber world for the looting of Western shipping. Another Barringer had served as Ambassador to Spain.

Gaston B. Means

W. C. Means—"the General," as he was called in later years—
made the most of his abilities and opportunities. He bought a
farm and added to it until he owned some three thousand acres of
land. He helped bring the railroad to follow The Great Trading
Path of Indians long gone. He became an important stockholder
in the Barringer cotton mill, and he was given credit in Cabarrus
County as being an enlightened and progressive farmer. It was
said that, in the 1850's, General Means introduced the first grain
mower that was seen in that section of the country.

General Means built a planter's house and established a reputation for hospitality that was unchallenged in the Concord area.
To maintain the huge plantation he required a small army of slaves,
and with them the General was no slacker in dispensing discipline.
Recalcitrant slaves were whipped. "Niggers" were made to tear
down a section of rail fence. He then shouted at them to place a
rail across an offender's neck and stand on either of the two ends,
while he wielded the lash against the arrogant chattel's back.

The General was every inch a southern gentleman, respected
by his peers—and perhaps feared by them even more than he was
respected. For the General was a violent man. From 1824, when
he had scarcely achieved his majority, until 1879, the year before
his death, General Means was engaged in almost constant litiga-
tion. The first encounter of this Means with the law began with an
assault and battery charge, brought by the State of North Carolina in 1824. The last suit was brought two years before his death.
In the years between, the General lived in almost constant friction
with his state and his neighbors, and on one occasion was ordered
by a court to stay off a neighbor's property, where he had been
trespassing repeatedly and annoyingly. Altogether, the Cabarrus
County records show General Means involved as defendent in
thirty-one civil and criminal court actions.

The General's fifth son, William Gaston Means, was born on the
plantation in the winter of 1850. W. G. inherited the graces and
attitudes of the wealthy southern planter, for by this time the

13

General owned nearly all the land between the Southern Railway station in Concord and Coddle Creek, to the west. He was the largest landholder in Cabarrus County. The General's children were educated under private tutors during their early school years; then, following the General's military inclination, W. G. was sent to the Horner Military Academy at Oxford, Mississippi, to prepare for college. In 1876 he graduated from the University of Virginia, then studied law in the offices of two prominent North Carolina attorneys.

[handwritten marginal note: Actually Oxford, N.C. The school moved from Oxford in Co. (County) to Charlotte in the late 1800s]

W. G., known as "the Colonel" in his mature years, settled in Memphis, Tennessee, to practice. In 1874, he married Miss Coral-lie Bullock, a member of a Mississippi family which claimed a governor among its members, and also kinship, through marriage, to the family of Theodore Roosevelt.

In the last years of the 1870's, as the General aged he became more irascible than ever. (Sixteen of the court actions against him were brought between 1876 and 1879.) William Gaston Means was persuaded to desert his law practice in Memphis and return to the plantation outside Concord to manage his father's affairs, and there to raise a growing family, which finally numbered four boys and three girls. At the plantation on July 11, 1879, Gaston Bullock Means was born.[1]

When the General died in 1880, his plantation was broken up into smaller farms, which were shared among the children. Like so many huge landholders who depended on cotton and slave labor for their wealth, the General had not fared well during the days of Reconstruction. W. G. Means was his father's executor, and he concluded the business of the estate, then moved into Concord to earn his living in the practice of law. The white frame house into which he moved his family on North Union Street was large, as it had to be to raise seven children, but it was not as pretentious as the houses of neighbors, for the Means family was no longer wealthy. The house was three stories high, with a sharply angled roof and a railed porch across the front. In the manner of

Gaston B. Means

Concord's fashionable Union Street, the Victorian house was set well back from the roadway, protected from street dust by an ample lawn. This was the house in which Gaston Means was to grow to young manhood, and it was to be Gaston's single haven during all the rest of his life.

Although reduced in circumstances, the Means family continued to be important in the affairs of Cabarrus County. Colonel Paul Barringer Means, Gaston's uncle, served in the State Senate and became an important figure in North Carolina politics. Another uncle, George Means, was active in Concord's local politics, and W. G. Means was mayor of Concord for many years. If W. G. was not considered to be an absolutely first-rate lawyer, he was high in the second rank, at least, and he became attorney for a young cotton manufacturer named James W. Cannon, who deserted the dry-goods business to open a factory in the town.

Concord was a God-fearing, churchgoing town, heavily influenced by the Lutheran faith the Germans had brought to the area, but also a center of Presbyterians, Baptists, Methodists, and smaller sects. W. G. Means and his family were Episcopalians. Gaston grew up, a strong, sturdy boy, and a regular Sunday scholar in the All Saints Episcopal Church. Many years later, asked to describe his moral training, Gaston Means said it was "perfect, as taught under customary methods."[2]

Perhaps the training was perfect, but apparently the boy did not respond to it wholeheartedly. Means also recalled, in later years, an incident that seemed far more in the Gaston Means character than the picture of an Eton-collared boy in a pew at the Episcopal church.

In 1886, when Gaston was seven years old, one of the ladies of the church called on his mother one day. She came to pick up the little cardboard missionary box which Mrs. Means kept, as did most of her fellow parishioners, in the hope of bringing clean faces and salvation to the unwary Hottentots.

Mrs. Means knew exactly where the box was to be found. Just

15

that morning she had put a quarter dollar in the box, and had left the receptacle atop the bureau of the rear upstairs bedroom. She had quite forgotten that it was the end of the month—the time when the ladies of the Women's Missionary Society called to collect the little boxes.

Gaston's mother greeted her caller and then hastened upstairs to find her offering. But when Mrs. Means picked up the cardboard box, she saw that it had been cut open, and her contribution—nearly three dollars in all—had been removed.

Mrs. Means called sharply for the colored housemaid, Lizzie, and asked if the girl had seen the missionary box. Dusting and cleaning every day, of course the girl had seen the box, but she emphatically denied having opened it or having taken the money.

Who else was in the house and had been there during that morning? Only Mrs. Means herself, and her seven-year-old son, Gaston.

Gaston was called into the room. He appeared downstairs with hands buried in the pockets of his short pants, bright eyes opened wide in innocence, two huge dimples in his cheeks giving him a cherubic air as he smiled and denied having seen either box or money.

Gaston's mother believed her son, as so many people were to believe him later, under the hypnotic influence of that cherub-face and open smile. Lizzie, the housemaid, was new, and her virtue was untried. Mrs. Means grew stern as she accused the girl flatly of theft and lying and discharged her on the spot. Little Gaston watched the scene gravely, with great interest, as the girl first denied the theft, and then burst into hysterical crying. The outburst did not move Mrs. Means. Within a few minutes, the wretched Lizzie had packed her bag and left the house forever.

From the safety of an upstairs window, the seven-year-old watched Lizzie shuffle down the walk and into Union Street, and as he jangled the new-found coins in his pocket he called her a fool. Years later, recalling the incident with pride, the mature

16

Gaston B. Means

Gaston Means said, "I think the sound of those coins in my pocket was the sweetest music I've ever heard."[3]

Gaston was a boy's boy. The name Gaston was far too unwieldy for everyday use, so from the time he entered school, at the age of five, Gaston Means was known as "Bud," and by that name he was always known in Concord.

Bud Means attended several schools in his early years, a church school, and a graded school, taught by a young man from Georgia, since there were no state schools in Concord at the time. During his school years, Bud Means showed himself to be a bright boy, although he did not exert himself in scholarship. He used his best abilities on the ball field, playing "one old cat" or "three old cat" with the other boys of Union Street and the surrounding "best" district of Concord.

From his earliest years, Bud Means was interested in money and he listened, fascinated, to the street-corner tales of prospectors who had struck it rich in the streams and hillsides around Concord.

Part of Gaston Means's inordinate interest in money even as a boy came from the irritating circumstances in which Colonel Means found himself. It was difficult to support seven children in a small town.

The Colonel had inherited his father's bad disposition, and, consequently, Gaston was to remember well the many arguments between mother and father over money matters. The Colonel was a disciplinarian, and while the four boys of the family respected him and feared him, Gaston Means, at least, did not grow up with any illusions, about his father, or about the world. "He was no more honest than any lawyer," Means later said of his father. "They're all grafters."

Yet the Means family was far closer than such a judgment might suggest. Colonel Means was a determined man, and a precise one, but, in spite of his hot temper, he loved his family and treated his wife and children with affection. He did not drink—

17

this was the major virtue attributed to the Colonel by one of his acquaintances. But such utterances were not made aloud in Concord, for the Means family was large, and its men were big and inclined to be quarrelsome. All Concord had a healthy respect for the Colonel and his family.

As a schoolboy, Gaston Means exhibited one characteristic which was to become his hallmark, first to bring him considerable acclaim in maturity, and later to bring the wrath of officialdom on his head and to cause untold confusion about the facts of his busy life. Gaston Means loved intrigue for its own sake. He liked hunting and fishing—stalking. On the ball field, few games ended without Gaston calling his teammates into a huddle to direct a strategy for victory. It made no difference to him if the strategy went beyond sportsmanship. Gaston liked victory as well when it was won through sharp practice.

Other boys in the neighborhood did not always approve of the Means tactics. One day, Gaston and his brothers Brandon and Afton were playing ball with a group of youngsters on the spacious lawn of Judge Montgomery, the town's most successful lawyer, when one of the three Means brothers picked a fight with a youth named Joe Fisher. Immediately all three Means brothers set upon the Fisher boy, but Joe Fisher had a baseball bat in his hand. He began to slug the brothers and would not stop until other boys ran down the street and found an adult who broke up the fight.

Townspeople said the Means boys were all "meaner than hell," a characteristic they traced back to the old General. But it would be incorrect to assume that all Concord, or even most of the white citizens, disliked the Means family. From the General, W. G. had inherited the southern gentleman's charm, and he passed this along to his sons—particularly to the dimpled, easy-natured Gaston. The Means boys might be bullies, and they might take scarce cognizance of the rights of others or even of the law, but they were disarming and friendly to their neighbors when not aroused. Gas-

18

ton grew up with characteristics as different as the brass of a Chinese gong and the poise of a Swiss diplomat, but the two disparate qualities served him well for more than forty years.[4]

Gaston Means's love of intrigue flowered during his formative years in Concord. By the time Gaston was ten years old, one of his uncles, George, was working with the United States Secret Service in Washington during the Cleveland administration, and Gaston decided to become an "investigator." The boy's father did not seem to disapprove. Quite to the contrary, when the young Means took to hanging around the courthouse and local gossip centers to pick up information about cases in which his father was involved, W. G. did not send the boy back to his school books, but encouraged him—or so Gaston said. He bragged that his father sent him to "shadow" jurors in cases in which the elder Means had a stake. As the boy grew toward manhood he found a temporary job as a reporter for the local daily newspaper, the Concord *Standard,* which further whetted his appetite for "investigation."

Two of the Means girls, Kate and Belle, were to become schoolteachers in Concord, and were to be loved and respected. The boys were to follow their own bents. One, Frank, took the unusual step, for a small-town southern boy, of moving to Yankee territory in Providence, Rhode Island, where he became an electrician. He stayed in the North.

Gaston was the only one of the Colonel's other three sons to go to college. Gaston convinced his father that he wanted to study the law. Occasionally in later life he was mistaken for a lawyer, because he had a superficial command of legal language (which he had picked up the hard way).

In 1898, then, as he was completing his high school work, it was decided that Gaston—Bud—would go on to the University of North Carolina at Chapel Hill to take a pre-law course.

It was a busy year in Concord. The Daily *Standard* carried reports from the Spanish-American War fronts in the Philippines and especially in Cuba, where local boys were stationed at Camp Co-

19

lumbia, near Havana. The two local banks in Concord were both booming, and business had not been better, altogether, since before the beginning of the War Between the States. The Colonel was immersed in his law practice, which was expanding healthily, and he spent a good deal of time in Charlotte on legal matters. A rumor flitted along Union Street to the effect that another cotton mill was to be organized in the Concord area, but this did not bother either Colonel Means or his client, J. W. Cannon, whose mill had begun to be very profitable with the manufacturing of "Cannon cloth," a rough fabric that was the local genesis of "turkish toweling." If "Cannon cloth" was not to appeal to the nation at large for several years yet, the housewives of Cabarrus County and nearby areas of North Carolina had already discovered its usefulness.

Concord maintained a dual standard of morality. As always in its history, the churches held strong influence on the town. Public drinking was frowned upon, but privately many churchgoing citizens kept ample supplies of "white lightning" and less potent spirits and imbibed them joyfully, if carefully. A vigilante organization, the White Caps, attempted to keep vice within bounds, raiding Negro bawdy houses—even those owned by white men— and frightening the visitors half to death with their shouts and shooting on the raids. Gamecock fighting was a favorite sport among the lustier townsmen, and several members of the Means family raised gamecocks.[5]

From this mixed atmosphere of church pew and cockpit, Gaston Bullock Means set out, in the autumn of 1898, for the University of North Carolina, an old and respected school. It had opened its doors in 1795, and boasted the first astronomical observatory in the United States. Chapel Hill was all that Concord was not— cultured, calm, and gay.

When Bud Means arrived at Chapel Hill, he joined a class of 129 freshmen, in a university whose total enrollment was less than 450 students. The course was classical, without much leeway allowed for undergraduates, and much less for freshmen, for freshmen were regarded as the fair game of the three upper classes, and the faculty worked the youngsters hard in basic subjects to ground them for their further studies.

Bud Means mixed well at the university. He was a pleasant companion. He was no student. His refusal to take academic life seriously became apparent in the first year, when his grades were so far below average that he ended the year with deficiencies in mathematics, history, and physics. But he was popular in his class.

Gaston Means was nineteen years old in 1898, and now he had the build of a football player. Yet he played freshman football without distinction and without much interest. His major interest at Chapel Hill was to be a "good fellow" among the others, and here he succeeded thoroughly. He was elected to Zeta Psi fraternity, and later to Theta Nu Epsilon, a sophomore secret society which was notable for its dedication to high jinks and for its nearly intolerable initiation cruelties.[6]

In the summers, Bud Means returned to Concord, where part of the time he worked at the Cannon cotton mills. As a college man, he was regarded with a good deal of awe by the younger boys of Union Street. A number of these boys, including the son of the Cannon family, were to be found on most days during the summer months playing ball on the playground of the Concord High School off Union Street. On his way home to dinner each day from the Cannon mill, Bud Means passed the school grounds, and nearly every day he took a detour to the playground.

Without a word he would walk up to home plate, take the bat from the unresisting hand of the younger boy who was "up" at the moment, and stand at the plate and "hit them," while the youngsters in the field shagged flies for him. None of the boys objected to this interruption of their game. Bud Means was their hero because he could hit the ball so far. So Means would stand at the plate before his worshipers, hitting flies as long as he hit them well. After a blooper, he would relinquish the bat to the boy who had given it up, and with a dimpled grin he would go home.

In his second year at the university, Gaston Means became more serious about his college activities, and a bit more serious about his studies. He managed to remove his scholastic deficiencies of the previous year, and he enrolled in courses in philosophy and geology. In other aspects of college life, Means made more of a name for himself. He was elected to the Dialectic Society, one of two debating groups on the campus. He was a member of the Historical Society. He played on the class football team and played center on the scrub football team of the university. The scrubs existed to train the varsity. Means's team that year lost its one official game to Horner School by a score of 10-6.

Means's picture appeared in the school yearbook, *The Hellenian*, in 1900, in a group photograph of the members of Zeta Psi fraternity. The picture shows Gaston Means as a pleasant-faced young man, dressed in the four-button jacket and high collar of the day. But there were notable differences between Bud Means and his fraternity brothers. All the others wore their hair long. Bud Means wore his cropped nearly to the skull on the sides, with a shock of long hair running straight down the middle of his skull, in the fashion known to a later generation as the "Cherokee cut." The others wore dark neckties; only Gaston Means sported a tie marked with flamboyant figures.

Gaston's college neckties were in character. Even as a boy, Bud Means had liked to be a center of attention. "He wore a plug hat," said J. M. Baker, a Cabarrus County man. "He always wanted to be noticed."

Means was not much more successful in football during his second year at the university than he had been during his freshman year. He was shifted from center to guard on the scrub team. Coach Reynolds noted in a critique of all players published in the student newspaper, *The Tar Heel*, that Means failed "to charge low and hard enough." In other words, Gaston Means was not as aggressive on the football field as a youth must be to be a first-string player. That year he played left guard during part of one game with the Deaf and Dumb Institute of Morganton.

22

Gaston B. Means

As the end of Gaston Means's sophomore year neared, it seemed that Gaston lacked determination and direction. He was ambitious, he wanted wealth and to make a name for himself, but he was not willing to exert a supreme effort, either in athletics or in scholarship. His grades during that second year were only slightly better than those achieved during his freshman year. It could not be said that Gaston Means excelled in anything the university found worth-while. He *was* still a "regular fellow," and was very popular with his fraternity brothers and classmates. But even other students noticed differences. Louis Graves, later a reporter on the New York *Times*, recalled that Means was immensely likable, but that he also had one strange characteristic. "He used to sit in restaurants and watch people and write himself notes about them," Graves said.

So the older Gaston Means was still the romanticist and "investigator" that the younger Bud Means had wanted to be.

In the autumn of 1900, Gaston Means returned from Concord to Chapel Hill to begin his junior year at the university. There was a change in the football program that year. The university brought in a new coach, Charles O. Jenkins, from Yale College, to add some expertness to the Carolina team. Means was not mentioned in the rosters of football lineups that year. He did not complete the year, but left Chapel Hill before the examinations at the end of the first semester.[7] He had been disciplined by a faculty committee for some minor offense. He was not expelled; no mention of the offense or any note of bad conduct appears on his university record, but before Christmas, 1900, Gaston Bullock Means left the University of North Carolina. He never returned to finish his studies; still, he was not forgotten at Chapel Hill. Later, in a way, he was to become one of the university's most notable alumni.

II

When the twenty-one-year old Gaston Means left the University of North Carolina in the autumn of 1900, he did not leave education behind him, but instead of acquiring schooling he began dispensing it as superintendent of the graded schools in the mill town of Albemarle in neighboring Stanley County, a few miles from his home.

It was not then necessary for a teacher in a small town in North Carolina to hold a college degree or even a teacher's certificate. Public education was still a novelty and in the mill school it was enough that Gaston Means was the son of a friend of the owner of a large cotton mill.

Apparently it was a necessity for Bud Means to find a job. His brother Brandon had been sent to the William Bingham School at Mebane, North Carolina, and from time to time during Bud's college years Brandon had come up to Chapel Hill to visit him, especially during football season. But with the departure of the elder brother from the university, no more of the Means boys were to attend college, and from 1900 on, Gaston Means was to be on his own in the world.[1]

For two years, Gaston Means supervised thirty-two teachers in the Albemarle school system. He lived in Albemarle, although it was only a few miles from Concord, since the automobile was still in the experimental stage, and no one in his right mind even dreamed of commuting along the muddy roads between towns.

Gaston Means lived at the old Hearn Hotel in Albemarle. He was no teetotaler, but he was not a heavy drinker either, and he confined his ambitions to getting ahead in the world along respectable paths.

In 1902, the young Means joined the Cannon mills as a salesman. A bright future in the textile business seemed to be open for him. Cannon soon sent an assistant named J. C. Leslie and Gaston Means to New York City to organize a sales office, and the young salesman began to travel. For a time he lived in a rooming house on the west side of New York City's Fifty-eighth Street, where a group of young North Carolinians had found quarters. He traveled for the Cannon company to Chicago, Philadelphia, Boston, St. Louis, and even to San Francisco.[2]

Now, it was not long before Gaston Means showed a penchant for the good life, which he was able to live as a salesman for the Cannon company. Among the young North Carolinians on Fifty-eighth Street, he was probably the most prosperous of all. He was earning $5,000 a year plus travel expenses. He dressed nattily in tailored clothes and imported shoes. He moved out of the rooming house and into an apartment at 105 Street and Columbus Avenue.

One day, on a New York street, Means encountered a young newspaper reporter named Phillips Russell, an acquaintance from the days at Chapel Hill. Gaston invited Russell to live in his apartment for only a nominal share of the rent. He explained that he was gone all during the week on selling trips, and that he wanted company and someone to occupy the apartment to protect it against burglary. Russell joined him, and for a few months the pair lived together. On weekends, when Means was in New York, they would go out to dinner at a nearby restaurant. Means would spend most of the dinner hour gazing around the restaurant and making notes in a little black book. When Russell asked what he was doing, he would reply that he was just checking on people.

One evening, as the two young men sat in a restaurant, Means started suddenly, and asked Russell to pay the check, then meet him outside. A man had just entered whom he did not want to meet. He arose and ducked out the back door of the restaurant. When Russell met him a few minutes later in the alley, Means paid his share of the bill cheerfully enough, but maintained a mysterious air about his strange affair in the eating place.[3]

Full-grown, Gaston Means in his middle twenties was nearly six feet tall. He weighed two hundred pounds and he prided himself on his strength and toughness. If he was overbearing, which he often was, that annoying quality was forgiven by his friends because Means had a sense of humor broad enough to cover even his own weaknesses. He liked to tell a story on himself. One of the stories he told involved an encounter on a New York City streetcar.

One evening during the rush hour, Means was riding across New York City. In the early 1900's, the smokers among the passengers congregated on the back platforms of the cars where they could puff their cigarettes and cigars in a common cloud of tobacco smoke without distressing the ladies inside.

On this evening, a man next to Gaston Means carelessly trod on the North Carolinian's toe. Means called attention to the fact and awaited an apology. But no apology was forthcoming, whereupon the Means temper, never very well under control, emerged in harsh words and threatening gestures.

The stranger seemed to be as large and strong as Gaston Means himself, but this did not bother Means. He had always been able to take care of himself. As the car came to a stop at an intersection, Gaston Means invited the large stranger to get off and settle their disagreement in the manly fashion.

The other man agreed and off they went, to square off in the street. Gaston threw one punch—and that was all. The other man's left hand struck him in the stomach, and as Gaston doubled over, a right cross slapped his head back, and he went hurtling like a stone to the ground. When the ambulance came, Means recalled with a dimpled grin and a hearty baritone laugh, he discovered, and only then, that the man who had trod on his toe was a professional fighter of considerable renown who kept a saloon on Twenty-fourth Street and acted as his own bouncer. He named the man, but in true Meansian fashion he named him differently every time he told the story, it seemed, and finally, in one version, his opponent became the heavyweight champion of the world.[4]

Both aspects, the willingness to tell a story that involved his own rash action and the embroidery of the story over a period of time, were parts of Gaston's character. He did not seem to care if he appeared brash and ignoble, as long as he appeared strong and virile. And truth was always submerged beneath the vigorous imaginative touches Gaston Means gave to every story.

If Gaston Means was almost universally popular among his male acquaintances in these days of young manhood, the same could not be said for young women who knew him. He gave too little and asked too much for the respectable girls he knew, and as with all his acquaintances, he presumed a great deal. For a time, in his eight-year stay in New York City, Means lived in another gathering place of young southerners, a French pension on West Sixteenth Street, operated by a M. Delaure. While he was living there, he sought the acquaintance of business girls in the house, and invited them out to dinner.

He had taken one girl to dinner and a show and afterward, instead of taking her back to the pension, he stopped at what she called a "fast" hotel. The girl dropped his arm and scurried for home, hysterical in the face of his open proposition and the necessity of finding her way, unescorted, through the New York streets at midnight. Twenty years later she was still incensed.[5]

But if Means's life in these years was reminiscent of the plot of

28

Gaston B. Means

Bertha, the Sewing Machine Girl and he of the villains in that and
other morality plays, still the sowing of wild oats was looked upon
benignly in the impersonal metropolis. Means had no reported
encounters with the law until 1910, and that case involved a civil
suit.

Several years after his arrival in New York, Means met Edith
Catherine Poole, an art student. She was attracted to Means's big
blue eyes, dimples, and manly bearing as much as he was to her
face and figure. It was not long before they were living in an
apartment as man and wife.

After a time, Miss Poole demanded more than the appearances
of marriage, but Gaston Means balked at the responsibilities, perhaps not entirely unwisely, since both he and Miss Poole were
treated for a period by a Dr. Cowles for venereal disease. He
promised her marriage, but he did not marry Miss Poole, and, in
1909, when he was transferred by the Cannon organization to become head of the sales office in Chicago, he refused to take her
with him.

Miss Poole was a very angry young woman, so angry that she
sued Gaston Means for breach of promise, demanding $25,000 to
salve her injured pride. Means hired Alfred W. Haywood, Jr.,
another North Carolinian, to defend him in the case. The defense
demanded the right to examine Miss Poole before the trial, to
ascertain a number of facts that Means said only Miss Poole could
prove.

Miss Poole claimed that on July 12, 1909, Means had definitely
promised to marry her. Means claimed that, although he did not
know it at the time—between June 6, 1909, and July 12 of that
year—Miss Poole had been unfaithful to him with a number of
men. He learned that she was unchaste and further than that, she
drank to excess.

Miss Poole's attorneys countered that while Means had submitted an affidavit asking a pre-trial examination of their client,
he had not offered a single *fact* to substantiate the need for it

beyond the facts contained in the pleadings. They said Means was attacking Miss Poole's character in the hope that she would abandon the case before her reputation was ruined.

The court held against Means, but Attorney Haywood appealed and the higher court ordered the pre-trial examination. That was the end of the case. If Gaston Means had hoped to embarrass Miss Poole, he had done so, and with enough of his characteristic vigor that she went out of his life, and Means returned to Chicago, and the Grand Pacific Hotel, to live in single blessedness.[6]

Although he lived in Chicago, Means did not forget New York for a moment, for the great city attracted him back with its opportunities for amusement and wealth. He no longer maintained a domicile in New York, but stayed at hotels or with his friend Louis Graves and Louis's brother Ralph, who was later to be Sunday editor of the New York *Times*. Means placed so little importance on his years in Chicago that later in life, in listing his residences, he ignored Chicago altogether and wrote simply that he had lived in New York City from 1902 to 1920, "in various hotels."[7]

He traveled widely, almost always by rail. And it was on a rail trip in a Pullman car that he was involved in an incident that was to make a drastic change in his life.

Salesman Means was journeying between Detroit and Chicago on December 8, 1911. He had taken an upper berth for the night trip, and after dinner he retired to his berth. Somehow, during the night, one of the chains that secured the upper berth was broken, and Means was thrown into the aisle of the car, where he landed on his head. Apparently he was badly injured, at least seriously enough so that he was taken to a New York hospital for treatment. Louis Graves visited him there and examined the head wound that Gaston Means displayed for his friend with his usual good humor and some trace of pride. The good humor did not extend to the Pullman Company, however. Gaston Means filed suit for $75,000 for his injuries. He collected $14,000.

Later, when Means's reputation was tarnished, his enemies claimed that he had sawed through the chain himself, and had

Gaston B. Means

feigned injury to collect easy money. But Louis Graves said Gaston was seriously injured, and Graves forever after believed that this head injury brought about a turning point in the career of Gaston Bullock Means.[8]

After Gaston Means left the hospital, he returned to his job in Chicago, where he divided his time between working for the Cannon company and chasing girls.

One day, in 1913, an acquaintance named John Glass told Means that he had just come back from discussing some hotel supplies with Burley and Company, and that, if Means had an eye for a pretty girl, he ought to find some way to visit that particular wholesale house. There was a new girl working in the store, and in the terms of that day she was "as pretty as a picture."

Means went. If he could muster no other pretext he could always tell a young lady that he was a hosiery salesman, and truthfully, for among the lines handled by the sales office of Cannon and Company were several varieties of ladies' hose.

Gaston Means did not make a very favorable first impression on the young lady. He learned that her name was Julie Patterson, and that she was the niece of the owner of the firm. But Julie Patterson was twenty-three years old, and Gaston Bullock Means was thirty-four. Furthermore, he was not a youthful thirty-four, but was growing bald, and sported more than the suggestion of a paunch. He asked her to go out with him, but she laughed at this "old man."

Gaston Means was a salesman. A refusal was only an invitation to persistence. As a salesman, he pursued the girl. He came back and repeated his invitation to dinner. She refused once more. He returned a third time, smiling and friendly as ever. Julie Patterson relented, at least enough to allow him to take her to the railroad station, from which she commuted each day to her uncle's house in River Forest.

Gaston was a cheerful and tireless talker. He told the girl of his experience as a man of the world. He boasted of the breach of promise suit and his skill in escaping Miss Poole, whom he now glorified as a "chorus girl." This alone was enough to intrigue

31

the sheltered Julie Patterson, who had grown up in the Convent of the Sacred Heart in St. Joseph, Missouri, and, from her protected position in her uncle's business, Gaston represented adventure in the unknown world beyond the family circle.

The suave Gaston had more interesting material at his fingertips. He spoke of his native North Carolina and the succession of mayors, governors, and generals who had borne the honored names of Means and Bullock. Then and forever after Means was to spin fascinating stories when he had a grain of truth with which to work. He required no more than a grain, and could manufacture a good tale without it, but his best efforts involved combinations of truth and imagination that soared wildly aloft, yet carried a ring of truth.

Means could hardly have found a more unknowing audience than Julie Patterson. She believed him when he said he had graduated from the University of North Carolina. It was an easy step, then, for Means to paint a picture of himself as a real educator—superintendent of schools in Albemarle. What difficulty would it be for such a man to secure the trust of James W. Cannon, and have the responsibility for all Cannon enterprises in the Middle West thrust upon his shoulders at a salary of $10,000 a year? The careful, scholarly Sisters at the convent had equipped her to understand what education means, but not to understand Means's education.

Later, Julie Patterson went to dinner with Gaston Means, who treated her more gently than he was accustomed in his dealings with women. He was first intrigued, then apparently badly smitten, for when he called and Julie was absent, Gaston talked with the family until she returned. The girl was flattered by the attention. She no longer saw her suitor's widening brow or the aging of the dimples or the broadening of his waistline. She began to think of him as more mature, more sensible, and more responsible than her other suitors.

"And suddenly," she said later, "I was in love with him. . . . I was wild about him!"

Gaston B. Means

The innocent Catholic girl and the man of the world were married on October 14, 1913, in the rectory of the Catholic church at River Forest.

There might have been a clue to the future for Julie Patterson Means in the manner of their first housekeeping, had she not been so immersed in the private world of the newly wed. Gaston Means, the important textile executive, rented a *furnished* apartment on Chicago's South Side.

Means showed new characteristics to his bride almost as soon as they were married. He became possessive and suspicious of her friends and outside activities, but this seemed a small price to pay for her happiness, since he showered her with kindness, and even his jealousy was a tribute of affection. As for himself, he went his own way without explanation from the very first moment of marriage, and his wife never thought of invading his privacy, or questioning him.

Julie Patterson Means brought her husband into a prominence in social life which he had not enjoyed since he left the family sphere of influence in Cabarrus County. In River Forest, Julie had met the widow of James C. King, a prominent Chicago lumberman. Julie was entranced by the widow: "She was a gorgeous creature of Gibson Girl type, with beautiful teeth, big brown eyes, tiny feet, and lovely ankles." The older woman responded gratefully to this girlish idolatry and, although she spent long periods of the year abroad, Maude King made it a point to keep track of Julie Patterson.

On her return from Europe in the spring of 1914, Mrs. King learned that Julie had been married and telephoned her in Chicago to invite the newlyweds to a dinner party on the roof of the La Salle Hotel. Gaston Means accepted the invitation gladly. They were shown great friendliness by Mrs. King and her sister, Mrs. Mary C. Melvin, wife of an osteopath in the Chicago area. Mrs. King seemed quite taken by Gaston, but Julie Means knew that Mrs. King's weakness was men, and she paid little attention.

Gaston Means enjoyed no immediate opportunity to capitalize

on the friendship of Mrs. King and Mrs. Melvin. On July 1, 1914, he left the employment of the Cannon cotton mills. He told Julie that he quit the job because he was not getting proper credit for the ideas he had contributed to the success of the business. But the initiative came from the Cannon company, where it was reported that even the topmost officials had tired of Gaston Means's tales. The last blow was a story that he passed himself off to business acquaintances as the son of James Cannon.[9]

Gaston chose a moment that was hardly auspicious to quit his job. Julie was pregnant. He had spent all the money he received from the railway accident of 1911, and at this time, unemployed, he found his creditors pressing him. He tried to renew a $1,500 note held by a Concord bank, and was refused, until his father and his brother-in-law, Joseph Goodman, agreed to endorse the note.[10]

In difficulty, it might have seemed sensible for Gaston Means to return to Concord, but Concord was a one-industry town—cotton milling—and having fallen out with the Cannon company, there was scant future for him there. He might have remained in Chicago, but Chicago did not offer Gaston Means what he sought. He headed, then, for the city of golden opportunity, New York, despite unproductive attempts to find a job there through correspondence.

Before he departed from Chicago, Means wrote to Mrs. J. C. McWhirter, who ran a boardinghouse at 15 West 107 Street, to arrange for room for his wife and himself. He was to pay $60 a month for room and board.

Julie was pulled from her comfortable apartment into a lodging house and from the Chicago friends into an unknown and uncaring city. She found the boardinghouse a nightmare, furnished with monstrosities; a bright green silk pillow decorated with a scarlet reindeer adorned her room.[11]

Failing in other efforts to find positions that suited him, Gaston Means turned to his first love—intrigue—and to a man whom he knew by reputation from his own family's connection with the

Gaston B. Means

U.S. Secret Service. William J. Burns, Chief of the Secret Service, had retired from government to form his own private detective agency in New York City. Gaston asked Burns for a job. He also offered a proposition: he would establish a "commercial department" for the agency if he could be cut in on the proceeds. Means had several ideas that interested William J. Burns. One was simple enough—a bank protection plan. Another was more ingenious— it involved a membership program for automobile owners who would pay yearly fees for protection and guaranteed investigation of auto thefts.[12]

On the strength of these ideas and his persuasive conversation, Means was hired by the Burns Agency at $25 a week plus commissions on any new business he brought into the office.[13]

So the year 1915 began with Gaston Means apparently once more on the road to business success. He and Julie were still living in the unsavory quarters of the boardinghouse. They suffered a tragedy in February, when Julie's baby was born dead. But Burns liked Gaston Means and believed in him, and Means was bringing new business into the firm, as he had promised.

Later in the year, Burns assigned Gaston to an investigation for the North German Lloyd steamship line. It was perfectly legitimate, for while the Triple Alliance and the Triple Entente were warring in Europe, the United States belonged to neither. American opinion favored continued neutralism in European affairs. When Gaston conducted the investigation quickly and well, or at least convinced the Germans that he had done so, he was employed by the Imperial German government itself as an agent.[14]

There is one story that the Germans first approached William J. Burns to work for them, but that Burns had already undertaken a commitment to work for the British, so he gave the German job to his trusted associate, Gaston Bullock Means. The relationship of Means and the Burns Agency during this period became vague, and remained so, particularly after the Burns records were discarded in moves from one New York City office to another.[15]

35

However complicated the relationships between Means and the Burns Agency during this period, there is no doubt that Gaston went to work for the Germans. He became "Agent E-13." He reported directly to Captain Karl Boy-Ed, assistant naval attaché at the German embassy in Washington, who was in charge of part of the Imperial government's espionage in the United States. Means's first job was to "plant" German agents in American shipyards where it was suspected that submarines were being built for shipment to England and France, in violation of the neutrality of the United States, as proclaimed by President Woodrow Wilson and by Congress in a resolution on March 5, 1915. That was a traditional assignment for an intelligence organization working in a neutral country.[16]

Gaston soon began to work on a better idea in behalf of the German government. A number of British warships were lying off Fire Island that winter, outside the three-mile limit that marked American territorial waters. The ships were stationed close to the American shore, with orders to seize or sink any German ship that might try to emerge from the port of New York and run the British blockade. The Germans would benefit if they could prove a plot existed among unscrupulous harbor captains to supply the British and thus violate American neutrality.

Proof would mean a major German propaganda victory, so the effort was launched. Means's first effort must be to sell Captain Boy-Ed and his superior, Franz von Papen, on the practicability of the idea, but once that was accomplished—and the German officers were eager to believe—he had clear sailing instructions from his employers and an almost unlimited expense account.

In March, Means moved his wife into a suite of rooms in the Hotel Manhattan (although he was not so incautious as to give up their rooming arrangement with Mrs. McWhirter), and he took office space at the Eastern Hotel at South Ferry, in the heart of the shipping district of the city. Then he set to work.

Means hired an unemployed tugboat skipper named Captain

Gaston B. Means

Thomas Wilson to look for tugboats, lighters, and crews to carry supplies to the British ships off the coast. Wilson tramped up and down the waterfront, looking. Since Wilson was an American, and nothing had been said about Englishmen and Germans, most of the seamen the captain saw were inclined to regard the matter as a simple shipping transaction. He saw Captain James H. Flannery, who maintained his own towing line at Coenties Slip. Flannery signed up for the job after Captain Wilson informed him that he was working indirectly for the British consul general, through a man named G. B. Means. In all, five tugs and lighters were laid on, five captains were hired at $140 a month, five engineers, five cooks, and five crews were assembled to man the boats. Captain Wilson, true to instructions, informed them all that they were to be paid monthly, and that they were to stand by, as of March 15, to start work at any hour—waiting for a wireless message to go ahead.

The five crews waited. Nothing happened. Captain Wilson came back to the waterfront. Some of the captains were uneasy, but Wilson assured them that the Dalzell fleet of tugs was already shipping supplies to the British, so it was obviously within the law. The plan had been changed, and they must wait until April 1.

Meanwhile, Agent E-13 was busy. Gaston found a captain named Peerless who needed work, and brought him to the room in the Eastern Hotel for a talk. When Captain Peerless agreed to supply the British, Means handed him an affidavit. The affidavit stated that Captain Peerless had already delivered a shipment of supplies to the British.

Captain Peerless wanted to know why he should sign such a paper. Because the British government was giving preference to those captains who had already worked for them, Agent E-13 said. So Captain Peerless, quite a yarn-spinner himself, and encouraged by Gaston, fabricated a story. In February, he had delivered supplies to the British cruiser H.M.S. *Essex* and a converted merchant ship that was carrying guns and flying the British flag.

37

The delivery was made at a point several miles off Sandy Hook. The captain signed an affidavit to that effect, and was then given a contract.

Other captains were shown the Peerless affidavit and the Peerless contract, and they were asked to sign similar affidavits attesting to their own previous work for the British. But the other captains balked. Since they had not shipped anything to the British, how could they swear that they had?

Captain Flannery suspected that something was not quite right, particularly when he saw the contract, which stated only that he was willing to do the work. The contract was not binding in any way on the British government. He also learned that the Dalzell tugs were doing no work for the British. Flannery then consulted his attorney, who informed him that he was clearly in danger of violating the laws of the United States. A worried Captain Flannery took a trip to the United States courthouse at the foot of Manhattan Island, where he told the whole story to Dudley Field Malone, Collector of the Port of New York, whose business it was to enforce Federal shipping regulations.

Collector Malone was an excitable man, an ambitious man, and a man of decision. He had been waiting for just such a chance to show how well he could enforce the Federal laws. When opportunity came, Malone lost no time. He sent a score of secret-service agents along the waterfront to investigate. He posted lookouts around the Eastern Hotel. The wires to Washington began to hum with messages.

Who was G. B. Means?, Collector Malone asked Washington. (Suspicious minds leaped to the conclusion that G. B. Means was a cipher "that means Great Britain").

The Collector placed himself on twenty-four-hour watch. One night, when the streets were quiet, he toured the harbor in a speeding torpedo boat, then boarded the destroyer U.S.S. *Parker* to search the outer harbor, then dashed out to sea with the destroyer's powerful searchlights ablaze.

The port's Neutrality Squad was alerted to cover the harbor from

Gaston B. Means

Newark Bay to Whitestone. A secret-service man was stationed at the Highland Light at Navesink, New Jersey. Every morning at dawn he scanned the horizon with a powerful telescope, looking for trouble.

On April 1, several of the tugboat captains descended on the Eastern Hotel, demanding to see Mr. G. B. Means. This was the day on which they had been promised work. Where was the work and where was Mr. Means?

The flurry of nighttime activity in the harbor had alerted Agent E-13. Gaston realized that his plan must be put into effect immediately or all would be lost. He was not ready, he did not have nearly enough captains or affidavits showing "past deliveries" to the British, but he put on his G. B. Means hat and traveled down to the customs house to call on Collector Malone. There Gaston, the patriot, told the story of the "British plot" to violate American neutrality, and produced his slender evidence to support the claim. A grateful Collector Malone doubled his efforts to discover the identity of the offenders. Means had let it slip that agents of a private detective agency—"one known all over the country"—had been working with agents of an organization of great power and influence, and had opened negotiations with dozens of captains and owners in New York, Philadelphia, and throughout New England to move supplies in the secrecy of night to the British fleet.

From midnight until five o'clock in the morning, Collector Malone went on the prowl. He began work at the upper end of Manhattan Island, passed down the Hudson River to the Battery, then to Hoboken, and finally out to sea, making a sweep within sight of the British vessels.

On Sunday, April 4, the newspapers discovered the story, and on Monday morning the report was emblazoned on the front pages. Collector Malone announced that he had discovered a plot to violate President Wilson's neutrality proclamation by establishment of an agency to supply British warships lying off Fire Island. He said he planned to take the case to the Federal Grand Jury.

Two days later, Captain Flannery told his story to the press. Captain Peerless admitted that his "affidavit" was a complete fabrication.

Sir Courtenay Bennett, the British consul general in New York City, showed neither guilt nor surprise when confronted with "the evidence." The British consul was shockingly calm, even for a British consul. The collector had evidently allowed himself to be entangled by German agents who were trying to stir up trouble between the United States and Great Britain, said the consul general.

Collector Malone changed his story. He had known all along that the "plot" was a German design to create trouble, and he had wanted it brought into the open. The collector's friend, the mysterious G. B. Means, was cornered by the press at the Hotel Manhattan. He announced that he represented a "large society" that was dedicated to the cause of peace.

"I am making it my business to see that the neutrality laws are being kept in all parts of the United States as well as the port of New York," Gaston said, pleasantly enough. In this important job he traveled to all parts of the nation. His headquarters was Washington.

Pressed for details by reporters, Gaston became secretive. He could give no particulars about the "organization."

Was his object to see if men were willing to break the law for pay? he was asked.

"Perhaps it might have been to find out whether they had been broken previously," Gaston replied, with dignity.

And was that the case?

"That, I cannot say. You had better ask Collector Malone."

The newspapermen did as Gaston suggested. They pursued the story of the plot for nearly a month before they tired of it and of Gaston's advice. Means gave up the office in the Eastern Hotel, but he retained the suite of rooms in the Hotel Manhattan. He and Julie stayed there, and there Gaston gave press conferences.

Gaston B. Means

The reporters discovered that of the "dozens of captains and owners" who had been approached by the "organization," only Captain Wilson, the contact man, had been paid. Captain Wilson had been paid ten dollars a day to spread the word about the great opportunity.

Gaston changed his stories almost as often as he changed his suits. One day he said he represented a detective agency. The following day he denied that he represented a detective agency, and returned to the tale he had spun about the "peace society." Since newspapermen were willing to listen, he expounded on his theme. On April 12, Gaston made a long, pontifical statement on the obligations of neutrals. He belabored the manufacturer who "puts money received for selling death-dealing instruments in one pocket and takes $5,000 from the other pocket to give to the Red Cross Society to heal the wounded. This, we claim, is hypocritical," said Agent E-13.

Gaston hastened to assure the reporters that *he* did not represent the Germans. As "proof" of his own neutrality he took full credit for causing the German cruisers *Prinz Eitel Friedrich* and *Kronprinz Wilhelm* to accept internment at Norfolk. Then he began talking about other violations of neutrality—but they were always violations by the British.

Gaston called the attention of reporters to plans by steelman Charles M. Schwab to supply American submarines to Great Britain. Schwab, he said, had made plans to build ten submarines for Britain. When Secretary of State William Jennings Bryan asked Schwab not to violate American neutrality, Schwab transferred operations to the Vickers plant in Montreal, in British territory. Means then produced a detailed list of the names of American boilermakers and mechanics who had moved to Canada to work in Allied shipbuilding plants—a clear violation of American neutrality.

As the month wore on and the reporters realized that Gaston's statements were undistinguishable from the official German propaganda line, the newspapermen became weary of the game. One accused him. He said Gaston was a German agent.

Gaston answered. "No, I am not connected with any German interest," Means lied. He called himself the "head of peace propaganda" for the United States. If reporters did not believe that he was an independent agent, then let them wait until the *Staats Zeitung* reporter came in. Means would raise that reporter's hair on end, for he would reveal the next big news break—which would involve the Germans, unfavorably. (Had the reporters waited, they might still be waiting for the *Staats Zeitung* man to show up.)

What were the results of the conflicting stories that Means was and was not employed by the William J. Burns Detective Agency? Burns said he had once employed Means, but not for long. Means denied that he ever worked for Burns, but said he was "allied with" Burns.

The long-suffering reporters were thoroughly disgusted with the performance by this time. At the end of April, Means lost his podium. The newspapermen refused to come to his "conferences." Means disappeared from the headlines. Reluctantly, Gaston moved Julie back to the "hateful rooming house" on 107 Street.[17]

Means continued to work for the German government during the spring and summer of 1915. He kept rooms at the Hotel Manhattan in the name of the American Peace Society. Julie Means was delighted with his new job, because Gaston was earning $100 a day as a German agent, or so he said. But he later said that during this period he earned $1,000 a week when he produced results—and that he never failed to produce results that were satisfactory to Captain Boy-Ed.

Means later told mysterious tales of meetings in secret, of bundles of currency left behind tombstones in Trinity churchyard, and of work for the Hamburg-American line as an employee of the Burns Agency. His tales were always exciting and filled with derring-do. Captain Boy-Ed asked him to secure supplies which were sent out to meet the various German surface raiders that operated in the Atlantic. Captain Boy-Ed did give $750,000 to the

Gaston B. Means

Hamburg-American line for the supply of raiders. The money was to be used to make fraudulent manifests, to bribe, and to do anything necessary to evade the American neutrality laws.

Did Gaston Means receive any of that $750,000? Perhaps, but it was carefully covered, because the United States government discovered the Hamburg-American line lawbreaking, and a number of American citizens actually connected with the work were convicted and sent to prison for their parts in it. Means was not included.[18]

Really, Gaston was a German propagandist. He hired a secretary for the "peace organization," a German-American girl named Marie Deutsch, whose father was working for the W. J. Burns Agency as a factory guard. Means was in communication frequently with John R. Rathom, editor of the Providence *Journal,* by letter and by telephone. He gave Rathom "information"—the same kind that he fed to any and all comers.[19]

Means was always to be vague as to the length of time he actually worked for the Germans. By the middle of 1915, there was reason for forgetfulness. The liner *Lusitania* was sunk in May, with the loss of life of 1198 persons, including 124 Americans. William L. Muller, German consul in Seattle, was arrested trying to bribe employees of a shipyard, and Muller was released by Seattle authorities only when Count von Bernstorff, the German ambassador, claimed diplomatic immunity to the State Department.[20]

No matter how his activities showed him to be in sentiment, Means was never pro-German. No matter what he might tell the press about the activities of the British, Gaston worked for pay. He boasted later that he worked not only for the Germans, but also for the British, the French, and the Mexican government during World War I, and that he, working for Germany, and William J. Burns, working for Britain, found it convenient to get together frequently to exchange information. He was pro-Means and pro-money.

Could the Germans be so naïve as to rely on a paid agent who played every angle? Apparently Means's abilities as a persuasive talker convinced Captain Boy-Ed of the North Carolinian's importance. Means claimed a close association with another North Carolinian, Josephus Daniels, Secretary of the Navy in the Wilson Cabinet, and with dozens of other officials and business leaders. Even the confused tugboat affair of March and April seemed to impress the German propagandists. Why not? Means managed to get a good part of their message across, in his own odd way. Later, the Germans prepared a list of prominent Americans whom they felt it was important to influence. There, among the Rockefellers and the Morgans and the Mellons, was the name of Gaston Bullock Means of New York and Concord, North Carolina.[21]

Working as Agent E-13, Gaston was certainly used by Captain Boy-Ed to do the German bidding in many ways, and he was regarded highly enough to be given an oil painting of the Kaiser to decorate his living room.

Means was also active in buying rubber and copper for the Germans and arranging for their shipment to Germany. At least, he said he did so. Captain Boy-Ed was besieged by German-Americans who wanted to see him, and Means took over the preliminary interviews of these people. Gaston met with them at the Savoy or Netherlands hotel or at the German Club on Fifty-ninth Street. He wrote articles for the German press about cotton, and he tried to buy submarine chasers and engines to be shipped to Germany.[22]

If all this activity was conducted from the office in the Hotel Manhattan, then Miss Deutsch was the busiest secretary in all the United States, for as he dictated, Gaston was still involved with the Burns Agency, and had branched out into an enterprise of his own which would have demanded the full attention of a lesser man. In the fall of 1915, he was preparing for a coup that would make him a millionaire.

III

In the summer of 1915, the fortunes of Gaston Bullock Means improved spectacularly. For a year, Gaston had felt his way in the fields of investigation and espionage. He continued his association with Burns, and suggested a new line of activity to the agency— the organization of a department to search out the hidden assets of firms that had gone into bankruptcy.[1] He worked with Boy-Ed and von Papen, but while he was conducting these programs, Gaston also stepped into the affairs of Mrs. King, apparently at the invitation of Mrs. Melvin, the managerial sister.

Means's first brief acquaintance with Mrs. King was interrupted when he and Julie had moved to New York City from Chicago. But, not many months after their move, Mrs. King and Mrs. Melvin appeared in New York City and looked up Julie Means once again, since Mrs. King regarded the younger woman as a protégée. Julie was grateful to the older women, because Gaston was spending most of his time downtown at the Hotel Manhattan and life in the boardinghouse was lonely. Mrs. King and Mrs. Melvin took Julie to tea and took her for drives in Central Park. As their association grew closer, it became apparent to all three ladies that Mrs. King had problems that Gaston Means might solve.[2]

Mrs. King had led a gay life since 1905, but three marriages, a succession of affairs, and constant doses of men and alcohol had left her in a condition that was described kindly as "confused." She returned from Europe just before the war with a divorce action pending against her third husband, trailed by a paramour who was doing his best to keep her out of the hands of her family or friends.

Mrs. King was born Maude A. Robinson in a small town in Illinois, some time around 1870. Early in life she married Edward R. Hull and lived in Chicago, where she studied singing. Near the turn of the century, the budding singer met James C. King, a lumber baron, who was then seventy years old. Not long afterward she divorced her husband and resumed her maiden name.

Maude Robinson then went to California for a winter. James C. King went to California, too. Maude Robinson traveled to Europe to complete her musical education. James C. King traveled to Europe that same year. Both returned to Chicago, and in July, 1901, they announced their forthcoming marriage. In a pre-nuptial agreement James C. King settled $100,000 on Maude Robinson, and she agreed not to make any claim against his estate. They were married in St. Joseph, Michigan. They were accompanied by Mrs. Melvin on the trip.

The Kings and Mrs. Melvin then made a voyage around the world. Dr. Melvin did not accompany them, but he did go with the Kings on other trips between 1901 and 1905. Travel was the Kings' way of life, because James C. King had the feeling that he was being followed, and he refused to settle down, so he lived in hotels and moved from one city to another.

The Kings spent the summer of 1905 at Mackinac Island, between Lake Huron and Lake Michigan, and returned to Chicago in October. There James C. King fell ill, and it became apparent that he would not recover. He decided to change his will to make further provision for his wife, but time was pressing, and King's

Gaston B. Means

lawyer, Noble Judah, advised him to make an outright gift to his wife instead of changing his will. So the old man gave Maude King the key to a safe deposit box that contained a quarter of a million dollars' worth of securities. Less than a week later, James C. King died.

After her husband's death, Mrs. King learned that her husband had been far more wealthy then she had ever known. She renounced the pre-nuptial agreement. She hired lawyer Americus B. Melville to negotiate with the estate for what she thought would be a fair settlement. King's will had not designated an executor, so an administrator had been appointed. No one questioned the will or Mrs. King's action; it was simply a matter of coming to agreement, and in time they did agree. In the agreement, Mrs. King was to receive $600,000 in cash or securities and the income on $400,000 for the rest of her life. The remainder of the estate was to go to establish the James C. King Home for Old Men, a charitable undertaking of which King had dreamed for years. The Northern Trust Company of Chicago was appointed trustee for the benefit of the home.

In 1906, the settlement was confirmed by the Illinois judiciary, and all concerned apparently parted happily. Mrs. King paid lawyer Melville a fee of $100,000 for his effort; she settled $100,000 on her sister; she also created trust funds for her mother and two brothers. After these generous payments Mrs. King retained property which brought in an income of about $70,000 a year.

Mrs. King then began to travel. She visited Paris and liked the city well enough to settle there for several years. She met an American doctor named Perry Chance, fell in love, and married him in London. The marriage seemed to be a happy one, but Mrs. Melvin took more than a normal interest in her sister's affairs, and some said she tried to separate the happy couple. In 1909, Dr. Melvin died, which made it possible for Mrs. Melvin to spend all her time with her sister. Dr. Chance and Mrs. King Chance were soon separated, and Mrs. King resumed her wandering.[3]

In November, 1913, on an Atlantic crossing, Mrs. King met M. J.

Marsh, an adventurous English bachelor who was traveling with his valet, and she fell easy prey to his advances. Prey is the word— for Marsh was the front man for a gang of English adventurers led by a London bookmaker named Leonard Davis. Later, New York police were to learn that Davis, Marsh, and company specialized in wealthy American women, and that earlier Marsh had married an aged American widow and had collected more than a million dollars from her estate when she died.

Marsh was an odd type for an adventurer. He was only five feet two and a half inches tall and he weighed 175 pounds. But the tubby Marsh wore an air that appealed to Maude King Chance. At this time, in 1913, she had conveniently subtracted a decade from her age, but her looks belied it. She was stout—140 pounds— and florid in the face. But M. J. Marsh had less interest in Mrs. King's personal dimensions than in those of her bank account. During their shipboard romance, she told him that she was traveling to Monte Carlo. When she arrived there, who should appear but M. J. Marsh, his valet, and his "sister," a female member of the ring who was born with the name Elsie Davidson.

This active group led Maude King Chance a merry chase across Europe. Finally they all turned up in London, where Mrs. Melvin hired Arrow's Detective Agency to discover the truth. When the detectives reported, Mrs. Melvin was horrified. She brought her sister home to New York City, installed her in the Hotel Nether-land, and sought the services of a doctor. The doctor discovered that Maude King Chance was suffering from heart disease, but that she was also "disjointed in her mental condition." The doctor visited them often, and, when the sisters moved briefly to Atlantic City, he called to treat Maude there. His report was more notable for frankness than for gentleness. He said Mrs. King Chance was "undoubtedly of unsound mind with a decided tendency to im-becility."

Mrs. Melvin seemed to be nearly powerless in her attempts to protect her sister from harm. The English gang followed the sisters to New York, and, in one of Mrs. Melvin's unwary moments, Marsh gained access to Maude King Chance, whereupon all Mrs. Melvin's efforts were undone. Maude went off with the fortune hunter. Marsh convinced his victim that all her relations were scheming to take her money away from her, and that he was her only friend. Maude moved out of her hotel and into the Hotel Manhattan with Marsh.

A Miss Anna Dolan, her nurse, was nearly frantic, and appealed to the doctor.

"My God, Doctor," she said, "she is absolutely insane and paretic; such a beastly state this gang has got her into. No one would recognize her."

Mrs. Melvin was distraught, but she did what she could do by herself. She called on an attorney, who employed detectives to watch Marsh. The detectives saw the pair in the public rooms of the Hotel Manhattan one night, drinking champagne from 10 P.M. until 12:30, and talking earnestly. They overheard Marsh telling Mrs. King that he would leave her forever unless she would go off with him, and they said that Mrs. King seemed half stupefied.[4]

Sometime during spring of 1914, Maude King Chance pulled herself together enough to make the trip west to Chicago, where she saw Julie and Gaston Means. But by summer she was gone again, this time to the West Coast, where she and Marsh took up residence as man and wife.

Mrs. Melvin and Maude's mother, Mrs. Robinson, were nearly frantic. They employed the Craft Detective Agency in San Francisco to try to break up the affair. In the event that Mrs. Chance returned to New York, the mother and sister made preparations to bring her before the New York State lunacy commission for hearing. They called on the Federal government, imploring the justice department to move under the provisions of the newly passed Mann Act, which made it a Federal crime to transport a woman across a state line for immoral purposes. But the justice department was loath to bring a test case that involved a wealthy middle-aged matron, when the law had been passed to stop white slavery.

Marsh and Mrs. King took a cottage in Pasadena, and lived the good life, or at least it should have been the good life, because between June, 1914, and autumn, Mrs. King spent all of her quarterly income of $24,000 and overdrew her Chicago account by an additional $30,000.

At this point, Gaston Means and the William J. Burns Agency came to the rescue. In the summer of 1915, Maude King Chance was saved from the adventurers, who were driven off with threats of exposure. Marsh and his friends disappeared, and negotiations for a French divorce were begun with Dr. Chance.[5]

Gaston stepped into Mrs. King's life that summer. Mrs. King's affairs had been in the hands of an Illinois trust company for nearly a decade, but now Gaston proposed to show the sisters that he could handle Mrs. King's business far more advantageously than an impersonal banker. Some of Mrs. King's money had been invested in stock of the Studebaker automobile company. During her travels, Mrs. King was advised to sell Studebaker stock and she had so instructed her Illinois banker. Since he believed in automotive stocks, the banker had bought her holdings for himself and had held them for several years. During those years the stocks rose sharply in value. Gaston convinced Mrs. King that the banker had used her investments selfishly, and he persuaded Mrs. King to order an independent audit of the funds held in trust. The audit showed only one clerical error, but Means first raised Mrs. King's doubts and then played upon them. Gaston concentrated on the matter of the Studebaker stock. He began a searching correspondence in which Mrs. King, Mrs. Melvin, the banker and the banker's attorney were all involved. Means here exhibited the special quality for which he was to become infamous, the one he had first shown in the breach of promise suit by Miss Poole four years before: the manipulation of suspicion.

The Illinois banker had been extremely close to Mrs. King. He had fallen in love with a stenographer in his office and had sent her to New York City to a finishing school. The girl was chaperoned in New York by Mrs. King and her sister. In the summer of 1915, the girl and the banker announced their engagement to marry in October. Mrs. King and Mrs. Melvin were to be honored guests at the event—so close was the friendship before the advent of Gaston Means.

Means insisted that Mrs. King was entitled to the profits made by the bank on the Studebaker stock, although she had ordered the sale years before. This idea had never before occurred to Mrs. King, and she was impressed with Gaston's shrewdness.

The amount of money was sizable—$10,000. Means's soft persuasion that Mrs. King was entitled to every penny of it convinced the sisters that Means was just the man to manage Mrs. King's financial affairs. Gaston thought so, too.[6]

That was a step in the direction Gaston wanted to follow, but only a step. Before he could go further, Gaston Means had to win the complete confidence of Mrs. King and overcome several important obstacles. The matter of Dr. Chance must be settled. The doctor was holding out for a large settlement. The susceptible Mrs. King was eager to agree because she had met another man she wanted to marry, Salvatore Giordano, an opera singer. She explained her problem to Means, who weighed all the questions and agreed to help her. The first step was for Mrs. King, Mrs. Melvin, and Means to go to Chicago to arrange her affairs. They left New York and traveled west in the first week in August, 1915. Just before the party left for Chicago, Means saw Giordano, and explained to him diplomatically that the singer's relationship with Mrs. King Chance had come to the attention of Dr. Chance, and that it might place an insuperable obstacle in the lady's path. In unpleasant accents Giordano told Means to mind his own business. But Gaston Means was not a man to be frightened by such a rebuff. The next day, Mrs. King telephoned Giordano and asked him for her sake to go immediately to Canada, to quell any rumors about their relationship.

Eager to please his lady love, Salvatore Giordano boarded a train for Canada. When he crossed the border, he began to think it over. He returned to New York. But it was too late. His bird had flown with Gaston Means, and Giordano never saw her again.[7]

In Chicago, Mrs. King and Means met with Mrs. King's banker and his attorney for several days. She agreed to settle with Dr. Chance for $50,000, and that obstacle was overcome. She also began to transfer assets held by the Illinois bank to New York City, where they could come under the watchful eye of Gaston Means. She made arrangements for the transfer of nearly $160,000 in securities and cash in the knowledge that, when she returned to New York, Gaston would help her invest it wisely.

Mrs. King was impressed with the masterly way in which Gaston Means dealt with the offending banker and with the lawyers. He knew her rights, and he insisted on every one of them. It was obvious that there was no intimidating Gaston Means.[8]

Mrs. King, from that point on, was to be clay in the hands of a master sculptor—or at least a master of the art of chiseling.

The total capitulation of Mrs. King was only a few hours away, and Gaston had already laid his plans for it. On August 9, the party left Chicago by train, arriving back in New York on August 10. En route, Means continued to gain Mrs. King's confidence. She began telling him all about her business affairs. By the time the journey ended, the conquest was complete.

Back in New York, on his way home, Gaston stopped at the Majestic Hotel to pick up a box of old papers that Mrs. King had left in the safe there. When he arrived at the rooming house, where he still lived, he sat down and began to leaf through the papers, Julie at his side. Suddenly, Means spoke.

"Well, sweetheart," he said, "here's where Maude gets all her money . . . it's old man King's will."

And sure enough, Gaston Means produced a will with the name of James C. King at the bottom, a will which left almost all of King's fortune of nearly four million dollars to Mrs. King.

Gaston Means lost no time in telling Mrs. King the wonderful news, and she was so overcome by it that she promised him a quarter of everything they collected. Also, henceforth he was to manage all her business affairs.

Since Gaston Means's relationship with Mrs. King and Mrs. Melvin was to be so personal, they decided all ought to live near one another. They took adjoining apartments, then, on the tenth floor of a new luxury apartment house at 1155 Park Avenue at the corner of Ninety-second Street. The total annual rental of the three apartments was $9,000 a year.

Mrs. King's apartment was at one end of the trio, Mrs. Melvin's apartment was in the middle, and the Means apartment adjoined hers. Since Mrs. Melvin did not need so much space as the others, two of the rooms that belonged to the Melvin apartment under the builder's plan were added to the Means apartment, and one of these Means furnished as an office, from which to conduct his affairs and those of Mrs. King.

Means supervised the furnishing and preparation of the apartments. He spent $16,000 for furniture and *objets d'art* for his apartment, and he also added little touches of his own, such as a listening device. Wires ran from his office, along the moldings, to microphones in the apartments of Mrs. King and Mrs. Melvin. If he was to manage Mrs. King's affairs, Gaston wanted to be sure he was familiar with all of them.[9]

In September, Means moved his trunks, his wife, and his portrait of the Kaiser into his eleven-room suite. He brought Marie Deutsch to work in the apartment. He sent to Chicago for Julie's father, W. R. Patterson, to come and assist him in the management of the King affairs. Patterson moved in with Gaston and Julie Means, to be near Mrs. King and Mrs. Melvin, for his job was to entertain "Maude and Maisie"—and be sure that no one else did. Means was well aware of Mrs. King's wayward memory and fickle heart, and he took no chances with such a valuable meal ticket.

Means also drew a formal contract with Mrs. King in which she promised in writing to give him $950,000 if they collected $2 million from her husband's estate. If the estate proved to be larger than $4 million he was to receive 22½ per cent of the total. Gaston talked grandly of an estate of $20 million and, impressed by the lordly command of finance exhibited by her new manager, Mrs. King began to advance him money.

The Means bank accounts in New York City had never been very impressive, partly because the nature of Gaston's activities led him to work heavily with cash and because after 1914 he did not maintain a bank account at all until 1916. Julie Means had an account at the Lincoln Trust Company, which had opened in 1914, the year Gaston gave up banking on his own. In June, 1914, Julie's account showed only one deposit of $300, but in August, after Gaston had found Mrs. King, Julie deposited $3,600, and in September she deposited $28,000 in her account.

During this same period, in August and September, 1915, Gaston continued to work for the Germans in his "peace" headquarters at the Hotel Manhattan. He was assigned to discover which wires of German firms and German agents were tapped by the United States government, and he went about it in a thorough manner, bribing the tappers. Captain von Papen asked Gaston to tie up the output of one factory that made Lewis machine guns, and mentioned a contract for 20,000 guns at $1,000 apiece.

Gaston boasted openly of his work for the Germans. There was nothing illegal about working for the Germans in 1915, and Gaston said nothing about the character of his work, other than that it was largely "commercial" and that he was "political secretary" to Captain Boy-Ed. He claimed later to have been paid $100,000 in one year by the Germans, and that year must have been 1915, when Boy-Ed and von Papen were in the United States. Means's handling of money lent credence to his claims; one night in a restaurant he paid a dinner check with a $100 bill, having first fumbled through a roll of $1000 bills and $500 bills to find something small enough for the purpose.

Not all this new wealth came from the Germans, however. In

Gaston B. Means

August and September, Gaston made a number of trips to Chicago with Mrs. King and Mrs. Melvin to wind up Mrs. King's affairs in that city. One draft after another was transferred to Mrs. King's New York accounts, until the total in cash and securities came to nearly $300,000, which represented all her resources except for the $400,000 trust held by the Northern Trust Company of Chicago, the bank which was entrusted with the estate of the late James C. King. There was no way Means or Mrs. King could get at that trust fund, because the principal did not belong to Mrs. King. On her death, it was to revert to the King estate and to be used for the purposes of the James C. King Home for Old Men. Gaston wanted Mrs. King to have that $400,000 and all the rest of the King fortune. He set out to secure the whole $3 million for her.

There was no hesitation now by Gaston Means in handling Mrs. King's affairs. The matter of the Studebaker stock transaction continued to be a subject of negotiation between Means and Mrs. King on the one hand and the Illinois banker on the other, until a few days before the October wedding. Means met with the banker and showed him a letter the banker had written some time before to Mrs. King. The language of the letter lent itself to *double-entendre,* and the banker was horrified at Gaston's indication that the letter might be shown to the prospective bride, if necessary. The banker paid $10,000 to Mrs. King for a release of all her claims against him regarding the stock transfer, but he did so protesting that he had no legal obligation to pay. To show how he felt about this blackmail, the banker broke off relations then and there with Mrs. King.[10] Such a breach was exactly what Gaston had wanted; he had not wasted his energy in trying to bring about the result.

One attribute of character which overflowed in Gaston Means was energy, and particularly when there was the smell of fresh green cash in the air, Gaston had not a lazy bone in his body. It had taken him no time at all to begin the campaign to win the entire King estate, and with his own stake in the future assured, he got down to work.

In October, 1915, the Means apartment at 1155 Park Avenue became as busy as a downtown office. Afton Means was summoned from Concord to New York to help Gaston. Henry Deutsch, the father of secretary Marie, was employed at various odd jobs. Mr. Patterson was relieved temporarily of the amusement detail and sent to Chicago to do research on James C. King, to find evidence to support the will case.

On October 15, Means hired the lawyer who had represented the banker in the $10,000 affair to represent Mrs. King in a contemplated suit to establish the "second will." In November, Gaston thought of a better course—he consulted Attorney Carl L. Schurz of New York, and set out to convince Schurz that a genuine case could be made for the existence of a second will. Not long afterward, Gaston summoned Attorney Americus B. Melville to New York by telegram, and dropped broad hints to Melville that indicated a second will had been discovered. Attorney Melville expressed disbelief, whereupon Means abandoned the conversation. Melville was never shown a copy of the "will," nor did Means actually make a flat statement that a will had been found. The Melville foray was a fishing expedition conducted by Gaston, who realized that if he was to make a case, he needed an attorney of impeccable reputation.

Melville's refusal must have convinced Means of the necessity to make a very strong appearance before trying his story out on a respected attorney. Gaston talked with Attorney Schurz from time to time, but he did not begin to make any moves yet, or really try to prepare Schurz to make a legal case. He was simply treading water in the legal department, while he and his agents worked to manufacture "evidence."

Gaston Means made a trip to Chicago that autumn, looking for one particular man who might be able to help him with a delicate phase of the matter of James King's "second will." In his most mysterious and official manner, Gaston began checking on a man who had been employed by a collection agency until he was arrested and convicted of a major crime. Means told no one why he wanted the man, but told various stories to newspaper reporters and others whom he sought out to question about the matter. The man had some valuable information, he said. The information was in reference to an estate. That statement, like so many to be made by Gaston Means, was partly true but completely misleading. The man he sought was a notorious forger, and a good forger was just the man Gaston Means needed at that moment.

During the autumn of 1915, Gaston Means, Afton Means, and W. R. Patterson collected affidavits and other material on James C. King, with Mrs. King footing the bills for this "investigation." Mrs. King wrote a number of checks to the order of Means, the largest of them for $25,000, and Julie Means opened another bank account with $10,000 in cash. These were not huge sums. For the moment, Gaston was going slow. Mrs. King handled her own funds. Means was engaged in a double-pronged attempt to increase her fortune; he was laying groundwork for the claim about the second will, and he was trying to build a case against the Northern Trust Company, to show that its officers had mismanaged the $400,000 set aside for the use of Mrs. King during her lifetime. If one attempt failed, he hoped to capitalize on the other.

In December, Means lost a valued employer when Captain Boy-Ed was accused of espionage and shipped home to Germany. Boy-Ed had called at the Means apartment frequently that year, and he had apparently been so pleased with Means's work that an addition was made to the Germanic collection—a portrait of Frederick the Great. Boy-Ed's departure made little difference in Gaston's efforts. Rudolph Otto replaced Boy-Ed as Means's superior, and Means then went to work to ship rubber surreptitiously to aid the German war machine. The rubber was shipped as "naval stores" from various points to Alabama and Georgia. There it was packed in barrels labeled "resin" and "tar" and sent to Norway and Sweden, and finally to Germany.[11]

On New Year's Eve, Means gave a dinner party at the Waldorf-

Astoria hotel for Julie, Mrs. King, Mrs. Melvin and a half-dozen acquaintances. Before the party left the table, over the wine Gaston Means arose and proposed a toast.

"Here's to the Kaiser," he said.

One of the women arose indignantly and raised her own glass.

"Up with the President and down with the Kaiser," she said.

Gaston smiled his dimpled smile and made no retort at all.

Later that evening, the party returned to the Means apartment on Park Avenue. Mrs. Melvin and Mrs. King excused themselves and went off to bed, leaving half a dozen guests sitting over drinks. The conversation turned to a contemporary poison murder case, which had been featured in the New York newspapers.

The host gave his opinion on the case. The murderer should not have used poison, Gaston said with authority. "He ought to have decoyed the old man into the woods and shot him, making it look like an accident."[12]

All those present knew that Gaston Means was an investigator, and they heard his views with respect. Since none of them was planning to murder anyone, the conversation quickly drifted on to other topics, before the party broke up and the others went home.

Gaston Means, investigator, had little time in the next few weeks to follow that particular murder case or any other, for he was deeply immersed in his plans to contest the King will. When it took longer than he had hoped to establish some of the factual background, Gaston again went to Chicago and then to Duluth, where James C. King had done much of his business in the years before 1905. Gaston was looking for various kinds of material, including a suitable piece of paper that had no watermark through which its age might be traced.[13]

In the beginning of their association, Gaston Means exercised considerable restraint in his handling of Mrs. King, but this restraint diminished rapidly. He had borrowed $25,000 from her in August, 1915, and later that year he made two interest payments on the loan, but no more. He collected $250 a week from her for his own expenses and she paid other expenses. Those extraordinary expenses were high, but that was natural since Gaston had assembled a platoon of workers.[14]

The loyalties of the workers were all to Means, naturally, since the workers were his father-in-law, his brother, and his own secretary and her father. In September, 1916, the loyalties were further cemented when Afton Means married Marie Deutsch. Then the entire Means organization was within the family.[15]

Gaston used various methods to obtain money from Mrs. King. She was an inveterate gambler, and he played dice with her in the evenings. Since Mrs. King consumed large amounts of champagne and liquor on these occasions, her handling of the dice was not as effective as it might have been. Means won $60,000 from her over a period of time, and collected the money in cash as he went along.[16]

Mrs. King's fortune in 1916 came under the complete management of Gaston Means. By the end of 1915, she had transferred everything to New York, as noted. But once transferred from Chicago, the money did not find its way into normal investment channels. The next year $20,000 worth of Mrs. King's New York Air Brake bonds was sold, and so were 150 shares of Brown Shoe Company preferred stock, worth $15,000. At this time, thirty mortgage notes worth $87,500 simply disappeared from the portfolio, and since no one in New York City other than Gaston Means was keeping close check on the securities, there was no one to raise an eyebrow. In blackmailing Mrs. King's Illinois banker for the $10,000 the year before, Gaston Means had gained more than one end. He had proved himself to Mrs. King and alienated from Mrs. King the one man who might have made Means's position impossible in a few short months.

Nor was Gaston the only drain on Mrs. King's wealth. She had settled $100,000 on her sister, Mrs. Melvin, in 1906, but Maisie Melvin apparently found it difficult to live on the income from that money. Late in 1915, Maisie borrowed $35,000 from her sister, most of which Mrs. Melvin placed in the hands of her Chicago broker—for Mrs. Melvin was also a gambler, and her métier was the stock market.[17]

So, late in 1916, much of Mrs. King's $300,000 had disappeared, and her resources were reduced to the income from the $400,000 trust held by the Northern Trust Company of Chicago.

All spring and summer, Gaston Means and his helpers prepared to prove that James C. King had left a second will. In November, Gaston was ready to move. Mrs. King and Mrs. Melvin closed their apartments at 1155 Park Avenue, gave up their automobiles, dismissed their servants, and traveled to Chicago, where they all took residence at the Chicago Beach Hotel. Mrs. King's mother, Mrs. Robinson, who was about seventy-five years old, had been staying in New York with Maude King, and she was urged at this time by Means and Maisie Melvin to go to Dr. Kellogg's celebrated sanitarium at Battle Creek, Michigan, while others conducted the business in Chicago. Mrs. Robinson did not want to go to Battle Creek, but Means was obdurate, so the old lady, her doctor, and her nurse went off to stay in a hotel in Battle Creek, and Mrs. Robinson entered the sanitarium for a few days.

In Chicago, Gaston Means installed all the ladies—and one new arrival—in the Chicago Beach Hotel. The new arrival was Julie Corallie Means, born in New York in September. To accommodate this household, Means took ten rooms at the hotel. The Means family had most of these for offices, sitting rooms, bedroom, and nursery. Julie Means was totally occupied in caring for her new baby, and Gaston, when he was at home, played the proud father. They called the baby "Sister." Her father doted on her; that much was apparent to anyone who saw this huge bear of a man play with his child, his blue eyes shining with love, and his dimpled cheeks wreathed in smiles.

Unfortunately, the press of business kept Gaston from spending as much time with his wife and child as he would have liked. Nor did he have very much time left for Mrs. King, so again he summoned W. R. Patterson to be sure that the ladies were amused—and watched.[18]

The Means entourage was short of cash on arrival in Chicago. Several checks drawn by Mrs. Robinson and by Mrs. King had been returned from their banks because of insufficient funds, and accounts that Means had established in his own name for the handling of Mrs. King's affairs were also low.

As a good business manager, Means set out to solve the financial problems of all concerned. He persuaded Mrs. King to sign a number of blank powers of attorney which would permit him to transfer stocks. He also took a trip to Battle Creek, to advise Mrs. Robinson on her financial affairs.

Mrs. Robinson had been given the Pasadena love nest that Mrs. King had shared with her English adventurer, and Means persuaded the old lady to take out a mortgage on the property. She signed the necessary papers, and most of the proceeds was actually deposited in her account.

But, on that same trip, Means accomplished other business, which concerned the trust fund established for Mrs. Robinson by Mrs. King back in 1906. The original sum of $100,000 had increased to $133,000. Mrs. Robinson did not later recall it, but, while she was signing papers for Means, she signed a statement revoking the trust. Perhaps her memory was failing, for later a notary public insisted that the papers had been read to the old lady and that she had signed in full understanding.

Gaston could understand her absentmindedness. He believed that Mrs. Robinson was in no condition to act for herself. He said so. In fact, he charged that Mrs. Robinson had been kept under the influence of drugs at the sanitarium, and that they had turned her into a drug addict. He tried to have two doctors certify that Mrs. Robinson was a drug addict, and thus incompetent, and to have a committee appointed to manage her estate. But here he failed, for while Mrs. Robinson was seventy-five, she seemed to the doctors to be neither insane, senile, nor addicted.[19]

Just before Christmas, 1916, Gaston Means returned to Chicago. Armed with Mrs. Robinson's papers and one of the powers of attorney from Mrs. King, he closed Mrs. Robinson's trust account. He sold the securities and deposited the money to an account for Gaston B. Means in the Illinois Trust & Savings Bank. In all, he deposited $105,000 in that account. Part of the remainder went for the expenses of the party at the Chicago Beach Hotel, and $10,000 went to Maisie Melvin, who immediately gave it to her broker. It was a very merry Christmas.

Once he had solved the immediate cash problems, Gaston Means was able to concentrate on business. He was eager to recoup Mrs. King's fortune in any way that he could, and he was ready to press the case for the second will of James C. King. One way to recoup quickly, given Means's claim to expert knowledge of textiles, was to play the cotton market, and this he began to do with a free hand, taking one small precaution: the cotton speculation account was carried in the name of W. R. Patterson, and all the transactions were conducted in Patterson's name.

Alas, the cotton market went to pieces at the end of January, 1917, and Gaston was wiped out. On the day the market finally collapsed, Means still had $35,000 in the bank account, just enough to cover a check written to one brokerage house, but Gaston was shrewd enough to get to the bank before the check cleared and draw out his balance. The check bounced, and Gaston Means owed the broker $35,000. If the house is in business, he still does.[20]

Mrs. King's business manager now began to suffer from uncomfortable feelings. Of all the moneys held by Mrs. King in 1915, all that remained was perhaps $50,000 in his hands, plus Mrs. King's monthly income from the $400,000 trust. The monthly income served barely to meet Mrs. King's daily expenses and it was obvious that, at the current rate of spending, the $50,000 of capital would disappear in a few months. Means faced certain embarrassment.

For one thing, he had neglected to tell Mrs. King of his decision to close out Mrs. Robinson's trust account. That account had

yielded Mrs. Robinson an income of $600 a month, and Means had
to pay that $600 every time it was due.[21]

Gaston had never informed Mrs. King of the low state of her
exchequer, either, and she went on blissfully spending as she
pleased. Since she now trusted her business manager to handle *all*
her affairs, Gaston had to find the money to pay the bills. Mrs. King
did not care about money; she quite enjoyed the freedom from
responsibility that Gaston Means had brought her. She turned
over the checks from the Northern Trust Company fund every
month, and Gaston Means deposited them and used the money to
pay the bills. If the bills could not be paid, Mrs. King would suffer
a terrible shock.

Faced with this problem Means did not panic. No Means or
Bullock knew the connotation of the word "panic," he said. Mrs.
King's business manager continued to do business as usual, working a little harder and a little more quickly to complete his case
for the second will. Locked behind the steel doors of the vault of
the Northern Trust Company lay the solution to all the problems
in Means's world—the millions of dollars of the James C. King
estate.

Gaston was a general who found it sensible to attack when he
was in difficulty. When Mrs. Robinson came down from Battle
Creek to Chicago to stay with her daughters, Gaston was all smiles
and attention. He went out of his way as never before to be sure
that Mrs. Robinson was comfortable and content.

"Mother, what is your income?" he asked her one day.

"Six hundred dollars a month," she replied.

"That is not enough. I am going to make it a thousand," he said.[22]

And so, without fail, the first of every month there was a check
for Mrs. Robinson for $1,000. She never thought to ask Gaston how
he had managed to increase her income by almost 100 per cent.
Her $1,000 check came regularly every month, and if it came from
Gaston Means's account now, instead of from the trust company,
what was the difference?

For many months, Gaston and his assistants had been collecting the evidence they wanted. One major point remained to be substantiated: just when the "second will" might have been drawn, and who might have drawn it. Means decided that the "second will" had been drawn at the Spalding Hotel in Duluth when Mr. and Mrs. King and Mrs. Melvin were staying there shortly before King's death, and that it had been drawn by a lawyer who was known to have done work for King. That lawyer was dead. So while there were many complications in proving that a will had been drawn at that time, the embarrassing presence of the lawyer in question was not one of them.

Means traveled to Duluth in March and began to investigate. Always the thoughtful husband and father, he telegraphed Julie in Chicago shortly after he arrived to tell them he was safe, and then he went to work. He discovered enough evidence to satisfy him that he was on the right track. But Gaston had no time to waste in Duluth, so he called Henry Deutsch to come from New York to do the work in Duluth, and then returned to the Chicago Beach Hotel.[23]

Mrs. King's business manager found it unwise to stray far from Chicago for any period of time. He had instructed Mrs. King and Mrs. Melvin to stay close to their rooms. He knew their enemies would do anything to balk his attempts to secure the entire estate for Mrs. King. He cautioned the ladies often, and they listened when he spoke. He also took great care to see that they were not disturbed. On one occasion, when the manager of the hotel engaged Mrs. King in conversation in the lobby, an irate Gaston Means broke up the talk and warned the manager that if he had anything to say to Mrs. King it must be said through her business manager. He was forced by busybodies to remain close to the hotel.[24]

Without Means's strong personality to maintain order, affairs in the Park Avenue apartment in New York had not gone well either. Henry Deutsch and his wife were living in the apartment, as were Afton Means and Marie Deutsch Means. But, with Means gone, there was little for them to do except take care of the Means files and forward messages, so the little family group fell to quarreling. When Henry Deutsch came west the situation worsened rapidly, and, on receiving a plaintive letter from his wife, Henry Deutsch wanted to return to New York.

Thereupon Gaston's reserves of courage nearly deserted him. He wrote his brother a plaintive letter, begging Afton to patch up the family differences and present a united front.

"I am staking my life on the proposition I am now working on." Means said. It was an overstatement of the facts but an understandable one, given the pressures and anxieties that Means carried after the cotton market collapse of that winter.

In the spring of 1917, Gaston consulted a number of handwriting experts. He bought tracing cloth, and he made photographic copies of the signatures of James C. King and the witnesses to King's will. He consulted the representatives of typewriter manufacturing companies, to check the brand and age of the machine on which the "will" was typewritten (and perhaps to discover the extent of the knowledge of the experts in these matters).

Early in July, the lawyers he had retained visited the Northern Trust Company in Chicago and disclosed the existence of the "second will" to officers of the company. Those officers were non-committal. They said they could take no position until they had seen the new will. Means then visited the trust company and brought the will with him.[25]

James C. King's "second will" was an unusual document. It was written on a single sheet of paper that bore no watermark, and the paper was ragged around the edges. The typewriting covered the entire sheet, without margins. The typing was not even original, but a carbon copy. Each character had been overwritten in lead pencil, a task that must have been done under a magnifying glass. The characters of the machine were so badly out of line and the typewriting was so distorted that the trust company's experts could not decide whether or not the machine had been manufactured before 1905. And the document was creased and re-creased, which gave it an aged look.[26]

The officers of the Northern Trust Company were not long in coming to a decision. They said the will was a forgery and that they would not accept it or pay a penny in compromise. They urged Means to file the will and try to probate it. Then they said good day to Mrs. King's business manager.[27]

If Means was dismayed by this turn of events, he gave no sign. He returned to the Chicago Beach Hotel and met with Mrs. King, who was surprised and apparently needed to be convinced that the matter should be pursued. She had given the matter little attention and was not familiar with the will, except as Means had told her of it. Now Gaston brought her dismaying news: the trust company was being difficult, but, far worse, her life was in danger. He said that those who had hidden the will in the first place to keep her from getting all the money were now determined to kill her.[28]

This news from her business manager was most disturbing, but perhaps not as disturbing to her as the news Mrs. King then gave to Gaston. She wanted to marry again, she said happily. She had met a young naval officer and she had fallen in love.[29]

Means assured Mrs. King that he would do all in his power to bring about her happiness, but that his first responsibility was to protect her life. He could not protect her in Chicago. She must disappear; she must go to North Carolina where he had friends and knew the countryside. There he could save her life.

On July 15, Means wrote his brother Afton in New York that all messages for the women in the group were to be "forwarded only to me." "Only to me" was underscored twice. On July 17, Means took Mrs. King away from Chicago by auto. It took two automobiles to carry the entire party and the luggage, for Julie Means and the baby went along, as did Mrs. Melvin, Mrs. Robinson, and W. R. Patterson.

The party headed south and stopped at the Grove Park Hotel in Asheville.[30] Gaston Means left them there and hastened back to New York City. The Northern Trust Company had been alerted to his plans. There was much to do and very little time.

IV

Gaston Means returned to 1155 Park Avenue to discover that the financial affairs of his multi-family ménage had reached a new low. The $9,000 rental on the apartments would soon be due. If he paid that amount, there would be very little of Mrs. King's money left. The large party in Asheville cost a great amount of money. In a matter of weeks he would have to either produce more cash or explain what had happened to Mrs. King's fortune.

Mrs. King's powers of attorney were of small value, because there was so very little left to sell. Her trust fund produced less than $20,000 a year income. She owned jewelry worth $23,000, but she had taken it with her. She held a $5,000 note from a friend, which Means could not collect, and one for $31,000 from W. R. Patterson, who had borrowed in order to go into the cotton market. If anyone knew how little his father-in-law's note was worth at that moment, Gaston B. Means, his employer, was the man.[1]

Some money was left in various bank accounts—Gaston's, Julie's, and the accounts held theoretically for Mrs. King. There was no use writing a check on Mrs. Robinson's New York account, as

67

several checks written earlier had been returned by the bank. So Means was reduced to working with the money at hand—perhaps $50,000—to see him through.

It was time for action, and Means believed he knew exactly how to deliver the master stroke that would both save him and make him wealthy.

In 1917 the most prominent attorney in the United States was Charles Evans Hughes, who had resigned a seat on the United States Supreme Court to run against Woodrow Wilson for the Presidency the year before. Losing by a narrow margin, Hughes had swallowed his disappointment and returned to New York City to practice law, where his services were sought by the most respectable of corporations. Those services were expensive, naturally, but Means was desperate and willing to pay to give the "second will" of James C. King the impeccable cloak of the counsel of Charles Evans Hughes.

Means had not sought out Attorney Carl Schurz of New York earlier without a plan in mind. Schurz bore an old and highly respected name among lawyers and statesmen, for the first Carl Schurz had been a leader in the Republican party and one of the dissidents who went into opposition against the excesses and corruption of the Grant Administration. Further, while Means had not the shadow of a chance of hiring the services of Charles Evans Hughes, Schurz might be able to get Hughes to work as counsel. For this contingency Schurz had been kept in reserve— and in the dark about the true nature of Means's "evidence" and the nature of the will itself.

Apparently it was Means's plan at this time to be prepared to probate the King will either in Chicago or in California, whichever seemed most propitious at the moment. That was feasible because the "second will" included bequests—small ones—to several California charities, and King had owned property in California.

Means had employed a Chicago lawyer. He had retained Carl

Gaston B. Means

Schurz, although he had given him almost no information for two years, and now, in addition, he wanted to secure the name of Hughes. He hoped to be able to get Hughes to take the case for a $2,000 retainer.

Late in July, Means conferred with Schurz and left his documentary evidence in the hands of that attorney. All this was done, of course, in the name of Mrs. King, with Gaston Means appearing only as her business manager.

A few days later, after several conferences, Attorney Schurz met with Mr. Hughes and gave him the facts of the case. Hughes commented on the many "extraordinary" features of the matter and did not seem to be overly impressed with the validity of the claim, but he did agree to reserve decision for a week, during which time he would investigate. If there was any question as to the facts or the character of any of the persons involved, he would have no interest, Mr. Hughes said. (It took far less than a detailed investigation for Mr. Hughes to determine that he wanted no part in this affair.)[2]

Gaston Means's problems were now so serious that only some extraordinary turn of events could prevent a crisis within a month. Just before the first of August, Means was forced to reach into his slender supply of cash and produce the usual $1,000 draft for Mrs. Robinson in Asheville. Means's account in the Corn Exchange National Bank was down to $4,000, from $18,000 two months before.[3]

In Asheville, Mrs. King was growing restless. She was used to big cities and bright lights and found the North Carolina countryside too tame. A telegram came to 1155 Park Avenue from the South demanding that Gaston "wire or phone encouragement immediately." Means did more than that. He went to Asheville to encourage Mrs. King in person, assuring her that in a few weeks matters would be settled and they could all return to Chicago for the probate of the new will.

While in Asheville, Means unfolded a plan to several other members of the party to keep Mrs. King under control. Gaston would return to New York to conduct his pressing business, he said, but he would send regular letters to Asheville. The others in the party (Mrs. Robinson excepted) were to read the letters, then place them in plain envelopes and slip them under the door of Mrs. King's room in the dead of night. This method of delivery was chosen for two reasons. It would impress Mrs. King with her business manager's extraordinary powers, and it would enable Means to date his letters from any place he wished to appear to be.

On his return to the Park Avenue apartment, Gaston began to compose the letters, and, knowing his subject, he dealt straightaway with the cause of Maude King's restlessness—the naval officer with whom she was infatuated at the moment—in letters that were cloak and dagger masterpieces:

Washington, D.C.

Just a line to state arrived here this morning. From information just before leaving North Carolina yesterday and virtually confirmed here, effort is being made to take our mutual friend to Canada and from Canada to England. I have not located his exact whereabouts as yet but expect to do so before the day is over.

Impossible for me to give you an address where you can reach me, but by my own methods I will be able to have notes slipped under your door or put where you can see them without anyone else knowing about it first.

Do not say anything to anybody when you find this note. I will try to get a note to you every day until I have located our friend, and later, just as soon as I know, will let you know when you can reach me by letter. Be very careful, very secretive, and let nobody know what you and myself are attempting to do for our friend.[4]

Means's second letter to Mrs. King was sent from "aboard revenue cutter somewhere in Chesapeake Bay." He reassured her that he would see that no harm came to their friend, and he cautioned her to remain where she was because he was trying to bring the friend to North Carolina to see her.[5]

Mrs. King was persuaded to enter the hospital in Asheville for a minor operation. Means hoped that this would immobilize her for a time. The delay permitted him a few more days of uninterrupted work with the attorneys. But finally there was nothing more to be done in New York City. Hughes's refusal put an end to that plan. Means went home to North Carolina to join the party there.[6]

There were several reasons for Means's trip at this time. His wife and child were with the party in Asheville. He was concerned about Mrs. King's restlessness, and he suspected that the Northern Trust Company had sent representatives to North Carolina to investigate the activities of the party. A few days after Means had presented the "second will" to the trust company, the bank's lawyer had telephoned the lawyer Means had engaged in Chicago, to ask if Mrs. King and Means proposed to present the will for probate. When the lawyer replied that the ladies had left Chicago, and that nothing more would be done at the moment, the trust company's attorney had said nothing, but Gaston Means was thoroughly suspicious. He was convinced that agents were trying to come between him and Mrs. King.

This was an excellent time for a North Carolina vacation. New York was in its worst season—summer. Means, furthermore, had been called to testify in a hearing held by the state controller's office. A complaint had been made against the William J. Burns Detective Agency, and there was a possibility that Burns's private detective license might be revoked. Means had already testified once in Burns's behalf, but it was 1917, the United States had entered the war in Europe, and he was not eager to air his past relationships with the Germans.[7]

In Asheville, Means made arrangements for his sisters Belle and Kate to invite Mrs. King to stay with them. He also arranged for his mother to join his wife and daughter at the Grove Park Inn suite at Asheville. "Old Seventy-Six," Gaston's name for Mrs. Robinson, was to be kept in Asheville, and in the dark. Means announced that it was necessary for Maude to accompany him to Concord to sign some papers, and that then they must go to Chicago and New York in connection with her business.

On August 18, Means and Mrs. King left the hotel and traveled to Concord, where they stayed in his father's house. On August 27, Mrs. Melvin left the Inn, telling her mother that she was going to New York. She, too, went to Concord.

During this week, Means bought a new automobile for Mrs. King in Charlotte. He paid cash and flashed a roll of bills estimated by the salesman to total more than $21,000.[8] He hired a chauffeur and almost every day took the ladies for rides around the country. Automobiles were new enough to Concord to create quite a stir. The town's leading citizens went for drives with them, including Judge E. B. Cline. This attention seemed to mollify Mrs. King and kept her from worrying overmuch about her naval officer. She never did show much concern about the second will of her late husband, a matter left entirely in the hands of Business Manager Means. She trusted him absolutely. As she enjoyed herself in Concord, she did not know that her New York bank had issued a sight draft on her, since she had been drawing on non-existent funds.[9]

Means was hopeful that he could divert Mrs. King long enough to "keep her from rocking the boat," and he so wrote to Henry Deutsch in the New York apartment.[10]

But, after a few days, the Concord pastorale failed to satisfy Mrs. King's yen for excitement. She had not spent so much time in such an unexciting place since 1905, the year James C. King died. What was there for a city woman to do in Concord?

Mrs. King could go driving, to be sure, and did. But the other forms of amusement were swimming, walking, and rabbit hunting. Mrs. King now weighed about 170 pounds, so swimming did not seem to be in the calendar, nor walking, since she never appeared in public except in high-heeled shoes.

Gaston B. Means

As she grew restless, Gaston Means wracked his brain to find ways to amuse her. They would have a barbecue. That seemed to Mrs. King to be an excellent idea since she liked people. The matter was under discussion for several days.

Eager to amuse his employer, Gaston Means tried one day to persuade her to go out with him on a mill pond in a flat-bottomed boat. But Mrs. King was afraid of the water, and would not go boating. On another occasion Means took her driving to a lake near town, where an enterprising garage owner had brought in several canoes for those who wanted to venture onto the water. Means spent several hours at this garage, ordering a youthful attendant to do one thing after another to the car, and while they were waiting, he tried, time and again, to persuade Mrs. King to go with him for a ride in a canoe. She would not do so, and, in the face of his persistence, she became absolutely stubborn about it. Much disappointed, Gaston finally gave up the plan that day, and went home without his canoe ride.[11]

On August 27, Means went to a hardware store in Concord and asked for a .32-caliber automatic pistol. Since everyone in town knew that the Means family had visitors, he explained that Mrs. King wanted a gun, and that she wanted a hand gun that could be carried in a dress pocket. The hardware dealer had nothing of that kind. Concord leaned more heavily to 12-gauge shotguns, .30-caliber rifles, and, where hand guns were wanted, to six-shot revolvers. An automatic pistol, basically a concealed weapon, had very little place in the Concord scheme of things.

The dealer, Monk Ritchie, offered to try to get such a gun for Gaston in Charlotte, and Gaston urged him to do so. But when Ritchie came back from his buying trip to Charlotte, he reported that he did not find what Gaston wanted there. Gaston then did buy the best substitute he could find, a .25-caliber Colt automatic, and a supply of steel-nosed cartridges. He was going to take Mrs. King out for a little target practice—another form of amusement that he had devised to keep her mind off other matters.

73

Means apparently tried the gun out once or twice himself, just to be sure it worked properly, before he offered it to Mrs. King to use. Two days later, Gaston visited the hardware store and asked the proprietor to clean and oil the gun, which Ritchie did. Gaston also complained that it had a tendency to "hang"—to jam. The hardware man looked the gun over and made the minor adjustments that were necessary. Those done, it should work like a charm.[12]

So Gaston Means took his automatic pistol and went back to amusing Mrs. King.

After dinner on the evening of August 29, the Means family and guests were sitting in the twilight and talking about a suitable spot for the barbecue. Someone suggested Blackwelder's Spring, a place a few miles east of Concord off the Gold Hill road. Mrs. King wanted to see it, and Gaston was, as always, agreeable.

"Let's take some guns along," Gaston suggested. "We may be able to bag a few rabbits."[13]

So Gaston found a pistol for himself and the little hand gun for Mrs. King. Afton came along, too. The Negro chauffeur, Earnest Eury, brought the car out in front and they got in. They stopped in town and picked up Captain W. S. Bingham, a cotton buyer and rabbit fancier, and set off along the road.

When they arrived at Blackwelder's Spring, Gaston and Mrs. King got out to look at the spring, while Afton and Captain Bingham walked on down the road looking for rabbits. It was an odd time to be hunting—by now it was quite dark—but they were out, and they had guns, and who knows what a rabbit will do?

Means and Mrs. King began walking to the spring.

"She walked with me down to the spring," Gaston said later, "carrying her new Colt .25 in her hand. I had a .32 with me. As we came near the spring, she handed me the gun. I said I wanted a drink of water from the spring. I placed her gun in the crotch of a tree and told her not to touch it. The tree stood on the edge of a marshy spot. It was muddy around there. She stayed back while I went toward the spring.

Gaston B. Means

"Just as I was stooping down for a drink of water, out of the corner of my eye I noted her reaching for the gun, and I called to her not to touch it, as it was loaded. Then I took a drink and the next thing I knew I heard a shot.

"I glanced around and saw her stagger. I jumped up and ran toward her and got there—it was only a few feet—just as her legs crumpled under. She collapsed in my arms. I called Afton and Bingham—and we called for the car. Putting her into the car with Afton I wrenched my back. We drove as fast as we could to the hospital in Concord but by the time we got her on the operating table she was dead."[14]

It was a terrible tragedy, but Gaston Means did not lose his head. Mrs. Melvin had gone to the movies, but Afton Means tracked her down and brought her to the hospital. When it was apparent that nothing could be done for poor Maude King, the body was taken across the street to L. A. Weddington's funeral parlor, and made ready for shipment to Chicago for burial. Gaston telephoned his wife at the inn in Asheville.

"Julie," he said. "Maude's been killed. Go tell Mrs. Robinson."

His wife called the hotel manager, who advised against bringing such shocking news to the old lady late at night, so Julie waited until the following morning to break the news, then rushed to Concord to see her husband.

The next day, Coroner Spears called a jury together and presented the case. The jury decided that Maude King had met death in an accident. So Means and Mrs. Melvin took the body to Chicago that night, leaving Concord on the Southern Railway, and they informed Maude King's two brothers of the accident. The brothers came to Chicago. On Monday, September 3, the remains of Maude Robinson King were buried in Chicago's Graceland Cemetery. The brothers went home, and Mrs. Melvin accompanied Gaston Means back to his home in Concord.

The newspapers reported the accident and the funeral briefly, and then only because Maude King had been a wealthy woman. The interest of most Americans was in the war news. President

Wilson had just rejected the offer of Pope Benedict to mediate between the Allied and Central powers. American troops had landed in France. General Pershing, in response to irritating public pressures, told the nation not to expect the green troops to be rushed into the front-line trenches. The Italians were breaking the Austrian lines along the Isonzo front. And Teddy Roosevelt, to whom Gaston Means claimed relationship, had just arranged to join the staff of the Kansas City *Star*—by agreeing to wire his comments on daily events to the newspaper.

Gaston Means was so little known to newspapermen at this time that he was erroneously identified as Mrs. King's lawyer, but newspapers did have the clippings from the 1915 New York harbor affair, and they noted that he had been "former political secretary to Captain Karl Boy-Ed."

Perhaps that odd and now unsavory relationship caught the eye of Chicago newspapermen, or perhaps they had heard something of Means's activities in other fields. The Chicago *Tribune's* reporters began to take an interest in the case, at any rate, and one of them began to ask questions.[15]

In Chicago, other people began to ask questions, too. Americus B. Melville, Mrs. King's attorney for many years, said he was sure of one thing: Maude King did not kill herself.

Attorney Jacob Newman, whom Means had employed in Mrs. King's name to assist in the matter of James King's new will, said he was puzzled. He knew of Mrs. King's long-standing antipathy to firearms, but he also knew that Gaston Means had "everything to gain" by Mrs. King's living and everything to lose by her death.

One of Mrs. King's brothers, William Robinson, told the press with finality that he was convinced the shooting was an accident, and that the case was closed.

The family was to take a different view a few days later, as Attorney Melville and others began to check into Mrs. King's affairs. Melville had drawn Maude King's will several years earlier —just before her meeting with Gaston Means. The will provided that the property was to be divided among the family and Mrs. Melvin was to be executrix of the estate. But what she was to execute remained to be determined, for Mrs. King's will was not readily found.

Northern Trust company officials saw some odd points in the affair, and they did not forget the will that had been presented to them six weeks before. They wanted to know where that will had gone.

A nurse who had attended Mrs. King off and on for many years told reporters that Mrs. King had said, weeks before, that her life was in danger. The fact that Mrs. King was shot in the back of the head puzzled many people. It seemed a strange place for an accidental wound.

For a week after the shooting little notice was taken of the matter, but on September 6, a great deal began to happen as parts of the puzzle fitted together. Mrs. Robinson recalled that both her daughters had gone off mysteriously with Gaston Means, and that Maude had taken all her papers with her on the day she left.

On the day that the body was shipped to Chicago, Undertaker Weddington, Gaston Means, and several others had first brought the casket to Asheville, and it was opened so Mrs. Robinson could take a last look at her daughter. But she got no satisfactory information from Means that day, and her suspicions were thoroughly aroused. She wanted to know where Maude's money was, so Mrs. Robinson decided to hire an attorney, P. C. McDuffie, of Atlanta, to investigate.

In Chicago, the *Tribune* reporter continued to harass the authorities about this strange case. Coroner Hoffman of Cook County received an anonymous letter from Concord.

"Everyone in Concord believes that Mrs. Maude King was foully murdered," the letter said. "It is the most dastardly thing ever committed in this place and we hope that Chicago, the home of Mrs. King, will take the matter up and see that the murderer gets justice. There are many motives for the crime and when you get busy you will find them out. If you will have her body examined you will see she could not have shot herself behind the ear. No one here credits the explanation of the crime and the good people of this place hope that Chicago and New York will combine in clearing this mystery."

It was a mystery as to who might have sent such a letter. By raising the question of motive, the writer indicated a greater familiarity with Mrs. King's affairs than anyone native to Concord enjoyed. The suggestions that investigation by northerners would be welcomed also indicated that the writer was someone foreign to Concord. It might have been the Negro chauffeur, Earnest Eury, or Mrs. King's nurse, who traveled with her much of the time, the nursemaid employed by Means to care for his little daughter, or any other person in service—perhaps Mrs. Robinson's maid—for Gaston Means was notoriously harsh with servants.

In any event, the anonymous letter provided enough new fuel to the fire of suspicion that, on the night of September 6, the body of Maude King was exhumed from Graceland Cemetery without family permission, by order of a judge of the Circuit Court, and a midnight autopsy was conducted by the coroner. The post-mortem examination indicated several facts which aroused the suspicion of Cook County officers. The coroner said he did not see how the wound could have been self inflicted. There were no powder burns on the head of Mrs. King. Dr. William Burmeister, a pathologist at Northwestern University, conducted the examination. He also discovered that Mrs. King's ankle had been broken.

Thoroughly suspicious, the assistant state's attorney sent a wire to J. S. Manning, the Attorney General of North Carolina, asking him to investigate the shooting further. That same day, in Chicago, Attorney McDuffie announced that apparently $510,000 of Mrs. King's money was missing, and that he had learned of heavy market speculation and losses by Gaston Bullock Means, Mrs. King's business manager. McDuffie had visited the Merchants Loan and Trust Company, where once Mrs. King had an account. All that remained there was the trust fund she had established in 1906 for her brothers. The trust fund had been changed significantly, too. Originally $200,000 had been put aside for the brothers, but in 1912, Mrs. King had asked that the fund be dissolved, as it had been drawn improvidently, and she established a new trust fund of $90,000. Erroneously, the newspapers now reported that this change was made at about the time she had met Gaston Means.[16]

The suspicions, once aroused, began to multipy and to reflect, even unfairly, on Mrs. King's business manager.

In Raleigh, North Carolina, once the telegram from Chicago had been received, Attorney General Manning called on the state's Solicitor General, Hayden Clement, to investigate the death of Mrs. King in Concord. Clement was a college acquaintance of Gaston Means. He had been a year behind Means at Chapel Hill, but he had known him, and, like most of Means's acquaintances in college, he had found Means to be engaging. But these considerations did not stop Clement in his investigation. He went to Concord.

In Concord, Clement encountered several puzzling bits in the story of Maude King's death. On the night of the shooting, when Afton Means had gone to the movie theater to find Mrs. Melvin, he had stopped to talk with an acquaintance in front of the theater. He had said, then, that Mrs. King was whirling the gun around her finger when it went off. The story that it was an accident, and that Mrs. King had dropped the gun or shot herself, did not agree in details. Also, a witness who lived near the scene talked of having heard two shots, not just one.

Aroused by the growing clamor, particularly in the Chicago newspapers, Mrs. Melvin sent telegrams to the editors of those newspapers, completely exonerating Gaston Means of any blame in the death of her sister. But now the hounds were loose. Hayden Clement, a slight and soft-spoken man, moved quietly around Concord, checking up on the stories of witnesses. He conferred on September 8 with Chief of Police C. A. Robinson and Cabarrus County Sheriff Howard W. Caldwell. He discovered a number of apparently different stories, but the most puzzling aspect was the complete absence of any motive on the part of anyone who might have been involved in the shooting.

When Gaston Means learned that he was under suspicion, he first expressed shock to his wife, then anger, and finally defiance.

"It's ridiculous," he said. "Somebody's back of this—somebody's trying to get me out of the way. Well, they haven't a chance. I'm innocent and I can prove it."

Means was quite right that somebody was behind the reopening of the affair. He suspected that the "somebody" was the Northern Trust Company of Chicago, but immediately, at least, it was not the company but Mrs. Robinson who told the press that she did not believe her daughter's death was an accident.

Hayden Clement continued his probing. He wondered why Means had taken the party to Blackwelder's Spring so late in the evening. It was not so late when they started out, Means said; besides, Mrs. King did not care much about hitting anything when she went shooting. She liked the noise and the excitement. As for the investigation, now that it was launched, he welcomed it.

"One can plainly see it meant everything to me for Mrs. King to live, and that since she is dead everything is lost."

That was the stopper for Hayden Clement. He wondered what the motive could be, if indeed there was a motive for Gaston Means to wish Mrs. King dead.

As Clement continued to ask questions, up North Mrs. King's brothers grew suspicious. Maude King's will was found in Chicago, but the money was not found, and the Robinson family, with the exception of Mrs. Melvin, joined the hounds. Maisie Melvin, staying with the Means family in Concord, believed in Gaston Means.

"Before God," she said, "that boy is innocent."

Means was thoroughly irritated, and while his lawyer father said mildly that the boys would produce the pistol and all other relevant material at a new inquest—if Clement decided to go ahead—Gaston Means spoke up harshly for the first time.

"There is going to be a day of reckoning for those who are

responsible for such insinuations," he said. "As a southern gentleman I brand them as dastardly and I mean to defend to the limit
the name of the woman who is dead and unable to protect herself."

It was always effective to bring the names of outraged virtue
and southern courtliness into such discussion, particularly when
outsiders were involved, as they most definitely were in this matter.
But Gaston's strong words had little noticeable effect on those
outsiders. Instead of narrowing, the circle broadened, as Means
discovered the next day when the newspapers reported that District Attorney Swann in New York City was opening his own investigation there. Alerted by the Chicago officers, Swann assigned
Assistant District Attorney John T. Dooling to look into the affair,
to see if a conspiracy had begun in New York City to kill Mrs.
King.

Almost immediately, Dooling decided that a conspiracy had
existed, and that Gaston Means was the principal conspirator. He
said Means had a "plan to break the King will with a forged
document and make Mrs. King worth $10,000,000 or so," that Means
had kept Mrs. King "in his power" for a year. Dooling theorized
that Mrs. King had come to her senses and demanded an
accounting.

These strong statements infuriated Gaston Means, but they also
alerted him to a new danger. If the New York District Attorney's
office was investigating with this conclusion in mind, many of the
papers in the Park Avenue apartment could hold evil connotation.
That night, Gaston dispatched Afton Means to New York, with
instructions to bundle up all the papers in the apartment and bring
them back to Concord.

And that night, in Asheville, "Old Seventy-Six," Mrs. Robinson,
collapsed when Hayden Clement told her that her $133,000 trust
fund no longer existed. She denied flatly that she had ever signed
any papers which revoked the trust. Gaston Means had asked her
to sign them, but she had refused, she said. The papers were
forged.

"Some of Means's dirty work," she said.[17]

81

Mrs. Robinson, who had apparently never been overly fond of Gaston, had turned completely against him long before this discovery. Means had tried to see her in Asheville several times, but she would not let him in the room. On September 7, she had finally granted him a personal interview—as long as someone else remained in the room with them. She recalled that after Maude's death, Means had suggested one night that he spend the night in Mrs. Robinson's room. She had not let him do so, she said, because she feared that he might murder her.

The tall, burly Afton Means—in many ways a carbon copy of his older brother—arrived in New York City on September 12. Assistant District Attorney Dooling heard that Afton was coming, and sent detectives to intercept him at the Pennsylvania Railroad Station. But whether by intent or accident, Afton Means missed the detectives and arrived at the apartment. The white-haired, lantern-jawed Dooling went to the apartment that day, and just in time, for Henry Deutsch and Afton Means had bundled up the papers and were preparing to ship them off to North Carolina.

Dooling held Afton Means and Deutsch, and spent the night reading Gaston's correspondence. Then, apparently addicted to trying his cases in the newspapers, the Assistant District Attorney announced that he had found evidence of larceny, forgery, perjury, conspiracy, and murder.

He found dice, and penciled notes about provisions of the "second will" in Means's handwriting, and a copy of the will itself. He found indications of Means's plunges into the cotton market, and the failures, not only in cotton, but in steel and other stocks. Gaston Means, it appeared, had a penchant for guessing absolutely wrong about the market. Dooling discovered that Means's judgment was so bad that he was successful only in one cotton speculation, and that he had earned only a little more profit for Mrs. King by a clandestine shipment of rubber overseas to Germany.

Dooling found tracing paper—which might have been used to

trace signatures. He found the dictograph and the wires and microphones in Mrs. King's and Mrs. Melvin's apartments. He found letters that showed how Means had smuggled liquor from wet New York City to dry Cabarrus County in his sisters' luggage. He found a large number of power-of-attorney forms which were blank except for the signatures of Mrs. King and two witnesses. (Handwriting experts said these signatures were forgeries.)

Dooling found letters from the Germans, and Means's two oil paintings. The latter, after the United States went into the war, had been removed from the apartment and stored in the basement of the apartment house, waiting for sunnier days.

While Dooling read, Afton Means paced the floor. He tried to telephone an attorney, but the attorney was not at home. Finally, Afton lay down on the couch and slept while Dooling continued his reading, all night long.

At 10:30 the next morning Assistant District Attorney Dooling bundled up the documents and Afton Means and took them down to the District Attorney's office. He secured subpoenas for both documents and Afton, intending to take them before the grand jury. He was certain that a case could be made against Gaston Means and others for conspiracy to commit murder, and he wanted to try that case in New York City.

In Concord, there was no such certainty about Gaston Means's involvement in any criminal action, but the investigators increased rapidly in number. Lawyer McDuffie came to town from Chicago, and visited Gaston Means at his father's house. He wanted to ask some questions about Mrs. King's fortune, he said. McDuffie was accompanied to the Means house by a man named P. C. Ambrose. And whom did Ambrose represent? asked Means. The Federal government, said Ambrose. He was a special agent of the Bureau of Investigation of the Department of Justice.

"I shall have to ask you to leave," Means said. "If Mr. McDuffie wants to talk to me he must be alone."

P. C. Ambrose went away. He did represent the Federal government in a way. He was an agent of the Bureau of Investigation, but at that moment he was on leave from the Bureau, and was acting in behalf of the Northern Trust Company, which had begun to take a very businesslike interest in the King-Means case.

McDuffie then asked Gaston Means to produce all the papers he had regarding the second will of Mr. King. Gaston gave him copies, but McDuffie was not satisfied with copies. He also wanted Gaston to make a statement about his relationship to Mrs. King and her finances.

Gaston suddenly realized that his memory was an almost total blank on that subject. With the necessary papers before him, he said, of course he could explain everything, because he kept complete records. He was perfectly willing to tell McDuffie anything he wanted to know. As to finances, he could account for every nickel of Mrs. King's money that he had handled since he was employed by her in the fall of 1914. At the moment, he did not have the papers available. They were in the apartment in New York. (He only thought they were.)

Gaston could recall that he now had some $50,000 or $60,000 in cash that belonged to Mrs. King, and that all bills and expenses were paid, as of that date. Attorney McDuffie asked Means for a list of Mrs. King's jewelry, and Gaston supplied it: four large diamonds and several smaller ones; a diamond brooch; a diamond solitaire ring; and a lorgnette on a chain with forty-three diamonds. There was other, less important, jewelry, but Gaston could not recall exactly what it was.

McDuffie went off to confer with P. C. Ambrose and the press, and Gaston Means went off with his father to Charlotte for the afternoon, in the automobile driven by the chauffeur.

On the next day, September 14, Hayden Clement made his decision. He had investigated, and there were far too many discrepancies in the stories of Means and the others for his liking. With the discovery of the papers in the Means-King-Melvin apartments at 1155 Park Avenue, a motive for murder had been found.

Gaston B. Means

Dooling had informed Clement—and Clement went to New York to confer with him—that Mrs. King had been worth $600,000 a few months before she took Gaston as her "business manager" and that, as of the day she died, her fortune had vanished.

Clement weighed all this information, and the stories he heard in Concord. He called on the coroner of Cabarrus County and asked him to reopen the case—the first step to an indictment. A few days later, before the coroner's second inquest, in New York City, Mrs. King's safe deposit box was opened by Assistant District Attorney Dooling, who was equipped with a court order. The box, which had once contained some $300,000 in securities, now held a half of a rubber band.[18]

V

The mystery of what had really happened to Maude King's fortune continued. Without his records, Gaston Means could not explain. Gaston had never regarded Maude King's supply of money as limited; he was the incurable optimist. He had convinced himself, in 1915, that it would be relatively easy to push the Northern Trust Company into a settlement with Mrs. King. After all, the company had already settled with her once—when Americus B. Melville broke the original will of James C. King. That question had never gone to court. Gaston saw no reason why the Northern Trust Company should take a different attitude in 1917.

There was one overwhelming reason for the bank's change in attitude. In 1906, the James C. King Home for Old Men was simply a dream, but in 1911 the home was built and, in 1917, the charitable institution had a huge stake in the maintenance of the status quo. Means had said in July that he really did not expect to have to go to court to settle the matter of the second will. It came as a shock to him to realize that the trust company was going to fight him every step of the way.

87

Suddenly the disposition of Maude King's fortune had become important, and Means's part in its disappearance was the subject for at least five separate investigations.[1] The State of North Carolina was conducting one investigation, to determine if the closed case of Maude King's death ought to be opened—in brief, whether or not to charge Means with murder or homicide. The State of New York was investigating, under the vigorous if opinionated John T. Dooling. Dooling already had all the information he wanted. He proposed to bring Means back to New York and try him on half a dozen counts.

The State of Illinois was investigating. Having reopened the King case, a grand jury met to consider evidence of crimes. Means's attorney, Jacob Newman, appeared and gave testimony about the second will and other matters. But, since there was so little documentary evidence still in Chicago, the Illinois investigation lagged.

The Northern Trust Company was investigating, determined to protect its interests, and those of the James C. King Home. P. C. McDuffie was investigating—trying on behalf of Mrs. Robinson and the Robinson boys to discover the whereabouts of Maude King's remaining wealth.

McDuffie's task was an enormous one, and he never could have carried it out had he not had considerable help from Assistant District Attorney Dooling, and indirectly, through his celebrated papers, from Gaston Means.

Mrs. King had been a profligate and empty-headed woman. In her youth she was a great beauty, but even James C. King did not ever believe she had an extraordinary amount of brains. His disposition of the fortune was an indication of that attitude. Maude had been trailed and protected for years by her mother and sister, until Gaston came along to take the sisters into his confidence.

Maude had managed to do away with a large share of her fortune before she ever met Gaston Bullock Means. She began with a total $600,000 in 1905, plus the income from her trust fund. After settling moneys on sister, mother, and brothers, and paying an

Gaston B. Means

enormous fee to Attorney Melville, Maude had only half of the $600,000 for herself, plus all the gifts of cash and jewelry that King was reported to have given her. So the improvident Maude had begun by giving away most of her money.

In spite of this generosity to her relatives, Maude's fortune in 1915 amounted to more than $300,000. She had paid off her third husband, discharged her debts in Chicago, and turned that amount into the hands of Gaston Means over a period of time. It was necessary to account for that amount, plus the $133,000 that had been removed from Mrs. Robinson's trust fund when it was closed out by Means. So Gaston Means, in two years, had in his hands nearly a half million dollars that belonged to Mrs. King and her relatives. The mystery was still what had happened to it.

It was no mystery, really. Gaston spent $16,000 furnishing his apartment, and perhaps $19,000 in furnishing that of Mrs. King. The latter turned over $35,000 in the autumn of 1915 to Mrs. Melvin. Another $35,000 in cash from the sale of stocks went into the account of Mrs. King and was dissipated before she stopped writing her own checks.

That accounted for $100,000.

Means won some $60,000 from Mrs. King over a period of time and for two years he drew an expense allowance of a minimum of $250 a week. The rental on the three apartment suites for two years came to $18,000.

That accounted for the second $100,000.

Mrs. King lent W. R. Patterson $35,000 (doubtless with the advice and counsel of Means). She lent $5,000 to a friend. She bought, or Means bought for her, a Fiat automobile for $9,000. Means claimed to have about $50,000 on hand in Concord.

That accounted for the third $100,000.

Means had on deposit in a Chicago bank about $5,000, and Julie had $5,000 in the Corn Exchange Bank in New York. And Means had lost more than $100,000 of Mrs. King's money in speculation in the cotton market.

That accounted for the fourth $100,000.

The remainder, the last hundred thousand dollars and the income from Mrs. King's trust fund, and Gaston's own earnings as a German agent—all that had gone for high living and the heavy expense of travel and employment of experts in the matter of the second will of James C. King. Further, in the large establishment at 1155 Park Avenue, there were ten mouths to feed, plus those of eight or nine servants. Means had borne a very heavy responsibility for two years. In a way it was remarkable that the money had lasted as long as it had—and it would not have lasted so long had Means not earned money from the Germans, and had not a few speculations and blackmailings, such as those of the Illinois banker, come to successful ends.

But, of course, one could not expect Mrs. Robinson or Lawyer McDuffie to look at it that way. McDuffie tried to get as much information from Means as he could, but failing in his attempts to find the cash, he went to Greensboro, where he secured an order from Federal Judge James E. Boyd to prevent Means or his family from transferring any money. Julie Means tried to draw out the $5,000 she had in the New York account on September 20, but the Concord bank would not honor her check. Later, she tried elsewhere to cash a $3,000 check, with the same result.[2]

September 22 was the date set for the reopening of the coroner's inquest into the death of Maude King. The date had been set in accordance with the wishes of Assistant District Attorney Dooling of New York. He was coming to help North Carolina Solicitor General Hayden Clement present the state's case. When he came, he brought New York Medical Examiner Dr. Otto H Schultz, to testify about the position of the wound in Mrs. King's head.

The Southern Railway train arrived at eleven in the morning. As the grizzled Dooling stepped off the train onto the platform he nearly fell into the arms of Gaston Means, whom he did not know. Means was waiting for his brother Afton, who had been released from New York City custody and had come home with Henry Deutsch.

90

Gaston B. Means

Afton and Deutsch were in the second section of the train, so the smiling Gaston waited on the platform for some time—and as Dooling walked away with Clement and others, Means was pointed out to him.[3]

When the Means party arrived, Gaston loaded them into his large automobile and drove back to the big white house on North Union Street. Large as the house was, however, it was not large enough for the entire household of Gaston Means. Mrs. Melvin was staying with Means, and a nurse was with her. Obviously, now that Maude King was dead and Maisie Melvin was her executrix, Means's loyalties lay with her. And Maisie Melvin believed in Gaston still, although no one else in her family did.

So Gaston made use of a brick house on Depot Street, not too far from the family place. There the overflow was housed—the Deutsches, and Afton and his wife.[4]

Brandon Means, the youngest brother, ran a pool hall across the street from the St. Cloud Hotel (where he sold whisky on the side), and that afternoon, Gaston and Afton went downtown to stand in front of the pool hall and talk to acquaintances.

Concord wore something of a festive air on this day. The mills had shut down since it was Saturday afternoon, and the mill workers and their families came to town, as did the local farmers and sharecroppers. The whole town was buzzing with talk about the King case, since it was common knowledge that it was to be reopened, and that Hayden Clement had brought a high-powered lawyer down from New York to help him.

Gaston drove up and down the street in his new automobile, smiling impishly and waving to friends. Afton stood on the curbing before the pool hall and hailed acquaintances, who greeted him warmly, not having seen him during the ten days he was held in New York City.

Was Gaston guilty or innocent? That was the question on the lips of all the people of the town.

The inquest was reopened, and the witnesses told their stories once again. But this time there were far more witnesses. Captain

William Jones of the New York Police Department testified that there was no "frizzle" of the hair of Mrs. King, which there should have been, if she were shot from close range. The Captain was an internationally famous pistol shot, and he now testified that Mrs. King could not possibly have shot herself at that point two inches behind her left ear—even if she had been left-handed, and she was right-handed.

Solicitor General Hayden Clement conducted the hearing. Clement and the others took a drive out to Blackwelder's Spring. They tried the automatic with the safety on and with it off, and it would not fire no matter how hard they dropped it. They tried to put the little gun in the fork of the tree, but they could not make it stay there. It kept falling out.

They returned to Concord, and to the hearing room. Witnesses came and went. Finally, Clement sent for Sheriff Caldwell and issued a warrant for the arrest of Gaston Means for the murder of Maude King.

Word of the decision reached the Means house on Union Street within a few minutes, and Means went quickly to his father's law office. W. G. Means went with him, and they began calling other lawyers for assistance. Two lawyers were selected to represent Gaston at the legal appearance he would make in the town's rambling courthouse the next day—Edward Cansler of Charlotte, and Lawyer Frank I. Osborne, one of the finest criminal lawyers in North Carolina.

When the sheriff arrived at the W. G. Means office, he was more shamefaced than a stern figure of authority. After all, W. G. was one of the most prominent citizens of the town, and Caldwell had known Gaston since he was a small boy. The sheriff's was an unpleasant duty, but he carried it out with as much grace as he could muster. Instead of carting Gaston off to jail, he remained with the party, because the lawyers wanted, now, to go to the scene of the shooting of Maude King.

By this time, the town of Concord was overrun with big-city

92

newspaper reporters. Not only had the Charlotte and Raleigh newspapers taken an interest in the case, but reporters were on hand from all the major newspapers of New York and Chicago—a fact the people of Concord did not appreciate.

The Means party set out by automobile for Blackwelder's Spring, and a procession of the autos of the press lined up on the Gold Hill road behind them. When the Means party turned off the road, and into the cleared area around the spring, Brandon Means sidled up to the reporters menacingly.

"Now you can go right back," he said.

The lawyers, more conscious than the poolroom proprietor of publicity, decided that the reporters could remain if they stayed out of earshot. The newspapermen stood back, and watched Means pantomime his actions of the night of August 29. Afterward, they all went back to Concord, where Gaston accompanied the sheriff to the two-story brick jail and was locked in a cell at eleven o'clock that night.[5]

The next day, the legal defense committee had risen to six. Julie Means and Gaston's sisters came to see him and bring his home-cooked meals. He remained in his cell and visited for a time with Julie and his baby daughter and other members of the family. He also read all the newspapers avidly, savoring every detail of the case and with his usual warm smile he greeted all the acquaintances who dropped by the jail to pay their respects.

Mrs. Robinson had come to Concord to see justice done, and she was staying at the St. Cloud Hotel. That night, Mrs. Melvin went to her mother's room to persuade her to drop her charges against Gaston, and the two women quarreled bitterly. So strongly did both feel on the subject of Gaston Means that they broke family ties that night.[6]

On September 24, Gaston was arraigned in the Cabarrus County courthouse. Now his lawyers were eight in number. At this preliminary hearing, Justice Pitts was to determine whether or not a cause for action existed. Lawyer Cansler wondered aloud why

New York and Chicago should be administering justice in Cabarrus County, and when he spoke the words "New York" his mouth twisted in a snarl, and his voice cracked with emotion.

The crowd at the courthouse that day was so large that not everyone could get in, and some stood in the halls outside or perched on the steps to gain what information and pleasure they could. They had come for a show. They got one. When the witnesses began outdoing one another in attempts to make telling replies to questions, the courtroom bubbled with laughter. At one point Charles Dry, a farmer who lived about 300 yards from Blackwelder's Spring, was asked how dark it was at 8:30 on the night in question.

"As dark as it was ever going to be," Dry said.

Someone giggled. Brandon Means shot up like a bullet, turned and swept the courtroom with a searching, venomous glare. Gaston Means wrenched his head around—unsmiling now—to identify the unfriendly one among the crowd. For a moment he showed the open hatred of the Means family for their enemies.

Lawyer Cansler tried to ridicule the testimony of Dr. Schultz of New York, and the doctor, who fancied himself as a professional witness, engaged in a verbal battle of wits with the lawyers for the defense.

Schultz gave edged answers to the searching and sarcastic questions of the lawyer. As one or the other scored a point, the crowd laughed and cheered them on. Justice Pitts became annoyed and threatened to bring the offenders before the bench and find them in contempt.

"Oh, let them go ahead," said Lawyer Cansler. "That is the way they went on when the Savior was crucified."

Solicitor General Clement leaped to his feet, objecting.

The defense lawyers tried to show that someone had paid the special witnesses from New York and Chicago to come to Concord to persecute Gaston Means. That was the kernel of the defense from that point on. They pointed knowingly at C. B. Ambrose, the man who wore the hats of government agent and private detective simultaneously. They questioned the motivations of Assistant District Attorney Dooling and the Chicago medical examiner.

The two sides might have fought the case for days, had not an event occurred, on September 25, which changed the minds of the defense counsel as to the best method of procedure. John Dooling told the newspapermen that he was going to seek extradition of Gaston Means to New York, to answer before a New York court charges of conspiracy to murder Mrs. King.

The defense counsel then hurried to bring the hearing to an end, and to retain the jurisdiction over Means within the hands of a North Carolina court. Attorney Cansler asked the Judge to hold Gaston Means for a grand jury rather than place him at the mercy of the New York City District Attorney's office. That was the Judge's final decision.

When the hearing ended, Means and Sheriff Caldwell walked out of the room, and the sheriff stopped to hand a paper to Dooling. Means leaned over to talk to Dooling, smiling his dimpled smile. Dooling recoiled and leaped to his feet as though confronted by a snake.

"Get him away from here," Dooling shouted to the sheriff.

The paper the sheriff had handed Dooling may have been the cause of this outburst. It was a court order to the New Yorker to turn over all the papers he had found at 1155 Park Avenue to Superior Judge Webb of North Carolina. Means's attorneys, acting in the name of Mrs. Melvin and Means, had informed the court that the papers were necessary to the Means defense and to the conduct of the business of the estate.

As Gaston Means and the sheriff were engaged in this scene, a few blocks down Union Street Afton stood in the lobby of the St. Cloud Hotel. He was talking to Mrs. E. P. Jones, the wife of the manager of the hotel. Afton demanded the keys to the rooms of Dooling, Dr. Schultz, and the other northerners who had come to Concord for the hearing. Mrs. Jones refused to surrender the keys.

If Afton intended to become ugly, he had no opportunity, for. at that moment the Dooling party arrived in the lobby and broke up the discussion.

The northerners went upstairs, while Afton waited for reinforcements. In a few minutes, along came Brandon Means, W. R. Patterson, Henry Deutsch, one of the Means lawyers, the sheriff, two deputies, and a policeman from the town of Concord. Trailed by the press, they all went upstairs to the room of Captain Jones, which Dooling and his associates were using as an office.

First in the door were Afton Means and the lawyer, demanding in loud voices that the New Yorkers hand over all the papers and waving a copy of the court order.

As Afton gesticulated, sitting on the bed next to Dooling was Attorney General Manning. Manning was composing by hand at that moment a letter to Dooling advising him not to turn the papers over to the Means representatives, because they were necessary to the case of the State of North Carolina against Means.

Afton told the sheriff to do his duty. The sheriff stepped forward, but so did three New York policemen in the room, and they warned the sheriff that they were armed and would not let him take the papers.

The Means move was blocked, it seemed. Afton stood in the room for a moment, irresolute, then turned on his heel and walked out the door. The others followed.

In a few moments Afton was back with a deputy, and he called on the whole group to surrender to arrest.

"We're going to get the papers one way or another," he said. Furthermore, the officers from New York were breaking the law, since it was against the law to possess a revolver in North Carolina.

As the two groups argued, a bellboy came into the room carrying a long blue envelope, which he handed to Assistant District Attorney Dooling.

"Ah," said Dooling. "This clinches the case."

Gaston B. Means

Afton was so upset by that remark that he abandoned the argument and left the room.

What was it that had clinched the case in the mind of the Assistant District Attorney from New York?

Nothing at all. Just some personal papers that had followed him from the city. They had nothing to do with the Means case, and Dooling had made the remark only because he understood the effect it would have on Afton Means.

Nor were there actually any important papers among the crowd that day. Dooling had brought two large boxes, one labeled "valuable papers," but this was strictly for show. The box held clothing. He had brought a few copies of documents, but the originals were all safely held in the office of the District Attorney in New York.

Cheerily, before he left Concord for New York City, Assistant District Attorney predicted that there could soon be "other arrests," and Afton Means, Henry Deutsch, and W. R. Patterson must have shuddered in unpleasant anticipation.[7]

But there were no more arrests as Concord waited for the calling of the county's grand jury and the establishment of the winter term of the state criminal court. The lawyers of the town, always a close-knit group, enjoyed some excitement when Lawyer T. D. Manners of the Means counsel was involved in a fist-fight with County Attorney Williams over the rough treatment accorded witness Charlie Dry in the courtroom on the day of the hearing. Soon that blew over, and before long every attorney in all of Concord was allied with the defense of Gaston Bullock Means. It was a remarkable record of solidarity, and one that extended throughout the town. After the preliminary hearing, Concord began to take a defensive attitude toward the case and a protective attitude toward Gaston Means. He might be a "son of a bitch," as some of the people of Cabarrus County certainly believed, but he was "their son of a bitch" and no one appreciated the attempts by New York and Chicago Yankees to invade the South once again. They did not even like the way the Yankees spoke the name of their town: Conc'-ord. In Cabarrus County the name was always pronounced Con-cord, with equal accent on both syllables. And when the Yankees called it Conc'-ord in their way, the Cabarrus County men and women spoke up:

"We might have been defeated, but we were never conquered."

There were some among the citizens of Concord who said that the Means family had the whole town frightened. Reporters who wanted to interview businessmen about the case discovered that they would discuss Gaston Means confidentially, but neither publicly nor for attribution. But fear, important as it was in the attitude of Concord, was not the most important factor in the public attitude toward the coming trial. Loyalty was. It was a question of loyalty to the man and to the region, and a question of showing the North that Cabarrus County could take care of its own problems without any assistance from New York.

Means remained in jail through the rest of September and October. Bail could have been arranged, but his lawyers told him not to seek bail. They preferred to see him as the mistreated symbol of northern authoritarianism. If he got out of jail, it might turn some of the farmers and workmen from the mills against him. Gaston in jail was a martyr. Gaston out might have been a menace.[8]

Businessmen came to the jail house in the afternoon and evenings to pay calls on Gaston Means. His wife and child were regular daily visitors. Wife, mother, sisters all combined to cook for him.

A few odd events occurred during the waiting period. On the night of October 2, thieves entered the apartment of Josephine Foraker in New York City. Mrs. Foraker, daughter-in-law of the one-time senator from Ohio, was the lady who owed Maude King $5,000 on the personal note. Mrs. Foraker had gone to parties in the apartments of Means and Mrs. King many times, had played dice with them, and had lost money to Means. Among the items stolen from Mrs. Foraker's apartment were all the papers which bore on her financial dealings with Mrs. King, including a diary.[9]

On October 29, the fall term of Cabarrus Superior Court was convened. The presiding judge was Gaston Means's old friend, Judge E. B. Cline, who had enjoyed the summer auto rides in Gaston's new car.

Two days later, when Means was indicted by the grand jury, Solicitor General Hayden Clement asked Judge Cline for a change of venue. He said public sentiment in Cabarrus County was so overwhelmingly in favor of the defendant that a fair trial could not be held there. He offered an affidavit which showed that, since 1914, three bills for murder had been presented in the county, and that in each case the defendant had been acquitted. If one wanted to commit murder, apparently, the best place in the United States to do it was Cabarrus County, North Carolina.

Besides, said the solicitor general, the defense had so tied up the legal talent of the town that the state could not hire adequate assistance in such matters as jury selection, where the lawyer's knowledge of character and relationships is far more important than his understanding of the fine points of the law. Hayden Clement was hard put to find anyone in the area to help him prosecute the case. He never did find a Concord lawyer, for all were on the Means defense committee, but he did hire a lawyer from Statesville a few miles away.[10] Clement said the case had been so widely discussed in the county that he did not believe the court could find twelve men who had no fixed opinions.

Five of Cabarrus County's lawyers represented Gaston Means in court that day. They argued that Means had many enemies (which was true, although most of them were now intimidated) and that only half the lawyers in town were on the Means defense committee (which was untrue in implication if not in fact). Any friendship felt for the defendant in the area was canceled out, they said, by the prejudicial attitudes of the metropolitan papers. It might be impossible for Means to have a fair trial, but the problem was that too many had adjudged him guilty. Notwithstanding,

99

the lawyers were willing to try the case in Cabarrus County. They presented affidavits from fifteen important citizens who said they were sure Gaston Means could have a fair trial in Concord.

For reasons of his own, Judge Cline wanted to try the case. Hayden Clement believed that Cline wanted the publicity—for the Means case had attracted national interest the like of which had never before been seen in western North Carolina. So Judge Cline ruled against the attorney for the state, and set the date for trial at November 26.

Gaston Means was calm and smiling. Never did his confidence in acquittal seem to desert him, and he cheered his wife and other womenfolk when their spirits fell low. He read avidly; not a magazine or newspaper article about his case was missed. He continued to read, as he waited for trial.

On November 26, Means was brought to the courtroom on the second floor of the rickety old Cabarrus County courthouse and seated with his wife, who would remain beside him every day of the trial.

Solicitor General Clement expected a difficult time in getting a jury. The original panel consisted of thirty-six veniremen, but a special venire of 150 was prepared. On the first day, the jury was selected easily—too easily, Clement realized later. Clement did not know these people, and L. C. Cline, the Statesville attorney who was helping him, had not lived in Concord for many years. Eight farmers were chosen and three mill hands—all of them said they had paid little attention to the case and had no opinions.

The twelfth juror was J. Frank Goodman, a member of the board of county commissioners. Clement was enthusiastic about Goodman's selection for the jury, because he had heard Goodman, outside the courtroom, make a remark to the effect that Means ought to be hanged. From Hayden Clement's point of view that made Goodman an admirable juror, and he passed him quickly. Only when the defense passed Goodman immediately and without question did Clement realize that all was not as it ought to be. Later he was to believe he had been jobbed by the defense and Juror

100

Gaston B. Means

Goodman, whose name was very similar to that of Joe Goodman, brother-in-law of Gaston Bullock Means.[11]

The state had spared no expense in preparing its case against Gaston Means. Captain William Jones of the New York police came to be a witness, and brought samples of human skin to show the jury what powder marks looked like. Assistant District Attorney Dooling came down to Concord from New York to help with the case, and began to present a part of it for the state. Willard J. Rockefeller, manager of the Chicago Beach Hotel, appeared to testify that Mrs. King and Mrs. Melvin were constantly under the surveillance of Means or his employees. Dr. Burmeister, the pathologist, came from Chicago to show that it was impossible for Mrs. King to have fired the shot that killed her.

The state brought Attorney Americus J. Melville to testify about Means's relationships with Mrs. King. Melville did not advance their case much, because he said that when he met Means in 1915 Mrs. King said Means was saving money for her, and he never saw any indication of domination of Mrs. King by Means. Melville also recalled an incident in which an investment made by Means brought Mrs. King a $26,000 profit—and Means got $8,000 of it for his efforts.

Throughout this testimony Means sat in his chair at the defense table, smiling and unruffled, even when "Old Seventy-Six," Mrs. Robinson, was called to testify against him.

Mrs. Robinson's appearance caused an uproar in the courtroom. Maisie Melvin rushed to the entrance to try to prevent her mother from coming in to talk against the man she admired. Court officials restrained Mrs. Melvin. In the hall, Henry Deutsch raised his hands and shouted, "Don't take that woman in there," to the bailiffs who were escorting Mrs. Robinson into court. The bailiffs did take Mrs. Robinson into the courtroom. She testified that Means kept her away from her daughter. She said the signatures on the paper revoking her trust were forgeries. She said Means kept her locked up in the hotel at Chicago.

In cross-examination, the wily lawyer Osborne led Mrs. Robinson down the garden path, treating her as gently as though she were his own mother. Before he was finished, she had admitted that she could not recognize her own signature, and that Means did nothing to stop her from going driving in her own automobile in Chicago.

Broker John R. Todd from Chicago came to testify that Means had opened a margin account in cotton in 1916, and he had posed then as a German commercial agent. Means gave Captain Boy-Ed and the Hamburg-American line as references, and talked loftily of German affairs. The broker was impressed, and he paid for it. Means left him holding that debt of $35,000 and he and another broker a debt of $8,000.

On December 3, the state rested its case, and the defense began. The defense was significantly changed too. Now the contention was not that the gun had fallen from the crotch of the tree, but that Maude King had picked it up and accidentally shot herself. Half a dozen North Carolina doctors testified that it was possible for Mrs. King to have fired the shot. One, Dr. W. H. Wadsworth, tried to demonstrate, but could only put the gun in position with the aid of the defense counsel. On cross-examination by John Dooling, the doctors admitted that Afton Means had helped them in all their tests.

Colonel W. G. Means testified that Belle Means had burned the big picture-hat worn by Mrs. King, at his direction. The hat might have told the story of the powder burns, or lack of them.

The jury visited Blackwelder's Spring, and heard a great deal of talk about the two shots that were fired. (The mystery was cleared up by Captain Bingham, who said that he fired one shot from his rifle into the air when he reached the body of Mrs. King.)

Finally, Gaston Means took the stand in his own defense. He seemed completely at ease, composed, sitting with his legs crossed and with a bright gleam in his eye, and answering lawyer Osborne's questions in a booming and confident voice. It was as though he looked forward to the encounter—an actor whose stage was the courtroom.

Gaston B. Means

For six hours, Means testified about matters of his life and associations, without getting to the time of the crime. He said he had quit the Germans when he discovered that they were trying to foment war between the United States and Mexico in 1915—in what was called the Huerta Plot, an effort to restore dictatorship to Mexico. He then had gone to Washington and told all to the Federal authorities, he said.

Captain Boy-Ed had discovered that Means had thrown a monkey wrench into the German plans, and had fired Means—that was Gaston's new story, and, if it bore very little relationship to the stories he had told before about his friendliness with the Germans right up to the time Boy-Ed left the United States, then it must be remembered that this was 1917, and American boys were dying in the trenches of France.

Gaston explained away the strange letters with which he had beguiled Mrs. King that summer, and the reason for the trip to Asheville. These actions were part of a plan to keep Mrs. King from worrying and to keep the Northern Trust Company from harassing her. (Even as Means testified, it was said that the company's man, C. B. Ambrose, was sitting in the audience of the courtroom, dressed as a woman to avoid detection.)

Means explained that he had transferred Mrs. King's money to his accounts because suits were threatened against her. He had cut off Mrs. Robinson's trust only to give her more money every month than the trust company supplied. He had made money on some cotton speculations and had paid Maude King her share.

Direct examination was one thing; cross-examination was another, and particularly when conducted by that old lion, John T. Dooling, who began to hate Gaston Means long before he met him, simply because he suspected Means of breaking the law.

But on cross-examination Means comported himself as well as he had on direct testimony. Dooling grew excited and sharp in tone. Means answered in his booming voice, his tones running the register of emotion, from nostalgia to righteous indignation. At one point, the exchanges betwen Means and Dooling grew so heated that Means began to suggest that Dooling put his questions in a "more gentlemanly manner." The Judge admonished both men to observe the rules of the court.

"Gaston Means was the smartest witness I have ever examined," Hayden Clement said later.

Means *was* smart, and he was a consummate courtroom actor. For three days he was grilled by Dooling, but he remained fresh and confident throughout, although clashes between them were so frequent that Judge Cline ordered the sheriff to stand within the bar to preserve order. As Means made what he thought were important points, he gave knowing smiles to the jury. He denied that he had ever used loaded dice against Mrs. King, or that he had ever won any money from her in dice games.

Then where did he get all his money? he was asked.

From a man named Heller, he said, a German commercial attaché of some kind, a tall, handsome, military type who had an office somewhere around 11 Broadway.

Almost every day there was threat of an outbreak in the court, and after court had adjourned for the day. The threat was not against Means, but against this outside prosecutor, the "damned Yankee" who had come down South to railroad Gaston. Hayden Clement was conscious of the threat, and finally, in the midst of Dooling's spirited cross-examination, Dooling withdrew. It had been decided that he was doing more harm than good in the state's cause, because of the sentiments his northern accent aroused.

Means kept the courtroom in constant furor, and kept his attorneys worried. One day he arrived in court with a gun in the waistband of his trousers, withdrew it, and carelessly laid it on the table before him. When Judge Cline read of that in the newspapers he exploded, and then Means explained suavely that he had merely planned to use the gun to illustrate a point. (And where did the prisoner, confined to jail, get a gun, anyhow?)

The most damaging evidence was that of the state's witnesses which tended to show that Mrs. King could not have shot herself.

Gaston B. Means

The defense counsel were much worried by this aspect, particularly after their experts had been made to look ridiculous by needing help to show the opposite. One night at the Means home, however, Julie Means demonstrated how the shot could have been fired, and she did so effective a job that the defense put her on the stand for that purpose.

Means admitted that Mrs. King's assets had diminished during his association with her. He did not deny speculations or any other actions, but he gave a most convincing account of how he had done all in the interests of Maude King herself.

As the trial drew to a close, all the attorneys wanted to be heard in argument. On December 12, after seven hours of argument, there remained ten addresses still to be heard, four for the prosecution and six for the defense. But finally all the lawyers had their say, and the jury was instructed to find one of three verdicts, first-degree murder, second-degree murder, or acquittal.

Clement, in summing up, said he was sure that Means had killed Mrs. King, that he had premeditated the murder, and that he had found no other way out, having squandered most of her estate and knowing that a time of accounting was approaching. The defense attorneys said the death of Mrs. King was an accident. In the midst of their dramatic appeal, Belle Means broke down completely and had to be removed from the court.

The case went to the jury at 7 P.M. on December 15. Judge Cline made a clear and sharp charge to the jury, so straightforward that Means was shaken for the first time.

"I guess this is the end of me," he whispered to Julie at the defense table. She looked at him, and saw the glitter of a half-formed tear in his eye. "It looks like good-bye, sweetheart."

When the jury went out on this Saturday evening, there was no word for many hours. It was 9:30 on Sunday morning when the jury instructed Sheriff Caldwell to get Judge Cline to the courthouse. Cline hurried to the courthouse, where the jury was ready. He did not know whether or not the jurors had a verdict, and he warned the crowd that began to assemble in the courtroom that he would not tolerate any demonstrations or attempts to approach the jurors until they were discharged. Gaston Means was brought from jail, and his wife, father, mother, sisters, brothers, and friends came to the courtroom too, to hear the verdict. J. Frank Goodman, foreman of the jury, announced the verdict. They found Gaston Bullock Means innocent of the charges made against him and acquitted him. That was the end of it, and he could never be tried again for murdering Maude King.[12]

Means's smile broadened as he heard the news, and he was not again to admit that he had ever had a doubt about the outcome. He threw one arm around his wife and hugged her. She and Kate Means fell into one another's arms, weeping. Means found it difficult to reach the door of the courtroom, so many were the surrounding hands thrust at him in congratulations. The forces of the Yankee North had been defeated!

The prosecution was stunned. John Dooling, who had gone back to New York, began muttering that he intended to find a way to bring Means to trial in that state. Hayden Clement had no such idea. There was no more he could do in North Carolina, and the matter was ended as far as he was concerned.

Years later, it was rumored that the defense had not been entirely without weapons in the case—its weapons consisting of three jurors who had decided before hearing the case that they were favorably inclined to the defense point of view. Two of the jurors were intimidated, and one was bribed.[13]

But no matter, Gaston Bullock Means was a free man once again.

VI

Acquittal gave Gaston Bullock Means an opportunity to begin life all over again as an honest man, an important figure in his native community. For a brief moment it seemed that he might be ready to choose such a course. He bought a small herd of Guernsey cattle from Gus Archibald, a Concord man who had been experimenting with grain feeding for milk cows, and Means pursued the experiment for a short time—until the lure of the city proved too great. In a few weeks Gaston tired of farm work and sold the herd.[1] He moved North, to New York and Chicago, to pursue the fortune of James C. King, leaving Julie and his daughter in the care of his family.

Perhaps no other course was open to Means at this point in his life, given his temperament and background. He could not live without excitement and excitement cost money. He was thirty-eight years old, without visible source of income, and Julie Means was going to have another baby. He had no home except his father's house, since the owners of the apartment at 1155 Park Avenue had evicted the King, Melvin, and Means tenants on

107

September 1, for non-payment of rent. His furnishings were in storage in New York City, and the "second will" of James C. King was in the hands of the New York District Attorney's office, having been taken there from a safe deposit box where Means had kept it.[2]

The costs of the trial had eaten up most of the money that Gaston Means had in his possession. He had run up a $300 bill at George Richmond's general store, to feed the people in the house on West Depot. Apparently he was unable to pay the bill, for he did not pay it.[3] In January, 1918, Julie Means brought suit against a temporary administrator of the estate of Maude King in New York, appointed by a New York court, to secure the $4,907 that remained in her account in the Corn Exchange Bank. She had written a check on the bank in favor of the Cabarrus Savings Bank of North Carolina, but the New York bank had refused to honor the check.[4]

In a way, Gaston Means's hand was forced by the New York authorities. Means had at least thought about filing the "second will" in California, but this plan was forestalled. The New York officials sent the "second will" to Chicago. There, on February 5, the Attorney General of Illinois filed a petition with the Probate Court of Cook County. The state authorities wanted to clear up the matter, because as long as this document was outstanding, the interests of the James C. King Home for Old Men were threatened. This action forced the hands of Gaston Means and Mrs. Melvin. They must either attempt to support the claim in Chicago or let it die. So Mrs. Melvin filed her own petition, asking that the old will be set aside in favor of the new one, which made her the principal beneficiary.[5] When Gaston Means had said that Maude King's death meant the end of all his efforts he had been quite wrong, knowingly or not. For if the new King will was valid, Mrs. Melvin would have charge of the three-and-a-half-million-dollar estate.

To prepare for this legal battle, Means had gone to New York City early in the new year to find a new lawyer. Carl Schurz had withdrawn from the case. He found Colonel Thomas B. Felder, a

Gaston B. Means

displaced Georgian with a reputation that was already becoming unsavory. Then he moved on to Chicago, where Attorney Jacob Newman had also resigned the case. In Chicago, he employed Roy C. Keehn.[6]

Filed in the winter, the case was deferred until May, which gave Means time to go home for the birth of Julie's second child in April. The whole Means family escorted Julie to Mercy Hospital in Charlotte, and there the boy Billy was born.

Home again, Gaston did not waste his time. He did not feel that the acquittal removed the taint of criminality from him, so on May 1 he persuaded the prosecuting attorney of Concord to swear out a warrant for one "Otto Schumann, a German interned as enemy alien, with several aliases." Schumann, said the warrant, had murdered Maude King in an attempt to assassinate Gaston B. Means.

The warrant was accompanied by a statement from the prosecuting attorney. It said:

1. Gaston Bullock Means had severed his connections with the German government in 1916 because of its attitude to the United States government and the then strained relations.

2. In July, 1917, in New York City, Gaston Means called on German interests in connection with profits belonging to Mrs. King and himself that were in their custody—profits derived from shipments of rubber and copper to Germany long before the declaration of war in 1917. Means's profits in this transaction were $85,000; Mrs. King's were $145,000.

In this interview Means said he had completed his investigations and was going to offer his services to the government or accept a permanent position heading a newspaper, which would enable him to be of service to the United States since the time had come for every citizen to be of all possible service to his country.

Immediately afterward, he and the editor of the "leading newspaper" had planned to investigate where the German base on this side of the Atlantic (submarines) was located.

The German interests then knew that Means had full knowledge of their rubber and copper transactions.

3. Means made plans on the King will probate. He put all the facts in the hands of Mrs. King's attorneys. He made arrangements with Carl Schurz for Mrs. King to meet Charles Evans Hughes regarding the King will.

4. Otto Schumann then followed Gaston Means to North Carolina and followed him around on a motorcycle.

5. Means was also under surveillance by C. B. Ambrose, the agent of the Northern Trust Company of Chicago. Ambrose and Schumann, before August 29, met and had numerous conferences. Ambrose was reporting to W. S. Miller, attorney for the Northern Trust Company, while Schumann was spying on Means and Mrs. King for the German "interests."

6. On the evening of August 29, Otto Schumann on a motorcycle followed Means and Mrs. King, and turned up the plantation road that runs in front of the church and schoolhouse just above the spring, and to M. L. Cline's farm.

7. That in the church that evening there was a man and woman whose veracity in Cabarrus County will not be questioned, who saw Otto Schumann go up this road with his motorcycle, leave his motorcycle in the woods, and walk to the underbrush on the hill just above the spring.

8. That shortly after the shot they saw Otto Schumann come back to his motorcycle, get on it, and leave at a rapid rate of speed.

9. That Charles Dry and his wife testified properly at the trial that they heard someone run through the underbrush, and saw a light from what appeared to be an auto going over the hill. This was Schumann on his motorcycle.

10. C. B. Ambrose and W. S. Miller and the Northern Trust

Gaston B. Means

Company conspired. Ambrose made written reports to Miller, and they suppressed these facts. Ambrose was sent away by Miller, to avoid his having to testify at the trial.

11. There were eyewitnesses, as Ambrose publicly said.

12. From the underbrush above the spring, Otto Schumann, with a rifle equipped with a supplemental chamber, fired at Gaston Means as Means was getting a drink of water. The bullet hit a rock on top of the spring and glanced and struck Mrs. King. Mrs. King fell, crumpled up, mortally wounded, with her feet under her and that was when her ankle was broken.

13. That C. B. Ambrose was employed by the Northern Trust Company all the time he was in North Carolina and was not representing the Department of Justice, as stated by A. B. Bielaski, chief of the Department of Justice Bureau of Investigation in letters to Senators John Sharp Williams of Mississippi, Calder of New York, and Simmons of North Carolina.

14. That the Northern Trust Company was equally guilty with Ambrose in perpetrating a fraud on the courts of North Carolina and the attorneys who prosecuted Means and that Ambrose was the instigator of the proceedings against Means as agent for the Northern Trust Company.

15. That Gaston Means was the victim of the Northern Trust Company as a result of the malicious reports given to the press so effectively by the agents and representatives of the Northern Trust Company, which reports and statements concerning Means were not based on facts and emanated from Chicago and New York City.[7]

This incredible statement, from which emanated the words of Gaston Means in every sentence, was filed as a court document, by an American lawyer, and accepted by Police Justice A. B. Palmer of Concord. The statement was a tribute to the Means family influence in Concord. It accomplished precisely what Means wanted. The story was picked up by the newspapers of New York

111

and Chicago and told in detail. Had Means made such charges,
he would have laid himself open for a half dozen libel suits. (About
the only person named who could not have sued was the non-
existent Otto Schumann.) But Means had not made the statements; they had been made in a document supplementing a warrant by an officer of a court. Perhaps those concerned could have
sued anyhow, but the difficulties were apparent.

If anyone believed all the statement, they would believe that the
patriotic Gaston B. Means, target of an assassin, had first been
cruelly hunted, then misused by authorities who were led by the
very organization that was now contesting Mr. King's second will.
The statement explained what had happened to Mrs. King's fortune, and showed Gaston Means as a man badly sinned against.

Two weeks after the issuance of the warrant, it still lay idly in
the hands of the Concord police, but Gaston Means was in Chicago,
ready for the opening of the second will case. Means's father died
that month, following an operation for gallstones, and with all the
family around him, he was buried in Oakwood Cemetery, beneath
a huge tree, in a plot on the side of the hill. His was the first grave
to be dug in the family burying ground he established there. At
the funeral services in All Saints Episcopal Church, every member
of the congregation was honored as a pallbearer. W. G. Means had
long been an officer of the church, as well as of his town, and the
funeral was a large one.[8]

Gaston took Julie and the children to Chicago for a time, but
when it became apparent that the will case would drag out for a
year or more, he moved the family to New York. They spent a week
in the house of William J. Burns, then moved to Staten Island,
where Means rented a house.[9]

Gaston Means spent the summer of 1918 commuting between
New York and Chicago, where he was a key witness, as well as the
manager of Mrs. Melvin's attempt to probate the new will. He
told now of having received $85,000 at one time and $92,000 another time from the Germans for his efforts in their behalf, and of

having delivered $1.3 million in cash to Captain Boy-Ed one night.

Asked for what Means was paid so highly, Gaston said: "I made the money the way lots of other Americans did, some of them the biggest lawyers in New York. I can easily tell you the place where I called for it—right in the Trinity churchyard at a designated tombstone."

That was the kind of story the newspapers liked, and they gave prominence to Gaston's tales. He told the court how Captain Boy-Ed had been deported—which everyone in America knew if they read the newspapers. But the way Means told the story, it seemed that he was revealing secret information.

"And now, for the first time," he said, "the public knows why Captain Boy-Ed was sent back to Germany."

Means dropped many names in his testimony. He said he had conferred (over the German affair) with Joseph P. Tumulty, secretary to President Wilson; with Secretary of the Navy Josephus Daniels; with J. P. Morgan; with John R. Rathom, editor of the Providence *Journal.* He had (said Means) given information which resulted in the arrest of a German agent named Werner Horn en route to blow up a Canadian bridge, and had warned of plans to destroy government buildings in Ottawa. He repeated the claim that the German government owed Mrs. King's estate a great deal of money—now the amount had become $167,000.

Mrs. Melvin's attorney, Roy Keehn, tried to connect the Northern Trust Company with the prosecution of Means for murder in the Maude King case. He called as witness a photographer who had made pictures of the will for John Dooling, a typewriter expert who had been asked by Dooling to look at the will, and another expert. He hoped to show that the bills had been paid by the Northern Trust Company.

The photographer said he had been paid, although he did not remember by whom. The typewriter expert said he had been paid by the New York District Attorney's office. The other expert said he had never been paid at all.[10]

In midsummer the case was recessed until fall, and Means went home to Staten Island, to seek work in New York again with his old friend William J. Burns. This period was probably the happiest in Julie Means's life, or so she said. She had two children to keep her company while Gaston was away, and when "Bud" came home he always brought gifts. One'time he brought the children a handful of hair nets, and they found them to be wonderful toys. His gifts were small ones, because they had very little money. Gaston was spending heavily for the services of handwriting experts and others who could help substantiate the claim that the second will was valid.[11]

At issue in the will case were the dates and signatures of the witnesses to the will. Mrs. Melvin testified that on October 9, 1905, James C. King called her husband, herself, and Mrs. King into his room, read his new will, and then signed it. Dr. Melvin and Mrs. Melvin signed as witnesses. Byron L. Smith, head of the Northern Trust Company, also signed the will, but not on that day. He had been out of town, and signed later.[12]

Sadly, of all those who signed the will, the only living witness was Mrs. Melvin (and the Northern Trust Company's experts said that Mrs. Melvin's was the only unforged signature on the will).

Dates and names—they accounted for the intensive efforts of Gaston Means and his relatives from 1915 to 1917 to establish the whereabouts of all these witnesses to James King's signature, and the story that Smith had signed the will later was the result of necessity. It had been impossible to locate all the people in the right place on any date before James C. King died.

As Gaston Means could understand from the attitudes of the opposing counsel and the court during the first phases of the trial, another problem existed now, and that involved the good character of Means and Mrs. Melvin. During the recess, Gaston set out to build his good character, and in the only way he understood, by an act that was impudent and daring.

The first step involved Roy Keehn, for Keehn was not simply a

114

lawyer but an official of the Hearst newspaper organization in Chicago. Means sought Keehn's ear for one of the long, confidential conversations he enjoyed so much and manipulated with such thespian dexterity. In the course of the meeting, Means unfolded a story about the "secret papers" of Captain Boy-Ed. The papers had not been destroyed, as a student of history might expect, but were secreted in the United States. Means himself had possession of the Boy-Ed papers. They were in his home town of Concord.

Means proposed that if Roy Keehn would finance his efforts and put him in touch with government officers, Means would turn the papers over to the government in such a way that the Hearst organization would have a sensational, exclusive story that involved some of the most important names in American public affairs.

It seemed too good an opportunity for any newspaper organization to ignore, a chance to help the government in the war effort, and at the same time to publish important articles and get credit for public service. Means's story had the ring of truth, too, for he had admittedly served as a German agent and was known to be intimate with Captain Karl Boy-Ed. Roy Keehn accepted the proposition and furnished Gaston Means with money. He also wrote to Secretary Joseph Tumulty at the White House. He said he thought he could get important papers for the government. Roy Keehn had every faith in Gaston Means, he told Tumulty.

"While Means has been tried for murder, accused of forging this will and of being a German agent, I have found him to be truthful, accurate, and absolutely dependable," said Keehn.

Tumulty sent the Keehn letter to Secretary of State Robert Lansing. Lansing replied that it seemed to him to be a matter for the Justice Department, and Tumulty then sent the correspondence to the Attorney General. John Lord O'Brian, special assistant to the Attorney General, replied to Tumulty, saying that Means's story was an old one. Up to that time, he noted, Means had never been able to make good his claims about "information."[13]

Working through William J. Burns and Lieutenant Colonel

Nicholas Biddle of military intelligence, Means and Keehn arranged a meeting with Biddle's subordinate, Captain Charles L. Lloyd. The meeting was held in Chicago, and there Means gave Captain Lloyd enough information to excite the interest of military intelligence. He promised, furthermore, to come to New York and Washington as soon as possible and get to work on the matter. Early in September, Means returned to Staten Island. He went away for a week—"to Washington," he said. In mid-September, Means told Colonel Biddle he was ready, and on September 21, Captain Lloyd talked to Means in New York.[14]

When Means wanted to impress someone, one of his most effective tricks was to increase the size of the bait for the fish who nibbled near his hook. He did so here, mentioning to Lloyd at that second meeting that he also knew of the existence of some papers belonging to the most important German in America—Count von Bernstorff, the Imperial government's ambassador until 1917. It would take some shrewd investigative work, Means said, but he felt certain that he could locate the von Bernstorff papers.

Yet, before they went further, Means said, one point must be clarified. As Captain Lloyd would remember, only two people in the United States besides Gaston Means had ever known of the hiding place of the Boy-Ed papers. They were Captain Lloyd and Roy Keehn.

For what reason, then, had an attempt been made since their first meeting to obtain possession of the Boy-Ed papers? Was Military Intelligence playing him false, or was Roy Keehn pulling some trick in behalf of the Hearst organization? Means was worried. He was being followed and he did not like it.

Captain Lloyd knew that Military Intelligence was not shadowing Means. He checked. Neither was the Department of Justice. At their next meeting, a few days later, Means told Captain Lloyd that he had been approached by a German on the Staten Island Ferry. The German had tried to bargain with him for the von Bernstorff papers, since Dr. Edward A. Rumely, formerly of the New York *Evening Mail,* was then on trial for his work for the

Germans in violation of American laws, and the papers would certainly incriminate Rumely. The German wanted Means to find and turn over to his people the von Bernstorff papers and any documents that might tend to show the ownership of the New York *Evening Mail* by the German government. Means mentioned the name of a lawyer whom Captain Lloyd knew to be connected with the Rumely matter. This verifiable fact stimulated Captain Lloyd's interest and his faith in Means. The next day Means said he had seen the lawyer, and an outright offer had been made to him: the Germans would give him money to go after the von Bernstorff papers. Means knew where they were, near Skylands, Virginia, in an old distillery in the "moonshiner" district. The Germans now offered him money to go to Skylands and get the papers. What should he do? asked Means. Should he take the German money and go, or not?

Means built the implication, without ever saying so directly, that the von Bernstorff papers under consideration were documents of the utmost importance to Military Intelligence. As Gaston expected, Captain Lloyd rushed to the office of Lieutenant Colonel Biddle, and the next evening Means was invited within the paneled walls of New York City's Harvard Club, where business was never supposed to raise its head, to discuss the business of securing the von Bernstorff papers. Military Intelligence had swallowed Gaston's bait.

Colonel Biddle and Captain Lloyd wanted Means to tell them where the von Bernstorff papers were located, but Means would not do that. He had already arranged everything, Means said. In fact, his own man had already left for Skylands, where he would secure the von Bernstorff documents and take them to Concord. It would be most unseemly for a stranger to be seen in the "moonshiner" country of Virginia. No stranger would ever find the papers, said Gaston Means. The man he had sent had been there before and would have no difficulty. He would go to Concord, where Means must go for the Boy-Ed papers. Then Military Intelligence would have them all. On Thursday, September 26, Gaston and Captain Lloyd left the Means house at 193 Franklin Avenue, New Brighton, Staten Island, to begin their trip to Concord. The next day, they arrived in the town and registered at the St. Cloud Hotel, then set out to find the Boy-Ed papers.

Means took Captain Lloyd by auto to Charlotte, and that same evening from there to Belmont. The auto pulled up before the Belmont Monastery, which also housed a Catholic school. Captain Lloyd waited in the auto. Means went inside the monastery and later emerged with a box two feet long and a foot wide. Gaston announced that the papers were not all there, that they had been rearranged since he last saw them, but that he knew where the rest of the papers were located. When his friend returned from Skylands, he would find the remainder of the Boy-Ed papers, too. There was no need to worry, Means added. He would take these papers home to his mother's house, where he planned to spend the night, and would bring them to the hotel for Lloyd to look over the next day. Lloyd objected: he wanted to see the papers then. Means was the soul of co-operation; he brought the box to Lloyd's room, where they opened it. The box contained more than a dozen red portfolios of memoranda, carbon copies of reports, and some original sheets. Since it was late, the two men decided to spend no time going through the papers that night, but to wait until morning. Means went to the big old house on North Union Street, and Captain Lloyd went to bed in his hotel room.

The next day, Means came back to the hotel, and he and the intelligence officer began to go through the papers. Lloyd glanced through them. He was not impressed. None of the papers were official documents, and none bore any signatures which would identify them as "Boy-Ed papers" of any official importance to the Germans. Captain Lloyd began to suspect that these were memoranda kept by Means when he was working for the Germans. In the bottom of the box he found a sheaf of private letters which had belonged to Means's father, letters that had nothing to do with German affairs.

Gaston B. Means

Gaston Means responded quickly to the suspicion he sensed in Captain Lloyd. Gaston extracted a number of the papers, which he said were the most important. He would dictate a full report on these when they returned to New York, but he could not do so until the other Boy-Ed papers were delivered to them, because important dates and much of the vital material were in those other papers.

Means left Captain Lloyd at the hotel that morning. He returned early in the afternoon and told the captain that he had heard from the agents who had gone to Virginia to get the von Bernstorff papers. The men had the papers, but they thought they were being followed, so there was no telling when they might arrive, Means said. In fact, it might be necessary for Gaston and Captain Lloyd to meet the men outside Concord. That being the case, Means thought he ought to make preparations. He needed a trunk and some suitcases in which to put the papers. Gaston said he wanted to measure the portfolios in which these papers were kept, so he took all but one set off with him.

Late in the afternoon, Gaston again came to the hotel, and he and Captain Lloyd went to a luggage shop. Captain Lloyd bought a large black trunk and four small suitcases that fitted into the trunk. Means then took all this luggage off to the house on North Union Street and put it in the carriage shed.

While he and Captain Lloyd were together, Lloyd questioned Gaston about the "men" who had gone for the papers. Means indicated, without really admitting it, that there was only one man, and that it was Afton, his brother. At other times, however, he said there were two men. When Lloyd asked more questions, Gaston grew irritable, and recalled promises made by Secretary Tumulty to Roy Keehn that no actions would be taken against Means or his agents in this affair. The best way to keep the others out of it, he indicated, was to keep their names secret. And that was what he proposed to do.

Captain Lloyd was stubborn, and he kept after Means. He

119

wanted to meet this other man. Finally, because Gaston wanted something more from Captain Lloyd, he promised Lloyd to arrange a meeting when the man returned.

What Gaston wanted—the object of his plan—was to secure a recommendation from Military Intelligence to Judge Horner in Chicago, a statement that would show how Means had assisted the government and would portray Means as an honest and upright citizen. After Gaston had promised to let Lloyd speak to the man who had gone to Virginia for the von Bernstorff papers, Means asked Lloyd to send a telegram to Colonel Biddle, stating that he had the papers. Captain Lloyd was cautious. He refused to send the wire until they had possession of all the papers. Had Lloyd sent the wire, Roy Keehn was waiting in Washington, and Means would have informed Keehn of the telegram, and Keehn would then have asked the head of Military Intelligence for the statement Means wanted for Judge Horner.

Gaston was disappointed when Captain Lloyd refused his request, but he swallowed his chagrin, and took the plan into the second stage. The following day was Sunday, on which apparently even secret agents did not work. Means spent most of the day at the house on North Union Street, and in conference in nearby Salisbury with a lawyer about his father's estate. Captain Lloyd drove to Salisbury with Means that day, but otherwise he whiled away the time as best he could. On the following day, Means arrived at the St. Cloud Hotel at about 10:30 in the morning, in a great hurry.

The papers had arrived, he said. In the dead of night his agent had tapped on his bedroom window and insisted on straightaway delivering the von Bernstorff papers. There was little more sleep for Means that night, for he had scarcely disposed of that parcel when the rest of the Boy-Ed papers were delivered to him.

Gaston realized Captain Lloyd was disappointed, of course, because it was impossible for him to meet the messenger, but there was nothing more to be done. Means had packed the papers in the trunk, and now they must make all possible haste back to Washington, Means said, to deliver them before something went astray.

Captain Lloyd and Gaston went to the carriage house behind the Means house, and there Means unlocked the black trunk, lifted a carriage robe which covered the four suitcases, and opened one of them to show Captain Lloyd the red portfolios packed along the sides. Means pulled out one portfolio.

"You see, this is the stuff," he said. The portfolio was marked "O'Gorman Case."

Before Captain Lloyd could be quite sure of what he had seen, Gaston put the portfolio back in the case, slammed the cover, and locked the trunk. Somewhere along the line he had also recovered from Lloyd the one portfolio Lloyd had kept out.

"We will take this down to the hotel where we can go through it," Means said. So they climbed into the automobile and began the trip back to the hotel. But, en route, Means had a second thought. They had to arrange for some conveyance to move the trunk. He did not think it would be a good idea to take the papers to the hotel. His implication was clear: they were being watched.

Gaston wanted to rent a room and dictate his reports. Captain Lloyd said he thought they ought to get out of Concord, and quickly. Means excused himself to run an errand, while Captain Lloyd went back to the hotel to telephone Colonel Biddle for instructions. It took the captain an hour and a half to make telephone contact with Colonel Biddle, but when Lloyd was through with his conversation, Means still had not returned.

When Gaston did come back to the hotel, he indicated that it was important that they leave for Washington that night. Colonel Biddle had given Captain Lloyd instructions to go to Philadelphia, but Means had taken matters in his own hands. He had checked the trunk, along with three trunks of his own, to New York, and he had also purchased their train tickets to New York.

This was the first news Captain Lloyd had heard of any other trunks, but Gaston assured him that the trunks filled with personal belongings provided a perfect cover for the trunk full of documents.

Gaston then dragged Captain Lloyd off to Salisbury again—this time while he talked to a lawyer about a claim against the Germans that he wanted to file in connection with work he had done for them. Gaston proposed to file the claim with the Alien Property Custodian, and, if it was accepted, to collect from German assets seized in this country. On the basis of his help to the government in producing the von Bernstorff and Boy-Ed papers, he asked Captain Lloyd to help him pursue that claim.

This was the second step in Means's plan—to use Military Intelligence to collect money from the Alien Property Custodian of the United States.

As Gaston conferred with the lawyer it grew late—so late that they could not return to Concord in time for the train North, so they boarded the train at Salisbury. Captain Lloyd was a careful man, and Means's actions worried him. After they found their spaces, Lloyd went back into the baggage car to check on the luggage. He did not find any trunks. He rushed back to their Pullman, where he told Gaston that they should get off at the next stop and go back. Means looked at Lloyd as though he thought the Military Intelligence officer was crazy. The trunks were checked through. The railroad had custody of them. What could possibly happen?

Captain Lloyd continued to worry about the missing trunks. He need not have, had he known the facts. As Gaston had suggested, the porter at Concord had simply forgotten to put them on the train, and they would be put on the next train.

But not knowing that, and beginning to know Means, Captain Lloyd was suspicious and restless.

On the trip North, Gaston began to talk about "publicity," and Lloyd recoiled. Means said that Roy Keehn was waiting in Washington, and that Keehn wanted a story for the Hearst newspapers about the discovery of the papers. Captain Lloyd said he could release nothing, and he began to fear that Means would get in touch with Keehn and release the story before Lloyd could deliver the papers to his headquarters.

When they stepped off the train in Washington, Means telephoned the New Washington Hotel and immediately went there, Lloyd tagging along, "to pick up a telegram." Gaston left Captain Lloyd downstairs and went to Room 709, where he said William J. Burns was waiting to see him. Since Burns had been a party to the beginning of this investigation, Captain Lloyd could not object. But when Gaston was slow in returning, Lloyd asked at the desk. He learned that Room 709 was the room of Roy Keehn.

Captain Lloyd was beside himself with worry. The trunks were in limbo, and Means was up to something strange, he was sure. But the papers were by far the most important matter, so the Captain rushed back to the Union Station where he made arrangements for the baggage master to hold the trunks when they arrived; otherwise, since they were checked through to New York, they would have gone on.

When Captain Lloyd returned to the New Washington Hotel, he found Gaston in the company of William J. Burns, Roy Keehn, and Captain Adams of Military Intelligence. Captain Adams announced that they were to go immediately to the office of General Churchill, the director of Military Intelligence. Captain Lloyd had planned to go to Philadelphia, to stop there at the Ritz-Carlton Hotel, where he would meet Colonel Biddle. Then he and Colonel Biddle could examine the papers and decide what action to take. But orders were orders, and, after placing one more call to Concord to try to find out what had happend to the baggage, Captain Lloyd reluctantly went to the general's office.

Means, or his friends, had been in touch with General Churchill beforehand. General Churchill had already been asked to tell Judge Horner of Chicago that Means had been of great assistance in bringing to light these important German papers. But General Churchill had not become the director of intelligence without learning some elementary caution. He turned Gaston over to a colonel, who began to question Means about Captain Boy-Ed's activities. The General waited, before he issued any statements to anyone.

The mystery deepened when Captain Lloyd finally completed his call to Concord, and the station agent said that Means's baggage had gone out on the train they rode. Lloyd knew the baggage had not been aboard. What was wrong? Shortly after noon the baggage master at Washington Union Station said the trunks had arrived, and that they could be picked up.

Captain Lloyd drove to Union Station to pick up the black trunk and Means's hand luggage, which held the keys. When the Captain arrived at the station, he learned there was a charge of $17.54 for excess baggage on the trunks, and since he did not want to pay for Means's personal luggage, he had the trunks weighed. One trunk weighed 165 pounds. The second trunk weighed 220 pounds. The third trunk weighed 260 pounds. The black trunk, the only one in which Captain Lloyd had any interest, weighed only 75 pounds.

When he learned this news, Captain Lloyd was truly disturbed. He paid the fees on the black trunk and Means's hand luggage and rushed to Military Intelligence headquarters on F Street. Then he walked into the room where a colonel was questioning Means. The colonel was busy—preparing a telegram to be sent to Judge Horner, reporting on Gaston Means's assistance to the government. Means wanted more. He wanted Captain Lloyd sent posthaste to Chicago to tell Judge Horner what a fine service Means had performed.

The Captain demurred. He wanted to see General Churchill before sending any message anywhere. The whole group moved into General Churchill's office, where the proposed wire was read.

Was there anything wrong with it? the general asked.

No, said Captain Lloyd, but they ought to look over the trunk before they sent the wire. The wire was delayed momentarily and Captain Lloyd asked Means for the keys to the trunk.

Gaston B. Means

"I don't want to bother about that now," Gaston said. "I must get this important telegram off for General Churchill to go to Judge Horner."

When Captain Lloyd insisted, Means could not help but give in. The keys were in one of the bags, he said. Lloyd looked through the bags. Not finding the keys, he forced the lock of the trunk.

It was empty.

Captain Lloyd brought General Churchill, who brought Gaston Means to look at the paperless trunk. What kind of a game were they playing?, Means wanted to know.

No game, said General Churchill, no game at all.

Gaston's telegram was not sent out to Judge Horner that afternoon. Captain Lloyd was dispatched, instead, to Concord to see what had happened. He learned that Means had brought the trunks to the station, and had helped weigh them. William Reade, the porter, had noticed that the black trunk was very light. The trunks did not go out because Reade went off duty, and the night porter forgot about them—that was the reason for the confused messages from Concord.

The night porter had also noticed that the black trunk seemed to be empty. It was unfortunate for Gaston that he had noticed, because under the Southern Railroad system, no weight was actually taken on the baggage, since it was being shipped collect, and the weights and overcharges would be collected at the other end. Means had pointed that fact out to the ticket agent. So had not both porter Reade and night porter Jess Whitmere wondered why someone was shipping an empty trunk, there would have been no way to know when it became empty. No other person approached the trunks at any time. One of the porters was in the baggage room at all times.

Captain Lloyd, then, had secured conclusive evidence that the trunk was empty when it was taken to the station in Concord.

The Captain had also asked Means to tell him the name of the man who had gone to Skylands, for Lloyd wanted to see if the man had really gone there. Means said the man's name was Henry

125

Freund. And who was Henry Freund and where could he be located? Means did not know, except that Freund lived in one mill boardinghouse or another. Perhaps he moved around a lot, as some restless men do. Sometimes he used the name Chester Wilson, and sometimes Means made contact with Freund-Wilson by addressing him in care of General Delivery in Concord.

Captain Lloyd searched around Concord and Charlotte for Henry Freund and never found him. Gaston said he was sure Freund would get in touch with him once he returned to New York City—and Lloyd felt it was quite important that Freund be found, to see if he had gone to Skylands and what had happened there—for Lloyd even then believed in the existence of Henry Freund.

When Captain Lloyd returned to Washington a few days later, Gaston Means was still there, waiting for his telegram to Judge Horner to be sent.

"As I have now done all that I could and have done my part with reference to obtaining these papers, are you now willing to send that telegram to Judge Horner with reference to me?" he asked. The Military Intelligence men said they would be glad to send the telegram, if Means would deliver the papers. Gaston repeated his question, and got the same answer. Finally, just as he was leaving the office, Means stopped at the door, and returned to make one final request that the telegram be sent.[15]

The telegram was not sent, but Means had not yet ended his efforts. Having earlier persuaded Roy Keehn that someone was trying to interfere with the search (as he had also told Captain Lloyd) Gaston now indicated that Military Intelligence had played him false and that they *had* possession of the papers. Keehn was inclined to believe him, for Means had laid the groundwork well for such belief. Roy Keehn wrote a letter of complaint to Joseph Tumulty, with whom he had originated the investigation.

"It is my opinion that Colonel Biddle and Captain Lloyd have the papers or know where they are. I have asked Means to make a complete written report, which I will send you. . . .

126

Gaston B. Means

"The fact that Captain Lloyd would permit such important papers to be checked as baggage on a night train and be shipped unguarded—and too, to check to New York instead of Washington, seems to suggest unfitness or crookedness."[16]

Tumulty, trying to get to the bottom of the affair, wrote to General Churchill. General Churchill replied, stating his belief that the trunks were empty when shipped.

Keehn asked that William J. Burns be invited to give his views. General Churchill agreed, and Burns indicated that Keehn had tipped off the Department of Justice, whose agents had then taken the papers. It was an interesting theory, said General Churchill, but it was nonsense.

Gaston then sought others for assistance. He went to John Rathom, editor of the Providence *Bulletin,* and asked for an introduction to Will Hays, chairman of the Republican National Committee. In a four-and-a-half-hour harangue, Gaston indicated that the "theft" of the papers was a Democratic plot. Those papers, Means asserted, would "lift the roof off" the Administration in the Congressional elections coming up in a few days. The papers proved conclusively, Means said, that a number of legislators had taken German money to represent German interests.

Editor Rathom refused to give Means a letter, for he knew Means too well from the days of 1915.[17] So Gaston went back to the trial of the King will case without the character references he sought. He had made a valiant attempt to accomplish much with his trip to North Carolina. He had tried to use the Hearst newspapers and Military Intelligence to win the will case, to establish a claim against German property, and to bring his personal effects from Concord to New York. Barring the moneys he received from Roy Keehn for "expenses," all he had accomplished, due to misfortune, was to bring his baggage to his new home.

VII

Gaston Means was never a man to take defeat lying down. Military Intelligence had abandoned him, but he was determined to win the Chicago case without help, if that was what must be done.

Almost as soon as he had seen Editor John Rathom in Providence, Means was in Washington again, this time laying plans for a coup against the Justice Department. His attorney—or an attorney who said he was representing Means in this matter—announced that they were trying to persuade Congress to investigate the manner in which C. B. Ambrose had used the name of the Department of Justice while working for a private firm during 1917.[1]

It was an issue that the Senate Judiciary Committee might well have shown considerable interest in pursuing. But the acting chairman of the Judiciary Committee, Senator Lynn Overman, was cautious, even though he and Gaston Means shared North Carolina citizenship. Means and his lawyer said Senator Overman would conduct an investigation. Senator Overman said that if Means wanted to protest to the Department of Justice about this matter, he would forward the protest (which any Senator would do at any time for any constituent.)

The lines of authority and responsibility of the Bureau of Investigation of the Department of Justice were very fuzzy in 1918. The Bureau was used as the Attorney General and the Director wanted it to be used, and under Director Bruce Bielaski, the Bureau's agents were not always careful in safeguarding the rights of the citizens whose lives they probed. Yet when the issue of government men on private service was raised openly, even Director Bielaski felt impelled to reply:

"Mr. Clabaugh, in charge at Chicago, allowed Ambrose leave because Means had been a German agent and we wanted to find out if there was anything of value to us in this case that touched on Means's connection with the Germans."[2]

Thus it was that Ambrose had been allowed to continue as an agent of the Department of Justice's Bureau of Investigation, and why it was possible for him to so identify himself in Concord. But even then the Bureau's chiefs realized that Ambrose had gone beyond the bounds of propriety, and he was sacrificed.

Senator Overman was not much interested in Gaston's troubles, but the Senator was interested in what Means might know about German activity in the United States. He was opening an investigation into the relations between the Brewing and Liquor Interests and German propaganda, and he called on Means to come and testify. Gaston was pleased to testify because he needed publicity —and he needed a podium from which he could shout to the world of the good citizenship of Gaston Bullock Means.

Means identified himself before the committee as a college man and former educator, and also as an expert on textile matters. When he had come to New York in 1903, Gaston said, he began writing for the trade press of the textile industry—and even more broadly for the New York *Journal of Commerce*. That, said Means, is how he met the Germans. In 1905, when he was traveling around the country, the Germans made arrangements with him to keep them informed of the activities of other cotton goods salesmen in America. It was all very logical and very commercial.

Means reported then to a man named Swartz, he said, and at least once each week he gave the fascinated Germans a report on cotton affairs. That is why he had not renewed his three-year contract with Cannon—a fact Julie Means would have been glad to hear, since his decision to devote his time to the Germans had uprooted her and caused her much unpleasantness. Shortly after he came to New York, Means said, he had been taken to the German Club on Fifty-ninth Street, and there he had met Captain Boy-Ed. From that time on he was a great frequenter of the German Club— according to his testimony—which made it difficult to understand why he could never remember whether it was located at Sixth Avenue or at Broadway.

Gaston said that he had broken with the Germans when they asked him to help find supplies for the German surface raiders that prowled the Atlantic and the Pacific during the war. Since that would have been a "breach of the United States government's laws," Means refused indignantly. He said nothing about breaching the laws as a party to shipping contraband materials to his German friends, or of breaching his moral commitments as a citizen by trying to foment trouble between the United States and England in 1915. That was to be expected. The postwar Gaston Bullock Means was a new Means.

The 1915 affair had come about, Means said, because Dr. Rumely had come to the William J. Burns Agency in the spring, wondering if any shipyards were building any submarines for any belligerents. Means had discovered that none were. The Germans were so heartened by that discovery that they had hired him to find out whether or not those British warships off the coast were receiving supplies from American sources—and the Germans were delighted to learn that the Americans were not giving anything to their enemies.

Through all this, Gaston's puzzling relationship with William J.

Burns kept cropping up. Burns had played an even stranger role during the early phases of the First World War than had Gaston Means. Apparently, according to such disparate sources as Means and the Office of Military Intelligence, Burns had worked both for the British and for the Germans at the same time. It was a neat trick, and it involved the best efforts of such trusted agents as Gaston Means. For the first time, it became quite clear just how close Means's relationship to Burns was; Means said he had been able to take temporary leaves of absence from the Burns payroll as he wanted to do so.

Means had also broken with the Germans, he testified primly, because they had tried to foment war between the United States and Mexico in the celebrated Huerta plot. William Burns at that time seemed to be working for the Mexicans, too, and Means had given him a verbal report on the whole attempt to foment revolution in Mexico, and then had prepared a report which Burns gave to Joseph Tumulty.

"And Huerta did exactly what I said he was going to do in that report," Means announced triumphantly. Since nobody in the hearing room had seen the report or knew exactly what Huerta had done, it was not too difficult to be impressive with the claim.

Means told the Overman Committee that Captain von Papen had collected data from the clearinghouse of the insurance companies of the United States. It was basically public information, of course, but few citizens realized that it was possible for the German government to trace German-American citizens through such a simple means as the insurance business. When Means discovered what von Papen was up to, he became upset and told the story to A. W. Haywood, his old lawyer friend, who was now with American Tobacco Company, and Haywood sent him to see Josephus Daniels, Secretary of the Navy. Daniels, unfortunately, never saw fit to give Gaston credit for his assistance in defeating the Kaiser, although Daniels had the highest respect for Means's uncle, Colonel Paul Barringer Means.

Gaston B. Means

After Means reported the Huerta matter to the Navy, Captain Boy-Ed fired him from the German service, Gaston said—which made the third different story he had told publicly about his relations with the Germans since 1916. But, except for breach of the neutrality act, espionage against his government, and violation of Treasury Department restrictions, Captain Boy-Ed had "never asked me to do anything that pertained to the breaking of a law," Gaston said. Apparently Captain Boy-Ed had not asked Means to blow up any factories.

"All of my work at that time was nothing in the world but commercial work," Means said. "I was with the Germans from a purely commercial standpoint—for the money that I could make out of it. I was pro-American all the time." (That is probably the one really truthful statement that Gaston Means made to the Overman Committee.)

Means told Senator Overman and his associates that he had finally proved his complete loyalty to the United States by turning over Captain Boy-Ed's secret papers to the government. Military Intelligence, unwilling to go into the strange concatenation of events that led to the "disappearance" of the papers, did not contest the Means statements. So it appeared, on the surface, that Gaston had done a great deal for his country in the past two or three years.[3]

There were a few indications, however, that those who knew Gaston Means no longer accepted him as a reliable witness. The Department of Justice's Mr. Bielaski said publicly that Means was "totally unreliable."[4] Senator Overman's committee listened to Gaston Means during most of one chilly morning in January, 1919, but then ruled that his "evidence" consisted largely of unsupported statements made by himself. Where he mentioned the names of others they were almost always long dead, or, as in the case of the Germans, long gone from the United States.

Possessed of such a reputation, one would expect that Gaston would give up his attempts to probate the "second will" of James

133

C. King. But it was Gaston's pattern never to do anything in the straightforward or obvious manner—and in the King will case it is possible to see why he followed this course.

Gaston Means was not, legally, the backer of the "second will." The backer was Mrs. Maisie Melvin, and, whatever Gaston's relationship to her might be, it was none of the business of the court. Means appeared in this case simply as a key witness. So, although the probate judge might refuse to accept the document offered by Mrs. Melvin, under Illinois law it was possible to appeal that decision to the Circuit Court and secure a new trial of the case. This ponderous legal machinery had been put in motion in the winter of 1919, while at the same time Gaston Means sought other, more immediate ways in which to mend his fortunes.[5]

Periodically Gaston worked for William J. Burns, more or less when he felt like doing so. The pay was not high, but it bought the necessities for Julie and the children, and the people he met gave Gaston an ever wider field in which to maneuver. The King will case ground along slowly, and Means earned money to support his part in it as best he could.[6]

In June, Edward W. Edwards, secretary of the Allied Printing Trades Council of New York City, took exception to Means's activities and those of William J. Burns on the labor front, and made a complaint before the state controller's office, which held the responsibility for regulation of private detective work. Burns went before this committee to testify once again for the honor of Gaston Means. If Means had once said that he received instructions from Burns in the matter of the Hamburg-American line, then Means was mistaken, but no more than that. For Means was a southern gentleman, who would not tell a lie. The short, plump private detective called attention to a suit Means had filed for a million dollars against those who had caused him to be brought to trial for the murder of Maude King.[7]

A million dollars was a great deal of money in 1919, and suits of that magnitude had not yet become common vehicles for press agents. The million-dollar suit attracted national publicity, and Means, in his usual manner, took the fullest advantage of the citizen's right to use the law. The suit was against the Northern Trust Company, and it was filed in Chicago. But Means also secured warrants, in Concord, for the arrest of John T. Dooling and William B. Miller, an attorney for the Northern Trust Company.[8] The charges were conspiracy and the subornation of perjury in the Means trial in Cabarrus County court. Means had not the slightest interest in pressing such a charge in North Carolina. As Dooling and District Attorney Swann said in New York the next day when they heard the news, Means was trying simply to discredit the New York witnesses in the King will case, and to bring enough unfavorable publicity down around the ears of the Northern Trust Company to force a settlement. Even in North Carolina this became apparent before midsummer, and when the matter was pressed before the grand jury on August 11, the jury refused to indict. So did a grand jury in Cook County, Illinois, when Gaston pressed his case there.[9]

Gaston did not give up. He went before a New York grand jury, trying to persuade this citizens' group that Assistant District Attorney Dooling had broken the law when he concerned himself with the death of Maude King and the trial of Gaston Means in North Carolina, and all summer and autumn Gaston raced back and forth between Chicago and New York, directing the King will fight with one hand and earning a living and slapping at his enemies with the other.[10]

As always, Gaston Means was exerting a monumental amount of energy, but this time with little success. In December, Illinois Probate Judge Henry Horner handed Maisie Melvin and Gaston Means a shock. He upheld the validity of the first will of James C. King, denounced the second will as spurious, and castigated Mrs. Melvin and Means for their fraudulent efforts to probate the will.

The Judge exonerated Attorney Roy Keehn from any attempt to impose on the court, but he leveled on Gaston Means and called his story of the finding of the second will a total fabrication.[11]

Others might quail under the angry denunciations of an arbiter of justice, but the charges of the judge rolled off Gaston's hide like raindrops off a rhinocerous. The faint-hearted among the corps of attorneys were discarded, and the battle was rejoined in Illinois' Circuit Court. As the moves were made to bring about a new trial, the indefatigable Mr. Means filed sworn complaints in Federal District Court in New York City against District Attorney Edward Swann, Assistant District Attorney John R. Dooling, his old nemesis C. B. Ambrose, and several lawyers and officials of the Northern Trust Company of Chicago. They were charged with conspiracy to bring about Means's conviction in the Maude King case and to defeat Gaston's efforts in the King will case. Means's suit asked a million dollars in damages, the same amount he tried unsuccessfully to secure in the Chicago suit. Again, within the privileged format of a court complaint, Means was able to make a number of propaganda points he deemed important. He charged that the alleged conspirators "fixed" Judge Horner in Chicago, and he called the whole group "a poison gas squad," which had forced him to spend $50,000, even to sacrifice a plantation in Como County, Mississippi, which he had inherited from his grandfather, in order to pursue his goals.

There were several good reasons for this chain of suits besides the obvious publicity attendant to them. Means had made his arrangement with Attorney Thomas B. Felder on a contingency basis, both in these suits and in the King will case. Neither Means nor Mrs. Melvin had the cash necessary to pay the heavy attorneys' fees that would otherwise have been charged. Means also succeeded in keeping the wrath of the New York District Attorney's office from descending on him by keeping District Attorney Swann and Assistant District Attorney Dooling constantly off balance. Swann testified before the New York grand jury in the spring of

1920 that, if Means had not made his charges, the District Attorney's office would have pursued cases involving forgery and perjury against Means. In terms of cash and even freedom, Gaston Means was in a position where he must keep moving furiously just to maintain his head above water.

As the second trial of the King will case neared, Attorney Thomas Felder was fortunate enough to discover a witness who had been overlooked in the previous searches. She was Miss Florence Isabel Lee, a showgirl. Miss Lee had known James C. King very well, and for some time before his death. She had met him at various hotels (where she was always escorted by her father, of course), and she had known him as a rich and friendly gentleman.

Sometime in 1904, Miss Lee said, she had decided to give up the stage and had thought of her acquaintance, Mr. King, who might help her with money to pursue her studies. Mr. King had been glad to do so, and Miss Lee had studied to become a stenotypist.

She met Mr. King on the street one day in the autumn of 1905, and he asked her to do a little confidential work for him. The next day King called at her boardinghouse and sent a taxi driver out to find a typewriter, when he discovered that she did not have one on hand. Neither did she have paper, so she used the backs of several old pieces of paper to do the typing he wanted.

What had she typed? Miss Lee could not remember. King had paid her $20, but otherwise she had paid no particular attention either to Mr. King or to what she was doing. She had written to lawyer Osborne, Gaston Means's attorney, when she read about the Means murder trial. But the judge, although he was Gaston's uncle, did not bother to reply for months and months. That was why her testimony was just coming to light.[12]

The remarkable evidence of Miss Lee was brought out in the New York newspapers in June, on the eve of the trial of the second will case. Attorney Felder told the story with a flourish, and added a few touches: he was planning to try to impeach District Attorney

Swann before the legislature; a plot existed in Chicago to arrest witnesses for the Means case if they showed their faces there.

District Attorney Swann invited Colonel Felder to bring his charge before Governor Al Smith of New York, and Judge Jesse A. Baldwin of Chicago warned Felder not to repeat the charge unless he wished to be cited for contempt. Against this background, the second trial began.[13]

David N. Carvalho, a handwriting expert, testified that the signatures on the will were all genuine—or, as he qualified it, they were genuine if the signatures submitted for comparison were genuine. (How complex the case had become and how wearying, but as far as Means was concerned it was worth every effort; the stakes had grown far greater: the King estate was now valued at $5 million instead of $3 million.)[14]

When the interesting Miss Lee was brought before the court, she told the same story she had told for Attorney Felder and the newspapers. A. F. Reichmann, a lawyer for the Northern Trust Company, cross-examined her and asked her why she could not remember the will if she had typed it.

"Great Scott, man," she exploded. "I can't remember everything. I am not a magician."

No, she was not a magician. She was a showgirl, and a forthright one. Sitting there, on the witness stand, she was asked about a particular show in which she had held a featured role. That show? It "opened in Peoria and closed in the summer," she said.

As to her personal life, Miss Lee had what she thought was a "marriage" to a Providence man, but the "supposed honeymoon" was spent in "punky hotels." That was the end of Miss Lee, and very nearly of the case.

It was apparent that Gaston now fancied himself as a witness of great talent, and he was just that, if one were looking for a show in court. Gaston had mastered the art of answering questions before a judge or jury. Gaston testified for several days, presenting the picture *he* wanted seen of his relationships with Maude King, and en-

138

Gaston B. Means

gaging in combat with Attorney Reichmann with evident relish:

> Q.: John T. Dooling prosecuted you for the murder of Mrs.
> King, did he not?
> A.: No. He prosecuted me for the *alleged* murder of Mrs. King.

Gaston produced a paper—an entirely new one—which showed that Mrs. King and Mrs. Robinson had given him control of the Robinson trust fund. Asked why he had not produced this document earlier, Gaston said he had been forced to "raid" Dooling's office in New York to find it hidden there in the files.

Mrs. Melvin testified. By that time, the lady was so thoroughly confused that her story conflicted with the story she told in the first trial of the will case. The first time she said that witness Byron Smith had signed the will not more than a week after King had signed it. The second time, she said it was "within ten days."[15]

Despite Miss Lee and the new "facts," Gaston Means's brave efforts on the witness stand, and the imposing figure of Colonel Thomas B. Felder as principal attorney for the appeal, Judge Baldwin was no more impressed with the case than had been Judge Horner. On December 10, Judge Baldwin sustained the Horner decision, and having done so, felt impelled to make one final remark.

"No fair consideration of this case can ignore the fact that Gaston B. Means is shown to be the controlling and dominating spirit in the attempt to establish this will. Indeed, the conclusion is irresistible that Mrs. King and Mrs. Melvin were singularly under his influence and were largely dominated by his strong personality and inflexible will."[16]

Even for Gaston Means, that statement marked the end of the affair. His damage cases against his enemies died of their own weight; no further attempts were made to secure "justice" by impeachment of the New York authorities; Mrs. Melvin and her family vanished from the life of Gaston Means, and all that remained

139

was Means's hatred of authority and his compulsive desire to gain great wealth.

In New York, the Means family now entered a period in which they were, as Julie said, "dead broke." Gaston had no resources, and what little money he obtained came from William J. Burns for "investigations." It was scarcely enough to keep the family in food and clothing. In the spring of 1921, disaster struck. "Sister," the five-year-old daughter and first living child born to Julie, fell ill and died. Julie was grief-stricken, but Gaston was nearly inconsolable. He lost weight, and his distress became so great that he decided to forsake the city of opportunity for the security of Concord, so as summer turned the family gave up the rented house on Staten Island and moved back to North Union Street, to live with Gaston's mother and sisters while this fourth child of the Means family paused once again to take stock and decide what to do with his life.[17]

Or so it seemed. Actually, there was no hesitation in the course of Gaston Means at this juncture. Summer had just arrived in Concord, and Gaston with it, when, on June 22, he went to the offices of the Southeastern Express Company. He took with him two Concord friends, Gus Archibald and Luther Weddington, and a wooden box eighteen inches long and six inches wide. There, as the agent, Archibald, and Weddington looked on, Gaston counted and wrapped $57,000 in cash. Then he put it in a wooden box and addressed the box to Roy D. Keehn in Chicago. The money, Gaston said, was a payment from the rubber deals he and Mrs. King had made with the Germans, and it represented part of her estate. He insured the cash shipment for the face value of the notes, and sent it off.

It was an odd shipment, but there was nothing illegal about it. Had it been made by almost any other person, perhaps there would have been no question in the minds of the officials of the express company. But Gaston Means had a reputation, even in Cabarrus County.

Gaston B. Means

The shipment reached Chicago, where it was delivered to Roy Keehn's office on La Salle Street. Since Gaston was well known in Roy Keehn's office, too, when the Chicago agent of the express company arrived, Keehn would not allow the agent to leave or to open the box until other witnesses were brought in to observe the proceedings.

The box was opened; Keehn picked it up and lifted out a block of ordinary wood.

"I thought so," he said. He put the box down, dismissed the witnesses, and went about his business.

Ten days later, Gaston appeared in the main offices of the Southeastern Express Company with his lawyer Jake Newell of Charlotte, and made a verbal claim against the company for the $57,000 that Means said was stolen from the box. But Means's reputation had advanced even to Charlotte, and Frank Shannonhouse, the general counsel of the agency, ordered an investigation before he would discuss the claim. In two weeks, the agents of the company convinced themselves that the claim was a fraud, and Shannonhouse advised Newell that Means was free to file a written claim. He encouraged Means to do so, in fact, with the indication that he would enjoy the subsequent trial of Means for fraud. So ended one more effort by Gaston Means to improve his fortunes.[18]

VIII

At the end of the summer of 1921, under the new Harding Administration, American government had begun to take the shape it would assume for the next two years of American history—that of a huge free-lunch counter. Gaston Means realized the opportunity for profit from his talents in the service of the Federal government. The Means family had influence with both Republican and Democratic politicians in North Carolina, so Gaston began to look for a government job. He did not want just any government job, obviously, but one in which he could use his experience as an investigator.

Gaston Means's reputation was against him, but in the appointment of William J. Burns to head the Bureau of Investigation of the Department of Justice, Means found a friend in high position. Burns could use Means, because he knew exactly the kind of work of which Means was capable. If there were informers to be bribed, or offices to be searched, or if in other ways the law of the land was to be breached by the secret investigating arm of the Department

143

of Justice, then Gaston Means was the best possible man to put on the job.

If Means appealed to Burns as a man of specific and valued talents, the Bureau of Investigation also appealed to Means. For here, Gaston could see in a glance, was the opportunity to get on the "inside" of the Administration. Gaston secured a recommendation from the Republican national committeeman of North Carolina, and Burns hired him as a Special Employee of the Department of Justice, for 90 days at a salary of $7.00 a day. The appointment finally came through at the end of October on this tenuous basis, but, at the end of January, his appointment was extended indefinitely.[1]

It might seem, to the amateur, that the office of the Commissioner of Internal Revenue would be the place for a man of ambition, ingenuity, and the morals of an alley cat. There was much to be said in favor of employment in the Treasury Department from the point of view of a man of Means's temperament, but he had no great opportunity there, and there was chance for different kinds of action in the Justice Department, or, as it was later to be known, the Department of Easy Virtue. Among the tools placed at Means's disposal by a benevolent government were the complete files of the Bureau of Investigation, an office and telephone, official stationery, an official badge, and an identification card. On the extended appointment, the pay was still low—$88 per week— but Gaston Bullock Means did not need the pay for long.[2]

Confident as he was in the success of the appointment, Means brought Julie and the children to Washington in September, and took rooms in a house at 1812 Newton Street. He was going to be with the Department of Justice, he told the landlady, and would want to remain with her for several months, until he could establish a more permanent home.[3]

Means went to work at the Justice Department around November 1, 1921. Ten days later, he was assigned to work with Captain Hazel Scaife on war fraud claims in an investigation of the air-

craft industry. Scaife was a thoroughly honest agent of the government, although far more naïve than his splendid goatee would indicate. Scaife was that anomaly in the Harding Administration—a
reformer. In casual conversation in the office, Scaife learned that
Means was once a German agent and asked him for information.
Means went to William J. Burns, who advised him to talk. So Means
did talk to Scaife, and as a result the Captain asked that Means be
assigned to assist him in his work.[4]

When a Depression struck the United States in the fall, Means
also was assigned to study the advances in prices from the years
1913 through 1920, in what came to be known as the Bread Investigation. It was in this connection, Means claimed, that he came
to know Jesse Smith, the right-hand man and apartment-mate of
Attorney General Harry M. Daugherty. Smith kept an office in
the Department of Justice, although he had no official position,
and Means went to see him, ostensibly because Smith had been in
the dry-goods business in the little town of Washington Courthouse, Ohio (but it was far more in character that Means would
have made Smith's acquaintance because he learned that Smith
was close to the Attorney General, and that Smith was already
reputed to be the "bag man" for the Ohio gang).[5]

During his first few weeks on the job, Means went to work, kept
his ears and eyes open, and his mouth shut, or as closely shut as
this talkative and easygoing North Carolinian could keep it. He
also took care to surround himself with friends. Miss Rella Lane,
the sister of his landlady, found a job as a stenographer in the
Department of Justice and Means took care to see that she became
the stenographer in his and Captain Scaife's section. He also made
himself most pleasant to Mrs. Jessie Duckstein, secretary to William Burns. Mrs. Duckstein was the wife of the confidential secretary of Edward B. McLean, publisher of the Washington *Post*, a
fact that did not escape Gaston's attention.

The Bread Investigation consisted largely of tracing the rise in
prices in various commodities, through checking the catalogues of

mail-order houses over a period of years and looking endlessly through yellowed newspaper files. But it was not very many days before Gaston submerged the Bread Investigation to the bottom of the pile and took up matters more to his liking.[6]

Late in the Wilson Administration, Means had encountered an attorney named Sidney Bieber in Washington. Bieber was well-known to the Justice Department, since he knew most of the shady characters in Washington. Their acquaintance continued in occasional meetings in hotels or on the streets of the city. When Means joined the Bureau, he invited Bieber to call on him. Bieber did so and was impressed when he walked into Means's private office, next to that of Chief Burns, and saw the now mountainous Gaston, heavy-bellied but still strong as a bull, sitting at ease and apparently in charge.[7]

Means explained in his most confidential manner that he wanted to make a showing "for the department," not for himself, and that Bieber could help him. Means needed general information about food prices. He also needed good "undercover" men. Bieber supplied both: pamphlets for the price information and his brother-in-law's brother, David Wolf, for the undercover work. Means hired Wolf at $11 a day, and Wolf worked for him for 102 days— without receiving a penny in pay. Thus Gaston had chalked up his first minor victory over the governmental system.[8]

The Bureau of Investigation used two methods of paying its employees. The most murky of these systems was the "blue slip" system, through which an employee of the Bureau drew a voucher which was cashed against a secret contingency fund at the disposal of the Director of the Bureau. Means collected David Wolf's "blue slip" money regularly and used it for his own purposes; at least, he never reported Wolf's "employment."

Sidney Bieber also assisted Means in hiring Clark Grier of Augusta, Georgia, as an "informant" or undercover agent. This was fast work, for Grier was appointed on November 29, 1921, and Means had officially been working for the Bureau only a month at that time.[9]

Gaston B. Means

Grier was a Republican politician from Georgia. He had known Means and the Means family for a number of years, not intimately, but more than casually. So, when they met again in Washington in 1921, they discovered they had a number of interests in common, not the least of which was an interest in money.[10]

Clark Grier was well acquainted with a number of bootleggers in Savannah, Georgia. Among others he had met Willie Haar, C. C. Tuten, and R. A. Bailey. In the winter of 1921-22, Grier appeared in Savannah, this time announcing that he was a special agent of the Bureau of Investigation of the Department of Justice, and flashing a card and badge, although none such had been issued to him. He told Willie Haar of his important connections with the Department, and how he could offer "protection" to the bootleggers if they wished to contract for it. In the Savannah Hotel, in agent Grier's room, money changed hands. It was paid to Grier in behalf of himself and Gaston Means, for Gaston was the originator of a plan to collect from the bootlegging crowd.[11]

Gaston began in a small way—contracting to sell Department of Justice reports and papers to the people involved. One of his tactics was to bring a man to the Bureau of Investigation offices, as he did George Remus, an Ohio bootlegger, in the autumn of 1921:

I was introduced to Gaston B. Means in the fall of 1921, when he claimed to be in a position to secure the return of certain papers used in the case of the *United States vs. Provenzani.* Ten thousand dollars was placed in escrow to be given him when he accomplished his word. He was to deliver over these papers, secure the transfer of District Attorney Dickerson from Chicago to North Carolina. He, Means, sent us copies of a letter supposed to have been signed by Assistant Attorney General Crim, transferring Dickerson. Needless to say, he did not deliver. At this time, when I met Means by appointment at the office of the Department of Justice at Washington, he showed me the file of the department in regard to myself and at that time tried to impress

147

me, and did impress me with what he could do. He told me at that time that he could handle anyone in the department in any matter, regardless of what it was, from the Attorney General down, including Mr. Burns. After meeting Means in the Department of Justice offices on a Sunday night at 8:20 o'clock, I later, in fact, several times thereafter, talked with Means at his Washington residence, and he was continuously telling me what he could do."[12]

Such practices had their pitfalls, as when distrustful men like George Remus put money in escrow, to be collected on performance. But, as he went along, Gaston learned these tricks, and was able to guard against them. He prospered, and, by the end of 1921, he was ready to move out of furnished lodgings and into the Bellevue Hotel, where he took a suite of rooms for himself and his family.

But Means also made one mistake toward the end of the year, which was to cause him much trouble.

One of Gaston's strongest qualities was loyalty. He was loyal to his friends, in his fashion, and, in reverse, he hated his enemies. In connection with the Bread Investigation, Means made several official trips to New York late in 1921. While in New York, Means could not resist telephoning John T. Dooling, his nemesis from the King trials. Dooling was flabbergasted by the call and sat down and wrote a letter to Attorney General Daugherty about it.

"Today he [Means] called me up on the telephone and said he was now at the Department of Justice and used foul and indecent language toward me and told that he was connected with the Department of Justice and would get me. . . ."[13]

Daugherty turned the letter over to William J. Burns, who hastened to protect his friend. Daugherty wanted to know if there was such a man in the Department. (Means, by this time, was passing himself off elsewhere as an intimate of the Attorney General.) Burns answered that there was such a man, a very reliable

man. Assistant Attorney General Rush Holland noted for the
Attorney General's eyes that Burns thought most highly of Means.
Burns, in fact, had sent a memo to Holland showing just how
highly he regarded his agent.

Burns said Means was wrongfully accused of the murder of
Maude King, and that her death was purely accidental; that he,
Burns, testified for Means when he was on trial for murder; that
Means was wrongfully accused of having forged the will of Mrs.
King; that a court in Chicago found that the will had been forged
but that the other parties interested had more money than Means
and bought their way through at the trial; that Means was not
appointed to the Bureau by Burns; that Means was one of Burns's
best men; that Dooling and Swann were both crooks of the first
water. In short, Mr. Burns told Mr. Daugherty that Means was a
much-abused and persecuted man, and that, in Burns's opinion,
Means was serving nobly in his position and should not be disturbed.[14] The report told as much to a discerning reader about
William J. Burns and his concepts of law and order as it did about
his subordinate.

District Attorney Swann also complained to Daugherty, and
Daugherty turned that letter over to Burns for answer.[15] Burns,
quite in character, said that he personally knew that Means was
not in New York on the day in question, and that Means had made
no long distance calls. He charged that Dooling was doing Means
a great injustice. There the matter seemed to rest. Means seemed
unaware of the storm raging about his head, and was attending
to business—his own business—as usual.

Gaston was running up a huge bill at the Bellevue Hotel. He
took the position that the only way to make money was to appear
to have it, and he spent with a lavish hand, although such a course
was certainly not indicated by his government pay: his check for
the two weeks ending January 15, 1922, was $112.70.[16]

In the course of the years since 1914, when he began working
for William J. Burns in New York City, Gaston Means had

149

developed a large speaking acquaintance in the underworld. He began, in 1921, to spread the word that he could "fix" Federal prosecutions, and that he could obtain favors and even make off with documents that might incriminate some of his old friends—all, of course, for a price.

Near the end of January, 1922, Means encountered Colonel Frank C. Morgan, from whom Gaston had rented the house in Staten Island in 1918. It is not exactly clear why Colonel Morgan was in Washington at that moment, although Means was to talk to him later about removal of liquor from bonded warehouses. At that moment, however, Colonel Morgan was an observer, not a participant in the real sense, in Means's affairs.

Morgan's room was on the same floor as Means's suite. One day, Gaston told Morgan that a friend was coming down from New York who wanted to take some notes on papers in Means's possession, and he asked if he could use Morgan's room for the purpose, since they did not wish to be disturbed.

Not long afterward, Henry Woodhouse of the Aerial League of America came to the hotel and asked for Means. Gaston and Woodhouse went into the Morgan room, where Woodhouse made notes on the papers. Then Morgan helped Means package up the notes, and Woodhouse left, after giving Means some cash and a check for $600.

Means did not want to cash the check, since as a government employee he had no business taking money from outsiders for a look at government papers. So Means had taken the liberty of having the check made out in Morgan's name. Morgan was surprised but agreeable enough, and then endorsed it, whereupon Sidney Bieber, the lawyer, happened by to cash it. Means took $500 and gave Morgan $100 for the use of his room.

The papers involved here were land claims against the Mexican government, which had arisen out of a long series of border incidents, including the Pancho Villa warfare in the decade just previous to the 1920's. For a time there had been a brisk trade in these land claims and a considerable amount of maneuvering, legal and illegal.[17]

Was it this incident, then, or the threats against John Dooling, or some of his opening maneuvers with the bootlegging crowd, that brought Means to his next step? It would be hard to say, except that Gaston always claimed that the next step—his suspension by the Department of Justice—was occasioned by no less an official than Andrew Mellon, Secretary of the Treasury. Perhaps this was true, and perhaps it was not, but, at any rate, Means was suspended quite mysteriously on February 9, 1922, by order of the Attorney General himself. Daugherty told Director Burns to suspend Means, and that was that. He would not discuss it. He simply said that he would investigate the charges that had been made, and let Burns know his final decision at a later time.

The suspension from the Department of Justice did not seem to hurt Gaston. At about that time, Captain Scaife quit the Department in disgust, because, Scaife said, the Attorney General refused to prosecute war fraud cases as he should. Means was frequently called by Scaife to go up on Capitol Hill with him and support Scaife's claims before various Congressmen.

Means then met Elmer Dover, Assistant Secretary of the Treasury. (At this time, Means's apartments at the Bellevue Hotel were searched from time to time, an indication of the suspicion with which every department seemed to regard every other.) Assistant Secretary Dover wanted some confidential information about David Blair, the Internal Revenue director, and he went to Means to get it, or so Means said, because Means had gone to college with Fred Coxe, a North Carolina lawyer who had helped arrange Blair's confirmation by the Senate. Dover, said Means, asked him to get some information about prohibition affairs, too.[18] That accounts for one of the strangest aspects of Means's career— a period in which he had been suspended by the Department of Justice, but was employed by the Treasury as a customs agent.[19] The Federal records show that this was the case, but, other than

151

Means's own story, there is little information as to why this was done.

Roy A. Haynes, the Prohibition Commissioner, wrote to Burns asking for information about Means and received, in reply, a glowing letter in which Burns described Means as "a resourceful, courageous, intelligent man." Haynes could not ask for a better agent, he said, " . . . Mr. Means has made some very powerful enemies by the courageous manner in which he has gone after crooks who have robbed the government. . . ." which accounted for Means's temporary suspension from the Department of Justice payroll.[20]

Armed with such recommendations it was not difficult for Gaston to move freely in government circles, suspended or not. He did not vacate his office in the Justice Department, a matter that caused considerable interest on the part of a slim young man in the Bureau named J. Edgar Hoover and one of the unimpeachable Assistant Attorneys General named Rush Holland. Holland became so interested in Means's continued presence in the office that he called Gaston in for a conference on March 24.

After the conference, Means reported to Burns that he had been called at his hotel at about 11:45. "As requested," he wrote Burns in a memo, "at 12:05 P.M. o'clock I arrived at Mr. Holland's office in the Department of Justice and was in a conference with him from 12:05 to 12:17, and present at this conference besides myself was Mr. Hoover and Mr. Holland."

Holland had called Means in to ask if he had been suspended, and if so, what instructions Burns had given him at the time of his suspension. Means said that Burns had told him to discontinue the handling of any new cases and to close as soon as possible any old ones, but Burns wanted Means to complete his work in connection with weekly charts and food charts he was preparing for the cost-of-living investigation, so the government would not sustain a financial loss by Means's dropping of that work.[21]

Gaston's report to Burns was typical of the man. Always, in

reports and testimony, Means piled up insignificant detail, which gave an air of truthfulness to statements that otherwise would appear most questionable. His use of the exact minutes—"12:05 to 12:17" when he was in conference with Holland and Hoover— was almost a trademark of Gaston's. And the use of such detail helped him immeasurably in covering up important facts he wanted to delete, and in the retailing of stories that were undoubtedly made of whole cloth.

For example, although Means had been in the Department of Justice for only three months by the month of February, 1922, and had not met Jess Smith before that time, Means later would tell a Congressional committee that he collected hundreds of thousands of dollars for Smith and turned the money over to Smith during those months, and that, in February, 1922, he had collected $100,000 one evening from a mysterious Japanese who appeared out of the murk of evening at the Bellevue Hotel.[22] Means could not remember the day, he could not remember how thick the stack of thousand dollar bills was, or very much else about that meeting. But when it came to a talk with an Assistant Attorney General, Means could remember the exact detail.

The confrontation called by Holland that March day was an indication of the turmoil within the Department of Justice during the Harding Administration, and even more an indication of the strange state of affairs in the Bureau of Investigation. William J. Burns tried to bring New York private detective methods into the Federal government when he became Director of the Bureau. He had no qualms about search and seizure, or the employment of known criminals and men of bad reputation, if they could secure the information he wanted in the service of the Department of Justice. It was true that it had been a long time since President John Quincy Adams had erupted in anguish at the breach of courtesy accorded him by the Congress a century before, and that the concepts of mutual respect and privilege between Executive and Legislature had been going downhill ever since 1825, yet they were never to suffer quite so much as in these two years of the Harding Administration. Burns had no qualms about searching a Senator's office, if he thought he might find anything there that he wanted. One department of government spied on another, and when Congress began to probe the affairs of the Justice Department, the Bureau of Investigation was turned into a protective counterintelligence organization.

Attorney General Harry Daugherty was responsible for this situation. Even had he been simply the shallow buffoon that his defenders would make him out to be, Daugherty must accept responsibility for the employment of William J. Burns, who in turn employed men of the caliber of Gaston Bullock Means to oversee the nation's internal security, men so remarkably arrogant that, even when taken off their jobs by the order of the Attorney General, they did not get out of the office.

Means, in effect, was not removed from the Federal payroll during his suspension, although he was not again to be a regular employee. Burns simply put Means on the "blue slip" system. He took the precaution of not drawing any blue slips for the time being—Means was not paid by the government from February 15 to May 29. But, at the end of May, Means received a check for $1,100 and during the summer and fall he continued to receive checks.[23]

Since he was relieved of routine work, Means was able to concentrate on the matters that interested him most, bootlegging and influence-peddling. The former activity took a considerable amount of planning, for, when total prohibition of the sale and consumption of liquor was pushed onto the people of the United States in 1920, it was necessary to establish a huge bureaucracy and a complicated set of regulations. The government realized, after prohibition began, that it was impossible to forbid the manufacture and sale of alcohol in America unless Americans were to cease manufacture of medicines, magnetic compasses, anti-freeze, and other products in which alcohol was essential. Also, liquor itself was prescribed

154

as a medicine by physicians from time to time, so Carry Nation and her associates could not hope to win a total victory, even though they achieved an end to the saloon. In bringing about this end, the unwary citizens and legislators of America created irresistible temptation for low-paid policemen who for the first time in their lives were shown by liquor lovers how they could become wealthy overnight.

There were several legal ways in which to draw liquor from the warehouses, which were bonded and watched by Federal authorities. Since the object of prohibition was to create national sobriety and not to ruin businessmen, it was recognized as only just that those who had been making liquor legally, or selling it, should be able to get rid of their supplies abroad. So, with the necessary papers, a businessman could withdraw liquor and ship it to Canada, Mexico, or elsewhere. Besides this, a druggist or manufacturer who was engaged in a legal business where alcohol was needed could withdraw liquor from bonded warehouses. First, he needed a basic permit, or a license to deal in intoxicating liquors. The permit did not allow him to withdraw liquor, but it did establish the amount he might withdraw during a year.

That seemed very simple in the beginning. But government soon established a complicated system of control, involving a number of forms to be submitted. Form 1404 was an application for a permit. Form 1405 was the permit. Form 1408 was a bond, which must be given by the man who received the permit. Form 1410 was a withdrawal application, issued by a state prohibition director and returned to him. Form 1410-A was the permit to purchase liquor. Form 1410-D was the verification of the purchase. Besides using these forms, the man who wanted to buy liquor, even legally, must meet other requirements regarding the payment of tax, fixing of tax stamps on the liquor, and transportation. Matters were further complicated by the establishment of "concentration bonded warehouses," which were brought into being to cut down on the number of warehouses that must be watched.

Immediately, of course, there arose a brisk business in the sale of Forms 1410-A to persons whose only claim to manufacturing was that they made cocktails for their own consumption. And it was in this atmosphere that Gaston Means found challenge and opportunity.[24]

Following the meeting with Rush Holland and J. Edgar Hoover, it must have seemed a good idea to Means and Burns that Means should temporarily stay out of the Washington offices of the Bureau of Investigation; so, during the spring of 1922, Means transferred most of his activity to New York City. He engaged in one or two further adventures in Washington that spring, such as the Case of the International Bankers. Waller International Bankers of Washington were under investigation by the government—or at least Means told a member of the Waller family with whom he had gone to college that they were. Means also suggested to this Mr. Waller the name of a lawyer in Washington whom it would be wise to see. Then Means hastened to the office of the lawyer and suggested that they blackmail Waller. Means would hush up the matter in the Department of Justice. But this lawyer was an honest man and wanted no part of such schemes. When the banker came to him, the lawyer advised the banker to go directly to the Department of Justice with his own attorney and report the matter to Attorney General Daugherty.[25]

Such a failure would tend to hurry a man out of town for a time, and, by late spring, Means was working in New York City, establishing the long lines that would begin to earn money for him in the future. He was also working at that time in Washington for Jess Smith, he said later, investigating a number of the members of the House of Representatives and the Senate who were attacking Attorney General Daugherty, and taking an occasional pay-off for Smith's campaign restoration fund. Means was later to make full use of the story of the fund, which he said was established by Secretary Andrew Mellon and Jess Smith and others to pay the Republican party's campaign debts.

Gaston B. Means

Commuting back and forth, since his family remained in Washington at the Bellevue Hotel, Gaston met many bootleggers and lawbreakers in the nation's largest city. Two honest public officials, U.S. Attorney William Hayward and his assistant John Holley Clark, Jr., were then investigating various cases of bootlegging and corruption in New York. The basic problem in the city in that period stemmed from the office of the state director of prohibition, where corruption seemed to be the rule rather than the exception. Means started off by securing a complete confession as to wrongdoing from Henry Grunewald, confidential agent for Director Day of New York, in the matter of the removal and disappearance into the maws of the speakeasies of 4,900 cases of whisky from the Republic Storage Warehouse during May and June. Means's feat impressed a number of persons, including another Assistant Attorney General, Mrs. Mabel Walker Willebrandt, who was then working closely with the Treasury Department to enforce the prohibition laws. With Mrs. Willebrandt's encouragement and backing, Means said, he spent the months from May through August in and around New York City, investigating everything that pertained to prohibition and its enforcement.[26]

Means was not idle in his own behalf during this period. The Bellevue Hotel was to be torn down, and he was forced to move during that summer of 1922. Gaston's blackmailing and eagerness to accept bribes for services he had no intention of performing were paying off that summer. True, he owed the Bellevue Hotel more than $1,000 when the hotel closed its doors and made ready for the wreckers in July, but Gaston was never quick to pay his debts. If a sign of his prosperity were needed, it was in the move to the Hotel Gordon, where, on July 19, Means engaged a five-room suite for his wife, nurse, child, his father-in-law, W. R. Patterson, and Patterson's second wife. On that same day, Means also took a three-room suite which he would use for his own offices.[27]

Gaston's exuberance in making rental arrangements had come about for several reasons. One was that Clark Grier had called bootlegger Willie Haar to Washington from Savannah, and had informed Haar that he was about to be victimized by the Department of Justice, acting in the name of the Treasury Department. Haar, it appeared, had grown forgetful about his income tax in these busy years of prohibition. Grier informed Haar that a friend of his in the Department of Justice, by the name of Gaston B. Means, could settle all Haar's income tax troubles and prevent the Department of Justice from indicting him. It would cost $10,000. Haar replied that he did not carry that amount of money about with him, whereupon Grier agreed to go to Savannah and collect it. So the agreement was made, and Grier was ready to collect $5,000—the first installment.[28]

Means had just met a short, fat man in his forties, a Chicagoan named Elmer Jarnecke, who had been spending a good deal of the past year in New York and Pittsburgh, trying to arrange for some bootlegging activities on behalf of himself and his partner. That was one of the reasons for the engagement of the private office space in the Hotel Gordon—Means suddenly realized that his business was growing so rapidly that he needed space for expansion, and a capable assistant.

Jarnecke was a man without education or culture. He had worked in Chicago for a number of years for the International Harvester Company. After fifteen years he was discharged when suspected of dishonesty, but not prosecuted. He had been a butcher and had gone into the wholesale poultry business, but it had failed. He had then made contact with a jeweler named Samuel Schmidt who was interested in liquor, and, on a trip East, Jarnecke had met Colonel Morgan, who was trying to sell some five hundred thousand cases of whisky that belonged to the Old Jordan Distilling Company. This was liquor that had been distilled before prohibition. There was no law against owning it, or warehousing it. The only difficulty for Colonel Morgan and his associates was to get rid of it, and Morgan wanted to do so legally, at least within the letter, if not the spirit, of the law.[29]

158

Gaston B. Means

After many negotiations during the winter and spring of 1922, Jarnecke learned of Means and came to Washington to see him. When Jarnecke arrived at the New Willard Hotel on July 12, he sat down and wrote to his partner, Samuel Schmidt, in Chicago.

Dear Friend Sam:

Arrived five hours late, and met two of the people and they are satisfied, but must meet the Department of Justice man Friday morning at 10 o'clock and then they will discuss the 200 propositions, they tell me they have a way that they will work it out without any wholesale drug house at a cost of possibly $30 or less and they surely are the berries, these fellows are as fine a lot as I have ever met and we are going to be in right at last. Will write you full particulars Friday evening. I invited them to take dinner with me Friday and Mr. Holmes is the man who will issue the documents.

Talk about duck soup? It will have to be turkey soup, and when I asked them about Morgan they said the colonel is o.k. but he can only do business one way and of course his hands is tide [sic], they say they started out the same as Col. Morgan but were soon convinced that no one would put up any such amount of money until they had some assurance of seeing the goods. Will write you fully Friday evening.

Sincerely yours,

Elmer.[30]

On July 14, Jarnecke did go to the Department of Justice, and there learned that the man he wanted was Gaston Means, not Holmes. Means was only too glad to discuss "200 propositions" or any other number, and soon the two were talking of many things. By the end of the day, Means had so impressed Elmer Jarnecke with his personal magnetism and exalted position in government, that Jarnecke's head was spinning as he sat down to write again to Samuel Schmidt.

159

Dear Friend Sam:

It is now 11 o'clock and the crowd just went home and hear [sic] is the proposition, we will be able to handle anything, either Boxes or Barrels, and either from Kentucky or Maryland or Pennsylvania. The price of all papers will cost us $20 and barrels will be figured at the price of cases, three gallons to a case. For instance a barrel containing 36 gallons will be 12 cases (cost us $240) with a guarantee direct from the head of the D of Justice that goods will be shipped to the man's warehouse and protected while in the warehouse. Of course he takes his own chance while delivering on the street. They say that no one could guarantee any more than this and if they do they lie. However this, I think, is better than ever.

All parties must come to this department in person and must see me first at the Willard Hotel. I will take them to the Department of Justice. There they pay their money and we are protected at whatever prices I say, and they will get their goods from whatever distillery they want. This has been changed this week so as to give all Distillers the same show. . . .

. . . Send your men hear [sic] as fast as you can and the Dough is ours. The Boss will leave Sunday evening and won't be back for a week, so shoot them to me and I will do the rest. . . . I cannot mention any names for I will lose all if I do but when they come I will show them the man and take them to him in his own office. . . . So hustle old boy. I brought you the bacon so it's up to you to fry it and get them to me an [sic] let all your other business go to Hell for this is where we will shine.

> Sincerely yours,
> Elmer[31]

The thoroughly dazzled Jarnecke now appended a "show letter" for Schmidt to use in rounding up prospects—patently a letter that was produced on directive from Gaston Means. Jarnecke, who always signed his own name, signed this letter "Mac," and now, although he had talked endlessly on the long distance telephone, he refused to talk further. In his use of the term "the Boss," referring to Means, Jarnecke let Schmidt know something that perhaps Jarnecke did not yet realize himself: Means had not only made contact to do some business, but he had found his assistant.

One of Gaston's peculiarities was the habit of coining new names for his associates, just as he had coined the title "Old Seventy-Six" for Mrs. Robinson. He referred to Burns constantly as the Governor, both in talking about him and in talking to him. Now he renamed Jarnecke, calling him Emil, and not Elmer. Perhaps Means thought the name more fittingly Germanic, or perhaps he unconsciously regarded Jarnecke as less than bright, which was the sad truth. Jarnecke did not object, nor did he complain too much when the glowing word pictures painted by Gaston Means were not backed by action.

A week later Jarnecke had been to Kentucky, and wrote Schmidt that one distiller wanted papers for 17,000 cases of whisky and would pay $25 a case for the papers, which meant $85,000 for Means, Jarnecke, and Jarnecke's partner Schmidt, whose cut was based on his financing of Jarnecke over a period of more than a year in "deals" that faltered, one after another. Jarnecke also informed Schmidt of the forthcoming arrival of two others in Washington who were coming with money, prepared to "do business."[32]

With such an eager assistant to leave behind, and one carefully cautioned to name no names, to never talk on the telephone, and to keep "the Boss" informed day and night, Means saw no particular interruption in his business life to go to New York and complete his part in the prohibition cleanup attempt there. His first line of approach was to make himself known to a number of bootleggers: Mannie Kessler, Morris Sweetwood, Emil Wormser, Charles Kurtzman. He went sailing with Kessler on his private yacht, and spent his evenings in speakeasies or with arms draped on the table of a hotel room, and a big black bottle sitting on the table.[33]

Willie Haar came up to New York, having paid his second installment of $5,000 for protection from indictment on income tax charges, then learned to his shocked disgust that the indictment had not been thrown out. Haar met Means at the Pennsylvania Hotel, in Grier's room. Gaston asked the bootlegger if he wanted a bottle of whisky, which Means said he had brought in by seaplane from outside the twelve-mile limit. Having softened his quarry again with another promise (and this one he could fulfill), Means gave considerable time to telling Haar that he was William J. Burns's right-hand man, and that, if Haar would come through with more money, there was no question about "fixing" his case. Willie Haar left the meeting sure that his future was secure, and that any indictments would be quashed. (Two years later Mr. Haar could be reached by addressing Prisoner No. 17523, Atlanta Penitentiary.)[34]

Armed with what seemed to be an endless supply of documents from high government officials, Means made a large splash in New York investigating and bootlegging circles. His truly positive achievement was to crack the bootlegging case that involved the La Montagne brothers, a firm of society bootleggers.

E. La Montagne Sons, Inc., was one of the oldest and most respectable wine-importing houses in New York City. At the beginning of prohibition they maintained a select shop at 280 Madison Avenue. After prohibition, when a good address meant less than nothing at all to a wine house, the La Montagnes moved to 632 West 34 Street, close to the Hudson River, where they set up operations as the Green River Distilling Company, and later as the Eminence Distilling Company.

In 1920, using permits they were able to secure from the notoriously corrupt New York State Prohibition Office, the La Montagnes disposed of huge quantities of liquor to speakeasies and society patrons. The following year, working through liquor brokers, they disposed of more—with permits acquired illegally—including quantities of wine and whisky sold to Vincent Astor, Robert Walton

Gaston B. Means

Goelet, Mrs. William K. Vanderbilt, Joseph Widener, and Whitney Warren.

In 1921, one of the members of the firm proposed that the La Montagne brothers go into liquor sales on a much larger scale. First, he said, they would buy up rabbis' permits from Jewish rabbis in the area. For income tax purposes they would charge the books with $2 less than the market price for each bottle of wine acquired. Then they would sell the wine at whatever price the traffic would bear. The profits would be divided secretly, and part of them would be used to finance a whisky pool. The rabbis were to get $7 per case for the use of their permits. The whisky pool would acquire druggists' permits, each of which called for delivery of fourteen cases of whisky.

During 1921, and most of 1922, the scheme worked very well. The records were locked in the vault of the Harriman National Bank, and the La Montagne brothers never delivered any suspicious bundles anywhere. Most of their deliveries were made by a truckman named Joseph R. Burrows, who maintained a draying stable next to the La Montagnes' new establishment on New York City's west side. Much of the "material" was to be delivered to the thriving cottages of Newport, Rhode Island, so Drayman Burrows packed the goods in piano cases and large packing cases before trucking them up through Westchester County and Connecticut. Small quantities were shipped in specially made cartons which were labeled "writing ink."

All went well until February 22, 1922. On that Washington's Birthday holiday, the La Montagne brothers were robbed of twenty-five barrels of whisky and several cases of bottled liquor. On February 23, when the theft was discovered, Rene La Montagne telephoned James Pershing, Assistant Prohibition Director for New York. He reported the robbery and then hung up the telephone, to wait for the arrival of prohibition agents to inspect his loss. Instead of prohibition agents of the usual variety, the man who appeared at the La Montagnes was Patrick McAllister, also known as McGee, a gentleman who shared a Fifth Avenue apartment with Assistant Director Pershing. Here was a golden opportunity, said McAllister. For $10,000 he would "write off" the robbery, he said, and provide permits for a new supply of liquor.

It sounded like such a good idea that, the next day, thirty-three more barrels and a number of cases were taken to the stable next door, and in the report it was claimed that fifty-eight barrels and thirty-five cases of liquor had been stolen in the robbery. Rene La Montagne swore to it. Thereafter the La Montagne brothers did more business with McAllister, and, each time, the "write-off men" of the prohibition unit came to take care of the problem.

The liquor from this profitable enterprise was delivered to the most respectable of addresses. New York's Racquet and Tennis Club received some 30,000 gallons. (Squash and tennis players do get sore feet and need alcohol rubdowns.) Then Gaston Means entered the case. On November 10, 1922, Means went to the office of Assistant U. S. Attorney Clark, escorting a cowed bookkeeper named Arthur Stevens, an employee of E. La Montagne Sons. Stevens made a complete statement about the company's financial affairs, and the statement was used by the U.S. Attorney to draw indictments of the brothers, Montagu, Rene, William, and Morgan. Faced with this evidence, the brothers pleaded guilty. It was an embarrassing trial for New York's social world, for many socialites were named as customers of this high-toned bootlegging firm. The staid officials of the First National City Bank were embarrassed to be named as recipients of some two hundred illegal cases of champagne.

Having entered a guilty plea, the brothers were sentenced: they must remain out of the liquor business for three years, they must make full restitution and payment of all taxes; each brother was find $2,000; Montagu was sent to Essex County Jail for two months and each of the other brothers was sentenced to four months. A slap on the wrist? Indeed, but the credit for the slap was always to be claimed by Gaston Bullock Means, and it was to remain for several years one of the most puzzling incidents in his career.[35] To be sure, the case established his reputation as an investigator. U.S. Attorney Hayward gave Means credit, and so did his assistant, Major Clark, and so did Assistant Attorney General Mabel Walker Willebrandt. But why did Means, of all people, turn the La Montagnes in?

The answer was simple enough, although it took time for it to emerge. Means had tried to blackmail the La Montagnes, and they refused to pay. Even after indictment, Gaston promised that the cases would be quashed if they would pay him $100,000. But the La Montagnes, defended by three of the most eminent counselors in New York, did not listen to Gaston Means, and thus saved their money and their time.[36]

Means, having turned in his acquaintances, announced suddenly, in the autumn of 1922, that he had been called back to Washington by William J. Burns. He returned to Washington in November, but did not again collect money from the Department of Justice. Gaston was convinced that he had found the way to fortune. As he told his new assistant, "our gold mine is going to be opened in a few days now."[37]

IX

Julie Means used a succinct if trite phrase to describe her husband's activities in the autumn of 1922. By October, she said, Gaston was "hand in glove with the bootleggers." Julie knew whereof she spoke. She recalled that on October 22, at the Hotel Vanderbilt in New York City, a bootlegger gave Gaston $5,000. On October 24, another bootlegger gave him $11,500. On October 31, another bootlegger handed over $13,800. All in all, that fall, Julie estimated, Gaston collected $50,000 from the bootleggers, and that accounts only for the transactions of which she knew.[1]

Since Gaston's business affairs were prospering, the living arrangements in the Hotel Gordon seemed cramped, so Gaston rented a house at 903 16 Street, N.W., hired three household servants, bought a Cadillac limousine, and employed a chauffeur to drive it. He moved his father-in-law into the new house in October to make it ready for the family, but he and Julie spent most of that month in New York City.

On November 12, when he announced to Major Clark that he had been recalled to Washington, Means might have said he was

167

summoned by William J. Burns to assist in the task of preventing Harry Daugherty's impeachment by Congress. After an uncomfortable summer, in which Daugherty's name had come before Congress time and again in relation to the government's failure to prosecute apparent malefactors, Congressman Keller had called for the Attorney General's impeachment. Daugherty claimed that the impeachment proceeding was a "red plot" of the labor movement. During the summer he had put down a series of strikes. In one case, trainmen of the Santa Fe Railroad had deserted their trains in the midst of the California desert near Needles, leaving passengers and valuable freight in the baking sun. While the strike was at its height, Daugherty employed a young U.S. Attorney from upstate New York named Hiram C. Todd to prosecute the striking trainmen. Within a few days Todd left for the West and after four months he wired the Attorney General that a jury in Los Angeles had brought in a verdict of guilty against all six of the leaders of the striking trainmen.[2] So Daugherty won the enmity of Labor, but he also defeated the Congressional committee that was trying to formulate impeachment charges against him.

In this impeachment struggle, Daugherty showed no hesitation in using the powers of the Department of Justice to serve his own ends. His loyal subordinates may have gone even further than he expected. Means had certainly done his part, working manfully to discover skeletons in the closets of the legislators who attacked Daugherty.

In August, Means met Laura B. Jacobson, who had been the secretary to Senator Kirby of Arkansas for fourteen years, until he was defeated in 1920 by Senator Caraway. Miss Jacobson had gone out of office with her employer on March 4. Now she had returned to Washington to visit friends and find a job. Since Senator Caraway was in Europe, Miss Jacobson dropped by the old offices in the Senate Office Building. The Senator's clerk, a lady from Alabama, was acquainted with Sidney Bieber. Through Bieber Miss Jacobson met Means. He told her he was working for the office of the Alien Property Custodian, and that he would employ her at $50 a week. Only later did Miss Jacobson learn that the job was investigating Senator Caraway, one of the leaders in the fight against Daugherty. Means promised that through Daugherty he would secure Senator Kirby's appointment to the U.S. Tariff Commission. The Senator had sought that job just as he was being forcibly retired from office, but the appointment had not been made, and he had returned to Little Rock to practice law. Miss Jacobson saw a way in which she could help her old employer and be assured of a permanent position in Washington.

So Miss Jacobson went to work at the Means office in the Hotel Gordon, investigating Senator Caraway for Means, for Burns, for Daugherty. The investigation, and Miss Jacobson's story, did much to explain the equivocal position of Gaston Means during this period. Gaston was a Federal employee, but he really was not. He worked for William J. Burns, but he did not work for him. Such "cover" was important, in case the Daugherty matter got out of hand.

Miss Jacobson did not like her part in the plot, and every day, when Means came to the Hotel Gordon, he was forced to reassure her that all was going well. Soon, he said, Senator Kirby would receive his appointment. In the meantime, she must say nothing to anyone or the entire plan might collapse. Naturally, Miss Jacobson kept quiet and kept on with her distasteful work, anxious lest she annoy Means.

Late that autumn, after his own extended trip to New York, Means sent Miss Jacobson to the northern city for a few days to seek information about Senator Caraway. While she was there in New York, the impeachment proceedings collapsed. Means telephoned to her to come back to Washington and send for Senator Kirby. Daugherty and Company were ready to give him the job on the tariff commission, Means said.

Poor Senator Kirby! Fourteen years in Washington had not improved the soil in which his law practice grew in Little Rock.

Yet, at his own expense, the former Senator boarded a train and went to Washington where he remained for nearly two weeks. It is inconceivable that a former Senator would spend so much time in the national capital with encouragement only from one Gaston Bullock Means. William J. Burns knew of the Senator's interest in the tariff job, and told Miss Jacobson that he had been asked by Means to intercede with Daugherty. But, again, nothing came of it, and the former Senator went back to Little Rock, poorer by his train fare and expenses and loss of time. Miss Jacobson continued to work for Means—or at least to report to his office, first at the hotel and later in the house on Sixteenth Street. She remained until April, 1923, although, after December 15, 1922, she did not receive any salary—just promises and soft talk from Means and his father-in-law, W. R. Patterson.

The campaign to impeach Attorney General Daugherty failed, but the bad odor surrounding the Justice Department grew stronger in the nostrils of Congressmen, and the campaign was later to affect the career of Gaston Bullock Means. In the autumn of 1922, however, Gaston was far too deeply immersed in boot-legging to pay much attention to government affairs. While he was in New York, Means had left Elmer Jarnecke to tend his office in Washington. Jarnecke telephoned several times to Theodore Stevens of New York. Stevens was later raided, and the authorities confiscated 250 gallons of alcohol on his premises. Jarnecke talked to August Jansen, proprietor of the Hofbrau House on Broadway, who was in trouble for liquor violations. He spoke to officers of the Baltic Bank, a notorious New York banking institution which catered to rumrunners. He also called Bill Dwyer, the man the Justice Department termed "the biggest rumrunner in the East."[3]

Gaston Means left such details to Jarnecke, for he was involved in more important matters. It was only proper that his assistant should separate real leads from false ones; Means moved in only where there was promise. Means had kept in touch with George Remus, the Chicago and Ohio lawyer and bootlegger. After Remus

United States Senate,

COMMITTEE ON MILITARY AFFAIRS.

Washington, D. C.
March 31, 1924.

Mr. Gaston B. Means,

903 - 16th Street, N. W.,

Washington, D. C.

Dear Sir:

You are hereby commanded to deliver to the Select
Committee on Investigation of the Department of Justice, all
of your records, files, diaries, reports and copies of reports.
and all papers in your possession in connection with the
Department of Justice, to be impounded.

Smith W Brookhart

CHAIRMAN, SELECT COMMITTEE
ON INVESTIGATION OF THE
DEPARTMENT OF JUSTICE.

Lord one thousand nine hundred and ....

Smith W Brookhart

Chairman Committee on

Sample genuine signature about same time.

no Typewriter of this style in my office.

An example of a typical Means maneuver—in this case a forged
document. Senator Brookhart's actual signature and his comment
about the typewriter used for the document can be seen at the
bottom.

—*Wide World*

Gaston B. Means after his arrest in the Lindbergh fraud. Also pictured are U.S. Commissioner Turnage, talking to the policeman, and J. William Tomlinson, attorney for Means. This is one of the earliest photographs of Means to be found. Though he had no aversion to publicity, he was rarely caught by photographers.

Commissioner Turnage reading charges to Means, who pleaded not guilty.

Some minutes later Means was still demonstrating his customary confidence.

—*Acme*

Means with Deputy Marshal John Clarkson and attorney Tomlinson before his hearing with Commissioner Turnage.

The press seems dubious but Means displayed his customary aplomb in an interview after his arrest. Professional bondsmen later refused to meet his bail, which was set at $100,000.

Gaston Means leaving the courthouse after the first day of the Lindbergh extortion trial. He appears purposeful, but somewhat less optimistic than usual.

Mrs. Gaston B. Means at the time of the trial.

Means with bondsman James Conroy after putting up the bail necessary for his temporary release from jail.

Dimpled, Means smiles happily for the photographers as if to assure them of his innocence.

Means, serving his sentence at Leavenworth, when he attempted to exonerate Bruno Hauptmann the week before the kidnaper was scheduled to die in 1936.

had refused Gaston's offers of assistance, Remus was convicted, along with twelve others, in a U.S. District Court in Cincinnati, of violation of the Volstead Act, and was sentenced to a prison term. Remus was well-to-do, and Means knew it, because Remus appealed his case as far as the United States Supreme Court. Ten days before the matter came before that high court, Means went to see Remus and told him that for $250,000 he could have Remus's case dismissed by the court, and Remus's bar association membership restored. Remus said no. Means returned to see him in Washington a week later and offered to fix the case for $125,000. The money, he said, was to be divided into four parts. One quarter would go to William J. Burns. One quarter would go to Attorney General Daugherty. One quarter would go to William Howard Taft, Chief Justice of the United States Supreme Court and former President of the United States. One quarter would be kept by Means for his bribery of a former President and an incumbent Cabinet officer.[4]

Remus did not bite at the bait. As a lawyer, he knew the incorruptibility of the Supreme Court. One did not need to be a lawyer to know the incorruptibility of William Howard Taft.

Means had no more time to waste on doubting Thomases; many other men in trouble could be found to accept his offers. Gaston left George Remus to the mercies of an unbribed Supreme Court, and Remus was sent to Atlanta to serve his prison term. Means returned to New York City.[5]

In Washington, Elmer Jarnecke was harried at this time by his old partner Samuel Schmidt, for Schmidt had invested $5,000 in support of Jarnecke during the lean period, and the Chicago jeweler wanted a return on his investment. Jarnecke was living at the New Willard Hotel and working in the office at the Gordon. Schmidt came to see him. Every evening Schmidt would accompany Jarnecke to the Hotel Gordon, and wait outside while Jarnecke talked to Means. Schmidt did not meet Means, but he was impressed by him, nevertheless, for Jarnecke told of Means's

181

prowess in bending the instruments of government about his fingers.

After several expensive weeks in Washington, in which nothing developed regarding his own interests, Samuel Schmidt returned to Chicago to wait a little longer. From Jarnecke, Schmidt had learned that vast changes were brewing in the government's method of enforcement of prohibition, and that Gaston Means was deeply involved in them.[6]

The Treasury Department faced innumerable difficulties that autumn in the enforcement of prohibition. President Harding was not pleased with the constant turmoil and complaint, and he was planning to discuss the matter with Congress. The newspapers speculated on the changes, the most common report being that the Justice Department would take over enforcement of liquor laws and control of liquor. Elmer Jarnecke and Gaston Means gleefully clipped all such news items and sent them out as advertisements of their wares.

A typical problem for the Bureau of Internal Revenue occurred when several thousand books of doctors' prescription blanks for liquor were stolen from storage in a building in Washington. So serious was the loss that Treasury Undersecretary S. P. Gilbert, Jr., undertook supervision of the destruction of all the old doctors' prescription blanks and the printing of an entirely new form. It was tiresome work. The members of the Destruction Committee discovered that they could do away with only two hundred packages a day, and they had forty million obsolete prescriptions to burn. The new form was printed on tinted paper at the Bureau of Engraving and Printing, but while the forty million blanks were out of service, only ten million blanks had been delivered to the prohibition enforcement officers in the various districts around the country. The whole system was threatened, as annoyed citizens pressed for change.[7]

After his return to Chicago, Samuel Schmidt received a short letter from Jarnecke. "The old man is feeling like a two-year-old

Gaston B. Means

kid," the note said.[8] The cause of Means's high spirits was a clipping Jarnecke had enclosed from the Washington *Post*, indicating that the prohibition department would be absorbed by the Department of Justice. From Jarnecke, Schmidt had learned that when this occurred, Gaston B. Means would be put in charge of enforcement.[9] The matter was settled, and Secretary of the Treasury Andrew Mellon had approved the change. When it came, prohibition would be handled by a committee of five, Means said. Three of them would be Senators: Cameron, Moses, and Watson. Old Mr. Volstead himself was another. Since he had been defeated for re-election and the Republican organization owed him employment, it seemed only logical that he should administer the bureaucracy created in his name. The fifth member of the committee was to be Gaston B. Means.[10]

Samuel Schmidt could see that Gaston Means was a man of importance in Washington, and he so informed an acquaintance, Isadore Padorr, whom he encountered one day in Chicago. Schmidt knew that Padorr was in the business of securing liquor permits and representing clients who wanted wholesale drug permits. Schmidt gave Padorr a letter of introduction to Elmer Jarnecke.[11]

Padorr was trying to secure some liquor permits for the Val-Dona Drug Company of Chicago. He had met Edward M. Salomon, the president of Val-Dona, earlier that year, after the drug house fell afoul of the Federal government. Val-Dona had been fined $38,000 by the Collector of Internal Revenue, and its permit for manufacture of extracts and other preparations that involved the use of alcohol was canceled when an analysis of the company's products proved them to be substandard. Salomon asked Padorr if he could get the matter straightened out, and Padorr agreed to try, for a price. Padorr then talked to local agents in Chicago and wrote to Washington, and before he was finished the matter was adjusted by the payment of a reduced fine of $5,000.

A few weeks later, Salomon approached Padorr to discuss the possibility of withdrawing liquor. He wanted a liquor permit, since the company had gone into debt during the six months in which it was not producing, and he needed to earn a large sum of money in a hurry. He proposed to put several new medicines on the market that would be notable for their alcoholic content. Padorr again agreed to help, and, armed with his letter of introduction to Elmer Jarnecke, Padorr went to Washington and registered at the New Willard Hotel, then went to Room 407 to see Jarnecke.

For an hour the two men talked about Chicago. Then Padorr got down to business. Usually it took about six months to obtain a liquor permit, but through the influence of a Congressman or a Senator it might be issued in a month. He wondered how quickly Jarnecke could work. Jarnecke was noncommittal, but that evening he took Padorr to the Hotel Gordon where they met Means. Gaston flashed his badge and what appeared to be credentials, and the two men, the broker and the fixer, sounded one another out. Then Padorr returned to Chicago to confer with his clients at the Val-Dona Drug Company.

Padorr was back in Washington within two weeks. Jarnecke now talked of a fee of $15,000 if he and Means secured the permit for the drug company. Padorr said the fee was too high. Finally, they settled on a fee of $8,000, which Means demanded in advance. Padorr later said:

"On November 5, 1922, I left Chicago for New York, where upon my arrival I met Mr. Jarnecke at the Vanderbilt Hotel and gave him the money; but, before I gave him the money, I asked to see Means. I told Means that I had the necessary money, as asked by Jarnecke, with instructions from my clients to ascertain what would be the latest date that they could expect to get the permits. Means then looked at his book and he said, 'Not later than November 20.' Whereupon, I gave to Jarnecke the $8,000."[12]

On November 21, from Chicago, Padorr telephoned Jarnecke in Washington, because the permit had not arrived. He wanted to know if the permit was coming, or if the money was going to be refunded.

Jarnecke replied that the chemists in the prohibition unit were still analyzing the formulas. Padorr gave that information to Edward Salomon and Salomon decided to go to Washington himself. So they went to the nation's capital, Salomon to the Willard Hotel and Padorr to the Lee House, where Jarnecke had moved. When the three men met, Jarnecke spoke up:

"You want to know about your Val-Dona permit. You wait here in Padorr's room and I will be back with the information. So far, the only information I have is just what I telephoned to Mr. Padorr in Chicago."

Jarnecke returned in an hour. He said he would take Salomon to meet someone at the Hotel Gordon, but he would say no more. A few hours later they all went over to the Gordon. Padorr waited in the lobby, while Salomon went up to Means's suite with Jarnecke, and later came down. Salomon seemed to be satisfied.

"I think you are on the right track," he said to Padorr, "but they're awfully slow."

Padorr did see Gaston later in the week, and Means told him confidentially that he had retained a specialist to put the permit through. When it did not come through at the end of the week, and Salomon grew restive, Jarnecke finally called them to come to the law offices of an attorney in the Southern Building. Padorr, Jarnecke, and Salomon went to the office and met Means there. Means disappeared into an inner office, then emerged with his hands filled with formulas and bottles of medicines. It was truly an impressive display. Means also told the three men that the formulas were still held at the Prohibition Unit's offices for testing, but that he thought nine of those submitted would be approved. He showed them the papers. Nine of the papers, sure enough, were marked "o.k." There were no initials or signatures on the papers, just the penciled notations: "o.k."

Salomon grew excited, and said he must rush back to Chicago to see his chemist and rearrange other formulas to meet the requirements of the Prohibition Unit. He took the papers off with him and disappeared.

If anyone wondered why Salomon was in such a hurry to return to Chicago, it was not Isadore Padorr. Two or three days earlier Salomon had gone for a walk with Padorr, and, in the course of their walking, the drug man had told the broker that he was going to be made Prohibition Director of Illinois. Padorr had scoffed, whereupon Salomon had grown annoyed. They walked for two hours, and during those hours Salomon spun castles in the air. He was supported in this, he indicated, by Major Haynes, the Prohibition Director, by Wayne B. Wheeler, counsel for the Anti-Saloon League, and by President Harding.

Since President Harding had never heard of Salomon and Padorr knew it, he wondered if Means had not something to do with this pipe dream. The next day, Padorr discovered that his assumption was correct.

Salomon had gone to see Means that day, and it was shortly afterward that he rushed back to Chicago. Besides conferring with his chemist, he was to raise $50,000, which would be needed to procure the directorship of Illinois. When he got back to Chicago, Salomon appointed several assistants whose services he would need as Prohibition Director, and made ready to take over. He sold out his interest in the Val-Dona Company, and took his family to New York for a short vacation. Just before Salomon left Chicago, Padorr saw him once again and asked him how the formulas were coming.

"To hell with the formulas," Salomon said. "I am interested in the directorship. I will be able to issue myself all the permits that I want."

Padorr, who had other business with Jarnecke and Means in New York, saw Salomon there a few days afterward, and still later he saw him in Washington. For a month, Salomon was certain that he was to be kingpin of prohibition in Chicago. Only when Means and Jarnecke avoided him and refused to talk to him did he begin to understand what had happened. Then he grew outraged, hired private detectives, and confronted first William J. Burns, then Gaston Means with Burns in attendance. Burns suggested that, if the story was true, Salomon should have Means arrested. In the beginning of 1923, when these meetings occurred, Salomon had no such ideas. He decided that the way to get his money back was to put pressure on Means, Burns, Daugherty, and yes, even the President of the United States. He invited Padorr to join him in the scheme. But Padorr had had enough and the "flu" at the same time. They parted angrily, Padorr to continue his "brokerage," and Salomon to continue his search for revenge.[13]

Means was very busy just before Christmas time, taking money to quash indictments and to help bootleggers receive liquor permits. A man named Friedman and an Arthur Johnson, identified as "a former secret-service agent," came to New York because they were under indictment for violation of the prohibition laws. Means agreed to have the indictments quashed for $10,000. The money was telegraphed to him from Cincinnati.

On December 4, Charles Haim of Baltimore gave Means and Jarnecke $10,000. Harry Steinfeld of New York gave Means $5,000. He had been brought to Means by Jarnecke's old friend Samuel Schmidt, and Means took that money to remove liquor from a warehouse in New York City. A Dr. Sacharoff of New York City paid Means $5,250 to fix the removal of 263 barrels of whisky, part of it from a distillery at Meadville, Pennsylvania. Dr. Sacharoff and a man named Harry Goldberg worked together with Means. Means made many promises that fall, but he was very slow in delivery. Perhaps that was because he was so very, very busy.[14]

Anyone who approached Means suspiciously, and many of these wary bootleggers did just that, was likely to be won over by Gaston's dimpled and sincere smile, and by his businesslike manner. Means smoked cigars and blew clouds of blue smoke in the air, as he expounded on the services he could perform for his clients. He often interrupted his talks to telephone William J. Burns at the Department of Justice, or at least to talk to someone he called "governor," to identify him as Burns, and to discuss matters of importance in the field of investigation.

187

Means improved his technique as he went along. By the end of 1922, he had fabricated a complex story that involved so many important administration officials it was difficult for Means's listeners to believe that it could be anything but the truth.

The Republican organization had emerged from the elections of 1920 with $1.8 million in debts, and needed $3 million more for the elections of 1924, said Means.

"We have had many meetings—Mr. Daugherty, Mr. Burns, and the Republican National Committee," he said, "and we decided that the only way this money can be raised quick is in the liquor game."

So Means, said Means, was the man who raised the money. When he raised it, it was split four ways, he said. But this time he described the split a little differently than he had to George Remus. The money was to be divided equally among Burns, Daugherty, the GOP National Committee, and Gaston B. Means. As to himself, Means was not over-modest. "A man, to raise this amount, has to be a pretty slick fellow, and no angel would be put on such a job. That is why I have it, and that is why they have confidence in me. They know what I can do."

During this frenzied autumn, Means and Jarnecke usually went on tour together. Jarnecke carried a briefcase that was divided into six compartments. In one compartment he kept fifty or sixty Department of Justice letterheads; in another compartment he kept envelopes; and in yet another compartment "reports" from the Bureau of Investigation, or at least reports that he convinced his associates were from the files of that organization. Means never carried such papers on his person. Jarnecke carried them always. Means never shared a room or a suite with Jarnecke. Always they were on different floors, and usually they stayed in different hotels. Means liked to keep his affairs to himself.

When he went to New York City, Gaston stayed sometimes at the Vanderbilt Hotel, other times at the Martinique Hotel. Wherever he stayed, he entertained lavishly, always kept quantities of liquor in his rooms for visitors to enjoy, and spoke freely of government officials in the highest circles.

He had long claimed that he was the collection man for Burns and Daugherty, but not so many persons knew, until he told them, that he was able to get anything he wanted from the Justice Department. Mabel Walker Willebrandt, he said, would "fix" any necessary pardon, if only the seekers were prepared to pay enough. Andrew Mellon, Secretary of the Treasury, would employ Means in preference to anyone else to move his own liquor, and the liquor of the banks in which Mellon was interested.[15]

So good an actor was Means, and so reasonable seemed his role, that scores of wily criminals were taken in by him. They were preconditioned, because they knew that skulduggery in the management of prohibition was an everyday affair. It seemed logical enough that Means, in his sensitive position, should be able to do those things he said he could do, and the criminal world, more knowing of the weaknesses of the Harding Administration than the electorate, was also more easily fooled. Means quickly achieved a reputation, by those who did not know him, as a miracle worker.

As had Dr. Sacharoff and Edward Salomon and others, one day Charles W. Johnson, of Philadelphia, heard of Gaston B. Means in a favorable manner. Mr. Johnson had been in the liquor business for a time until prohibition. He wanted to move some liquor, so he asked around for help in the anti-prohibition circles of New York. An acquaintance, Jacob Stein, was a disbarred attorney with good connections in the liquor business. He went to Washington and returned to tell Johnson that the "parties" could arrange for the removal of Johnson's liquor, but that they were not interested unless Johnson could show them the color of his money. (Means was becoming wary now. He had just gone through an unfortunate experience with the manager of Reisenweber's restaurant. He had promised to "fix" an indictment, and the manager had promised to pay $25,000. After one payment of $5,000, the manager had agreed to pay $500 a week, but fell behind on the payments. Means wanted to have Reisenweber's closed, and so he did nothing to stop the process of the law.)

Johnson promised to show money, and was then invited to go to Washington. He did so, around November 25, and Stein arranged for him to see Jarnecke at Lee House. He was glad that the liquor was in the Pittsburgh area, Stein said, because they liked working in that territory.

"Now you ought to know who is in back of this," Stein said to Johnson, indicating quite clearly, in a manner that had Gaston Means stamped all over it, that Pennsylvania's Andrew Mellon was the man behind the scenes.

Johnson, quite taken in, was eager to put up his money. He and Jarnecke sat down to discuss details. Jarnecke said he would have to have $2.20 per gallon for taxes and $4.20 per gallon for bond payment. That money would have to be paid in advance. Afterward, when the liquor was delivered, he must have $200 per barrel for delivery. Johnson nodded and went off to Pittsburgh to make the arrangements. He also went off to Pittsburgh to see the real owners of the liquor, a pair of well-to-do businessmen who wanted to withdraw the liquor for their own use. But Johnson did not tell Elmer Jarnecke that part of the story.

On December 4, 1922, Johnson was ready to do business. Jarnecke called Means "for an appointment" and they went over to the Hotel Gordon to meet the great man. As they entered, Gaston did not stir himself, but continued to dictate to his secretary in loud tones about something that seemed quite important—at least, he dropped a number of important names. Eventually, however, Means finished his dictation. He then told Johnson that these rooms at the Hotel Gordon were used as a private meeting place for Attorney General Daugherty, Commissioner Blair, and himself. And during the meeting, Means was interrupted several times by telephone calls from people he addressed as Mr. Burns, Mr. Daugherty, and by other prominent names.

Gaston B. Means

Shaking off these interruptions, Means turned a friendly eye to his guest and spoke frankly:

"Mr. Johnson, I understand you have some goods you want to get out; I know all about you and all about your troubles. Everything is all right to move these goods for you. Where are they?"

Johnson was wary. He wanted to be sure Means could remove the liquor legally. His friends wanted no trouble.

"Don't let that worry you. It is the government that is doing this," Means said. "I represent the Department of Justice and the Secret Service"—whereupon he flashed his card and badge. He then covered the same ground that he had covered with others, speaking of the large Republican debt and the need for cash payment. "You give me the designation," he added, "the location of the warehouses where you want the goods moved, and give me $6.40 a gallon and I will handle everything and deliver the goods into the warehouse you designate with government trucks and everything, and put a government seal on the warehouse and nobody can bother it."

"I don't understand how you can pay these taxes in Washington to remove the goods," Johnson said. "My understanding of the regulations is that you can only remove the whisky on 1410-A's."

Seeing that he had a more knowledgable man before him than usual, Means was quick to change his approach.

"That is right that the 1410-A's apply only after goods are tax-paid and going through the office of Mr. Haynes," he said, "but when you are dealing with Mr. Blair, as you understand, the goods, as long as they are not tax-paid in the warehouse, are under his jurisdiction, and he can do most anything he wants to in moving and handling them. If there is a warehouse which he deems unsafe for the goods, he could order the goods moved to a warehouse that is safe."

Means then grew mysterious. He would do no more than repeat what he had told Johnson, and he left Johnson to ponder on the strange actions that might be taken by the Commissioner of Internal Revenue, poking around personally in a Pittsburgh distillery to see if it was "safe."

But Means gave some apparent guarantees. He would take the certificates. He would take care of everything. If there were any questions, the distillery need only get in touch with Blair or Daugherty.

So the deal was made, and Jarnecke took the papers relating to the whisky that was located in the Sam Thompson Distilling Company in Brownsville, Pennsylvania. Johnson told Jarnecke that he had principals in this affair, and he needed a receipt if he was to give up cash. Jarnecke made out a receipt for $15,097.60 and gave it to Johnson, and Johnson handed over $15,097.60 in cash, with a promise from Means that he would get the money back if the goods were not delivered.

Means promised to deliver within ten days. He could not go to Pittsburgh immediately, he said, because he had to take a quick trip to Savannah to help Willie Haar with his income tax. He expected, however, to be back by the weekend and would take the liquor out either on Saturday or on Monday. Johnson went away pleased.

But by Thursday of the following week matters were far from all right. Johnson finally located Means at the Martinique Hotel in New York and demanded indignantly to know what had happened. Means was smooth. He had been delayed with Willie Haar's problems until Tuesday, he said, and then he had to come to New York to look after some important business for William J. Burns. He would be through with the work in New York by Friday, however, and dutifully promised to remove the liquor on Saturday. That was only a week late, and he would not fail. In case he was delayed, he would dispatch a man directly from Mr. Blair's office in Washington, with the stamps and papers, and would make arrangements for a fleet of ten trucks to go from Johnstown to Brownsville, to move the fifty barrels of whisky. Further, he introduced Johnson to Ed Flanagan, the man who would do the job. Johnson went off to Pittsburgh, mollified, to wait for Means as directed, and, as promised, on Saturday afternoon Flanagan appeared at the Fort Pitt Hotel and called Johnson. They talked several times.

Nothing else happened relative to the liquor that day, except that Flanagan spoke of the difficulties of moving the liquor, nothing serious, he said, but several petty problems. But the next morning, Johnson discovered that Flanagan had checked out of the hotel, and Johnson had no liquor, nor had he his $15,000. He called Jarnecke and demanded to know what kind of game they were working.

"Nothing is being pulled on you, Johnson," said Jarnecke. "Everything is all right; the old man is on his way to Johnstown to look after those trucks. They had an accident of some kind."

Jarnecke said there would be delay, but only delay. So Johnson waited. He spoke to Jarnecke later that day. The accident was more serious than they had thought, said Jarnecke. He had been in touch with Means, and Means was on the scene.

Sunday became Monday. Johnson called Jarnecke again, and Jarnecke again said everything was all right. Johnson waited until late afternoon, then tried to get Means at his home in Washington. But Means was not at home, the voice on the other end of the telephone reported. Johnson called Jarnecke, but Jarnecke was just leaving for Boston and could not talk. Washington would keep in touch with Johnson, Jarnecke said.

And that was the end of it. Johnson never heard from Jarnecke or Means or from Commissioner Blair or from Attorney General Daugherty. His $15,000 was gone. It was December 18, 1922, a week before Christmas, and Gaston B. Means was far too busy with Christmas shopping and Christmas cheer to attend to such mundane matters. He was "out of the city" to all his business associates.[16]

It was a very merry Christmas season for the Means family.

During the year they had acquired a huge and luxurious house in which they could place the expensive furnishings left over from Park Avenue days, now that Gaston had acquired the wealth to take them out of storage. The chauffeur was busy running Julie Means to the houses and apartments of friends, so the generous Julie could drop off little remembrances at Christmas time. On New Year's Eve, the Means family gave a gala party for a number of acquaintances, including Miss Rella Lane, who had been Gaston's secretary at the Department of Justice.[17] They toasted in the New Year with champagne, a fitting drink for a wealthy man who dealt in the liquor trade. Gaston Means looked forward to a bright and prosperous 1923. What man ever had his world more securely by the tail?

X

In Gaston Means's pleasant winter of 1922-23, when the money
flowed like whisky, Gaston and Elmer Jarnecke made two mistakes.
The first mistake was Jarnecke's, to sign the receipt for $15,097.60
in favor of C. W. Johnson, with a written promise that if the proper
papers were not furnished within ten days for release of fifty barrels of whisky, the money would be returned.

Means thought little of the incident at the time. When he had
said to Johnson at their first meeting that he knew all about him,
Means meant that he knew Johnson had been convicted of a liquor
offense in Pennsylvania, and, at the moment when they were
negotiating, Johnson was technically a parole violator and a fugitive
from justice in that state. When Johnson had gone to Pittsburgh
to wait for Means and the liquor delivery that never came, Johnson had registered at the Fort Pitt Hotel under the name Jamison,
so careful was he to avoid arrest by the state authorities. Knowing
that much, Means gave no further consideration to what Johnson
might do once he was bilked. If Johnson went to the authorities,
he was certain to be turned over to the state of Pennsylvania, and

195

equally certain then to go to jail to serve the sentence he had so far escaped. Johnson did just what Means thought he would do. He tried to force Means to live up to his word, but failing that, he gave up and disappeared. He decided that for many reasons it would be wise to take up residence in the Caribbean and he did so. He ran a boat between the Bahamas and Florida, and later opened a bakery in Havana.[1]

Such a denouement to a liquor transaction was frequent with Gaston Means. He had discovered the Achilles heel of the bootleg trade. He capitalized time and again on the "code of the underworld" and the helplessness of the underworld to cope with the renegade lawman. Although Means had taken $10,000 from Willie Haar, that unfortunate man had not complained to the authorities, and he was never to complain, officially. George Remus knew Means was a crook, but he said nothing about it to his jailers. Manley S. Sullivan, of Charleston, South Carolina, was indicted for violation of the prohibition laws. Federal agents tried to talk to him later about reports that he had paid Gaston Means to fix the case. But when they came to see him, Sullivan left town. Means obtained $15,000 from a man in Louisville, but the man never appeared to complain or reveal his name. Gaston took a large sum of money from Joseph R. Hayden, a man who lived at the William Penn Hotel in Pittsburgh, always paid his room rent a year in advance, and was widely known as a "sport" and a liquor supplier. But Hayden also had a reputation for walking with a closed mouth. He would not talk, one government man said, even if he lost a million dollars.

Means knew Eddie Donegan, who was convicted of conspiracy to defraud the United States government, sentenced to ten years in Atlanta Federal Penitentiary, and fined $65,000. Means offered to get Donegan off. First, he said, he would have Donegan put into the hospital as an orderly when he arrived at Atlanta, and then would have him appointed as special agent of the Department of Justice to obtain evidence against smugglers in Europe. Donegan would be sent to Europe. Means would substitute Donegan's name for the names of other operatives who were making regular reports to the authority, and, in six months, without doing anything at all, Donegan would be granted a pardon. Means wanted $50,000 for this service. The deal was threatened when Donegan's lawyer tried to reach Means at the Department of Justice and could not. The lawyer then interviewed William J. Burns, Mabel Walker Willebrandt, and others, and discovered that Means was not connected with the government. Means overcame that difficulty. He had the lawyer call the Department of Justice number from the house on Sixteenth Street, and someone answered who identified himself as Burns, and gave Means a clean bill of health. Someone also answered in Mrs. Willebrandt's name. Means showed letters signed by several important officials. The lawyer, once again, was convinced by Means's story that he was engaged in activity in behalf of the government. But Eddie Donegan, in jail in New York's Tombs, was warned by the grapevine that Means was a "wrong guy," and refused to go ahead.[2]

The one successful defense of the underworld against Means was the word-of-mouth warning that he would not produce what he promised. Neither Donegan nor the other victims of Means's confidence game complained publicly or officially. But when he had picked on Charles Johnson, Means had not fully realized that Johnson was simply a go-between, who hoped to earn $25 or $30 per case of liquor from the deal he made in behalf of the two wealthy citizens he represented. One of the men was John W. Hubbard, a steel manufacturer who owned businesses in Chicago, Cincinnati, St. Louis, and Pittsburgh, and who maintained residences in Pittsburgh, New Jersey, and Chicago. The other was Frank D. Saupp, a Pittsburgh auto dealer. Johnson had approached Saupp with a proposal to take liquor out of a warehouse legally and without trouble. Saupp had called Hubbard and each of the two had put up $7,500 on Means's demand for $6.40 per case for taxes and bond. Both men were wealthy enough to take the loss

197

without excessive pain, and they did not complain to the government, officially. Hubbard was acquainted with Arthur Sixsmith, however, a fact that Gaston Means could not have known. Arthur Sixsmith was personal secretary to Andrew Mellon.

One day, not long after the incident, Hubbard lunched with Sixsmith at the Willard Hotel in Washington, and in casual talk he mentioned the expensive joke that had been played on him. Sixsmith laughed and asked Hubbard if he would object to telling Secretary Mellon the story.

"No," Hubbard said, "but I don't think it would do any good."

"I would like to have him know it," Sixsmith said, and persuaded Hubbard to go back to the Treasury with him from lunch that afternoon.

Secretary Mellon, a man of little humor, looked bleak, and remarked that he did not see how he could do anything about it. Feeling uncomfortable about the position into which he had been pushed, Hubbard said he did not expect Mellon to do anything, but had simply come in because Sixsmith had asked him to do so. Mellon considered the matter for a moment, and then decided that he wanted an affidavit on the affair from Johnson. Hubbard was not anxious to go any further. He would have preferred to drop the entire matter, but Mellon was now aroused because of the implication of government agents, and to settle the matter Hubbard made arrangements for Johnson to appear at the Treasury.[3]

Gaston Means could not possibly have done anything to forestall that march of events, except, of course, either to have produced the goods he promised or to have kept Jarnecke from issuing any receipts to anyone. But Gaston did not expect that a victim would be acquainted with a Cabinet member, and particularly the Cabinet member entrusted with enforcement of the prohibition laws. Means, here, was truly a victim of chance.

Gaston's second serious error cannot be so lightly dismissed; it involved a serious misreading of the temper of the Department of Justice. Perhaps Gaston had become so bemused by the corruption he saw around him that he forgot there were still honest men in the Department of Justice who might be aroused to indignation when the scales of justice were tipped by an unwelcome hand. That was the cause of Gaston's second error. He conspired with his old acquaintance, Attorney Thomas B. Felder, to take money from not-so-innocent victims who thought they were bribing the entire Department of Justice.

Means had dealt with a number of attorneys in such matters, and had tested the corruptibility of several others who refused his advances indignantly. In Colonel Thomas B. Felder, Means found just the man for his purposes, for Felder was as corrupt as Means. Perhaps that is how these two formidable gentlemen reached agreement in the beginning, when Felder undertook the case of James C. King's "second will" after several other attorneys had refused to touch the matter, and one court had upbraided Gaston Means for attempting so crude a ploy.

Felder had been a member of the Georgia legislature, and at one time was closely identified with the prohibition movement in that state. He had a collection of letters of recommendation that spoke of him in the highest terms as lawyer and citizen, and were signed by such reputable officials as N. E. Harris, Governor of Georgia in 1917; William H. Fish, Chief Justice of the Georgia Supreme Court; and Walter F. George, then a Judge of the Georgia Court of Appeals. On the other side were Cole J. Blease, former Governor of South Carolina, J. Fraser Lyon, former Attorney General, and several other important South Carolinians who said Colonel Felder was a blackguard. "The worst scoundrel in this region," Blease called him. Blease and Felder had fallen out over the operation of the South Carolina State Dispensary, which in 1910, when Felder was involved in South Carolina, was the official purchasing and dispensing agent for liquor. The Dispensary was first operated by a board of three members, but the administration soon became so questionable that the board was fired and a commission of five members was established. In this attempt to clean house, Attorney General Lyon had employed Felder, then a member of an Atlanta firm. But, instead of the house becoming clean, the situation grew worse, and Governor Blease and others believed that Felder had attempted to bribe various officials for purposes of his own.[4]

Felder had been admitted to the bar before he was nineteen years old, and boasted that he was a member of the bar of some twenty states and had been admitted to practice before the U.S. Supreme Court. When he left Atlanta to practice in New York, five thousand friends gave a testimonial party for him in the Atlanta City Auditorium. He knew Warren G. Harding well (they were both prominent in the Benevolent and Protective Order of Elks). He also knew Attorney General Daugherty well. He and Daugherty had worked together during the Administration of William Howard Taft to secure a pardon for Charles W. Morse, a wealthy Wall Street man who had run afoul of Federal law and had been sent to the penitentiary. Daugherty and Felder secured a pardon for Morse on the grounds that he had a fatal kidney disease and wanted to die at home. (Morse ate a bar of soap, and a pair of gullible government doctors accepted the results as conclusive.) After Morse was released from prison he lived on for fifteen years more, having shown a remarkable recovery, and did not even reform before he died. Felder and Daugherty had to dun him for their fee.[5]

Means and Felder kept in touch with one another after the unfortunate ending of the King will case, and in 1922 they discovered how they might work together profitably. The initiative came from Gaston Means. The matter was one that was to become celebrated as "The Glass Casket Case."

Early in the 1920's, a company was organized in America to manufacture glass caskets. No longer would undertakers be forced to pry up the lids of coffins, as had Undertaker Weddington of Concord, when he and Gaston Means had taken Maude King's body to Asheville so her mother could gaze once more on the beloved features. Once the glass casket came into use, the body would be fully exposed to the eye and, tastefully adorned and cared for by skilled undertakers, the dead would depart the land of the living in better style than ever before. Glass caskets were fabricated and placed on display in various cities, as the company involved tried to interest bankers and the public in its product.

The manufacturer did interest the officers of the Crager System, a New York corporation which financed industries by the sale of stock. Benjamin Crager and his assistants saw great possibilities in the glass-casket idea, and they undertook to sell the stock to the public.

In their understandable exuberance about this product, the Crager salesmen indicated that the glass-casket manufacturing company was farther along in its industrial program than could be stated without mangling truth. The company was really scarcely in business at all. Federal officials took an extremely cloudy view of the transactions of the Crager Company in selling glass-casket stock, and when the salesmen made certain statements in letters to prospects, the Federal authorities decided they were using the mails to defraud. Some fifty or sixty Crager salesmen and officers were arrested in one day in September.

At this time, the Crager matter came to the attention of Isadore Padorr. Mr. Padorr was acquainted with Samuel Rosenblatt, one of the defendants, and when he read in the Chicago newspapers of Mr. Rosenblatt's trouble, Mr. Padorr was shocked and sympathetic.[6]

He called Mr. Rosenblatt and told him that he knew two men in Washington who had the highest connections and could find an attorney who would get the defendants out of the mess in which they found themselves. It was not a question of assuring acquittal, but of persuading the government to quash the indictments, or at least of saving the defendants from serving jail sentences. Padorr suggested that his Washington friends could "fix" the case.

The defendants already had counsel, Joseph Kostner, a Chicago

201

lawyer. Padorr, Kostner, Rosenblatt, and another defendant named Harry Sideman came to Washington, and there Padorr introduced them to Jarnecke. Jarnecke tried at first to get rid of Kostner, for Means did not want another lawyer involved in the affair. But Kostner would not leave, so Jarnecke passed the decision along to Gaston Means. In the beginning, Means would have nothing to do with Kostner. He did not like lawyers, he said. But when he learned that Kostner was also a Chicago alderman, he relented, perhaps seeing a new source of revenue for the future.

Jarnecke brought Kostner to the Hotel Gordon one evening in early October, 1922, and Kostner and Means discussed the matter, after Means had opened the conversation by talking informedly about the bootlegging situation in Chicago.

Means assured Kostner that the matter could be settled if the defendants employed Colonel Felder to help them. Kostner left that night for New York, taking the other Chicago men along to discuss the matter with several of the defendants in the case who lived in New York City. No money had yet changed hands, and no specific fees had been mentioned by Means, but Jarnecke, conferring with Means, had come forth with an estimate that the men ought to be able to pay $40,000 or $50,000. Padorr wanted to be cut in, however, and it appeared that Kostner might want part of the money, so Means raised the fee, and eventually it totaled $65,000.[7]

A few days later, Kostner returned to Chicago. Means had indulged himself in some wishful thinking about the case, and he had decided that since he had not heard from Kostner, he should take the offensive. He told Jarnecke to telephone Kostner.

"You had better call Kostner on the phone and tell him to get a retainer fee down here of $20,000 or everything is off," Means said.

"Suppose I send him a telegram?" Jarnecke asked.

"I do not want any more writing or telegrams," Means replied.

Jarnecke went back to the Willard Hotel and called Kostner as directed. Kostner said it would be impossible to raise so much money, and the conversation ended on an indefinite note. That evening Means took a strong stand, and ordered Jarnecke to tell Kostner that unless $10,000 was in Washington by noon the next day, all was off. Jarnecke did so.

The money did not arrive by noon, but Jarnecke had to travel to New York that day to meet Means, and he left word that all telegrams were to be forwarded to the McAlpin Hotel in New York. On the following day the $10,000 did arrive, and after some confusion, Jarnecke picked it up by identifying himself to the Western Union office.[8]

Jarnecke received $2,000 of that money, after he had turned it over to Means, and Jarnecke paid that amount out immediately to his old friend Samuel Schmidt. The other $8,000 went to Colonel Felder, as part of the fee for the case.[9]

A few days later the Glass Casket defendants came to New York to complete arrangements for their "defense." Means was to meet them that day, but he left the Vanderbilt Hotel in the morning, walked up Thirty-third Street toward the Waldorf Astoria, and told Jarnecke, who was with him, that he must go to the Waldorf to meet with Burns, Daugherty, and Andrew Mellon on some important business. Jarnecke would have to explain to the Glass Casket people and take them over to Felder's law offices. Jarnecke did not go with the defendants, but the defendants went to the offices, and were greeted there by Harold Spielberg, one of Felder's partners. Spielberg knew something about the case, but apparently not much. He suspected something, however, because he kept asking if they had paid any money to anyone. They denied that they had (as they had been instructed by Jarnecke to do), but Spielberg asked the question again.

Jernecke heard that afternoon what had happened, and at 6 o'clock he saw Means again at the Vanderbilt Hotel. Means flew into a rage when he heard the report of Spielberg's remarks. He tried to telephone Spielberg at the office, and when he could not find him, called Spielberg's home, where he was connected with the lawyer.

"I understand that you asked these people that came down to see Colonel Felder whether they had given anybody any money today," said Gaston. "Now I want to tell you not to be butting into any affairs that I have with Colonel Felder. When I send someone down to that office I want Colonel Felder to transact the business and no one else.

"Furthermore," Means said, "these men have been making money when you were carrying a pack on your back. I won't permit any Russian Jew to meddle in my affairs."

Means slammed down the telephone and sent Jarnecke to the McAlpin Hotel where the Glass Casket defendants were staying. He returned to the Vanderbilt, and then Means decided to go over with him to the McAlpin. "Let's go up and see the boys," he said. So they walked back to the hotel, and up to the room of Alderman Kostner. Means went on to the Pennsylvania Hotel for another meeting, but returned at about midnight, and spent another hour with the Glass Casket defendants.

The next day, despite all these attentions, Defendant Sideman was not quite sure how much he was being helped. "Now just what do you expect to do for this amount of money?" he asked Means.

"Well," Gaston replied, "there will be no indictments against you; all your books and papers will be returned to you. You will get a letter from the Department of Justice which will exonerate all of you, saying that a mistake has been made."

Defendant Samuel Safir wondered, aloud, if they could get back to work soon.

"Why, yes," Gaston said. "You can go right back to work. I am at the Department of Justice, and all these complaints come over my desk. I can either pigeonhole them, tear them up, or dispose of them some way, so that there will be nothing against you. . . ."

Defendant Sideman was not yet convinced.

"$65,000 is out of the question," he said.

"That is an awful amount of money, $65,000," said Safir.

"Well now, I will tell you," Means drawled. "My superiors have raised cain with me on account of letting this go so cheap. It should have been $165,000, but I have told you $65,000, and it stands at sixty-five."[10]

Mollified—or at least glad that the punishment was no worse—the defendants agreed to go through with the raising of the money, and returned to Chicago. At the end of October they returned to New York and went to Felder's office for a final financial conference. Felder's private office was an impressive room, equipped with comfortable chairs and thick carpeting. Above the shiny desk hung a picture of Attorney General Daugherty, and the defendants were allowed to believe that Daugherty's own son, Draper, was a constant caller in those offices. (Draper's case was a sad one: he drank more than was good for him and often caused his father considerable embarrassment by placing the elder Daugherty under serious obligation to outsiders.)[11]

Several of the Felder partners attended this meeting, although Felder was not there himself. But the meeting was not conducted by any Felder partner, but by Gaston B. Means. After the preliminaries, which consisted of handing around cigars and cigarettes, Means took charge, and asked the defendants if they were ready to turn over the money.[12]

There was some discussion then, and Means took Alderman Kostner out to a different room for five minutes of private conversation.

"Well, have you got the necessaries with you?" Means asked when he returned to the private office.

"Yes," said Kostner.

"Well, lay it on the table."

Kostner made a move toward his pocket, but was interrupted by Rosenblatt, who leaned over to whisper.

"You are not going to give up the money now, without getting some assurance everything is all right?" Rosenblatt asked.

Kostner gave him a reassuring look and put the money firmly back into his pocket.

Means was growing impatient, moving his balding head from side to side nervously.

"If you have got the money, let's count it now," Means said.

"You are not going to ask us for the money now, make us give the money now, are you, before that thing is dismissed?" Kostner asked meekly.

Means bridled. He was a very busy man.

"I am not going to fool around with this damn thing any longer," Gaston said impatiently. "I am late on an appointment right now. Either you pay over the money or you don't. I'll give you just about three minutes to pay over the money."

The defendants were near panic. Kostner turned to Rosenblatt.

"What do you say about that, Rosy?" he asked.

Rosenblatt turned to Safir.

"What do you think about this, Sam?"

Safir had nowhere to turn.

"I think we are at the mercy of Mr. Means," he said. "I believe we will have to turn over that money."

Kostner handed the money—$47,800—across the desk to Gaston, who counted it with the assistance of Felder's partners. Rosenblatt, still unhappy, asked for a receipt. Means directed the secretary to write out a receipt, which she did. Means then walked out with the others. The money remained in the office. Gaston rode uptown with the others, instructing the cab driver to stop at a place on Sixth Avenue, where he got out for a moment and came back into the taxi carrying a bottle of whisky. At the hotel, Means took one drink from the bottle and then handed it to the others.

"You boys can get the balance," he said.

Not long after this meeting, the indictment of one of the defendants, Samuel Getzler, was quashed by the government, and Getzler fled immediately to Europe to live. The money was divided several ways. Colonel Felder complained that he only got about $25,000 of the total $65,000 which was paid in—the last of it in small amounts. Jarnecke received somewhere around $10,000, but he had to split his money with Schmidt, his old partner, and Padorr, the man who had brought the Glass Casket defendants to them and who wanted a "finder's fee" for the service. Felder said that Alderman Kostner took a large part of the money; Kostner denied that he got any of it. Means denied nothing and said nothing.

Rosenblatt, the nervous defendant, did not like the way in which matters had been handled, and he kept calling New York to learn why the indictments of all of them had not been quashed as promised, and why he had no letter of apology from the Department of Justice.

Toward the end of November, Rosenblatt called Jarnecke, frightened by a rumor that a New York Grand Jury was preparing further indictments.

Jarnecke denied this.

Rosenblatt checked and discovered that his information was correct, and that the grand jury was meeting day after day. He became so worried he called Jarnecke in Washington every day, and finally talked to Padorr. Padorr shrugged and advised him to go to Washington, so, with Sideman, Rosenblatt did go to Washington and to the Lee House, where Jarnecke lived.

In November, life in Washington and in the Justice Department was complicated by the impeachment proceedings against Daugherty. Jarnecke and Padorr blamed everything on this impeachment matter. Daugherty could do nothing at the moment, Jarnecke said.

For a week Jarnecke stalled the Glass Casket defendants, but then they insisted on seeing Means, so were taken to the Hotel Gordon for a conference.

Means was the soul of compassion and courtesy. He was very, very busy with the Daugherty matter at the moment, but it was finally under control, he said, and now he had a moment in which to look into their problem. Excitedly, Rosenblatt told Means that he had heard that a true bill had been brought in against the Glass Casket defendants by a New York Grand Jury.

"It's a goddamn lie," Means said, "but if it is true, you don't have to worry about it. What do you want? Do you want an indictment and a *nolle pros* after that, or do you want to prevent an indictment entirely?"

"I don't want any further publicity to hurt myself and my family," Rosenblatt said, "and I feel Sideman and the other boys feel the same way about it. We have been hurt more by the publicity than the actual indictment."

"You go to Felder," Means said, "and tell him I sent you and tell him to stop that indictment, for him to get in touch with me."

Sideman and Rosenblatt hastened to New York that very day, and rounded up Samuel Safir and went to see Felder. As they came into the office they heard the switchboard operator talking. "Mr. Daugherty, I will see when Colonel Felder can see you." There was a pause as she spoke to Felder. "Two o'clock, Mr. Daugherty." Then they were announced and shown into Felder's office.[13] The lawyer was surprised, he said, to hear of the indictment. He would call Colonel Hayward and seek an appointment to stop this gross injustice, since he believed the defendants were all innocent as lambs.

"If any of you are convicted," he said, "I will go to jail for you."

When they met again the next day, Felder denied that the defendants had been indicted in New York, then admitted, under pressure, that it was so, but he blamed a Chicago lawyer and Crager himself, because they had stirred up "false propaganda" about Colonel Hayward, the U.S. Attorney. Colonel Felder persuaded the defendants to wait in New York for another week. Then, on the eve of their arraignment (which could never happen, he once said), Colonel Felder called the defendants to his office and persuaded them to sign a statement which said he was not retained in this case as a "fixer" but only as a lawyer, doing his duty to help his clients. Only Crager refused to sign the statement.

The defendants went before Judge Knox then, and were arraigned. They pleaded not guilty. Assistant U.S. Attorney McCoy made a motion to increase Safir's bond from $10,000 to $50,000, saying that this was the largest mail fraud case in the history of the post office in New York, and that he had heard that the principals were all preparing to flee to Europe. Felder argued the other side, but without much conviction, apparently, because the bond was raised to $25,000.

Felder called the defendants back to his office, and assured them that he would take care of everything. He would have the Safir and Rosenblatt cases fixed, and Sideman, Crager and the other defendants would be saved, too.

Means, from Washington, reported that the case was all but settled, and that only a few formalities needed attention. And then—a few weeks later, the defendants were indicted for the third time, in Pittsburgh. The end of December came, and Gaston Bullock Means went out of the lives of the Glass Casket defendants who were to be convicted and sentenced to prison for fraud. By the time of the convictions Means was not available for further consultation.

Isadore Padorr suspected that Jarnecke and Means were "running a fake game," and he tried to persuade Jarnecke to come back to Chicago with him. Jarnecke refused. He was not afraid. Means had arranged to cover every transaction by the invention of fictitious persons, he said. In the event of trouble, they would claim that all money had been paid to these people. Besides, Jarnecke said, Daugherty would never dare indict him or Means. Means had too much on Daugherty.[14]

In February, 1923, Gaston Means was busy with the bootlegging business again. Harry Goldberg had shown up and wanted the removal of Dr. Sacharoff's whisky. Dr. Sacharoff provided the necessary certificates, showing ownership, and Means and Goldberg went to Cleveland to stay at the Hotel Cleveland. Means had already collected $5,250 from Dr. Sacharoff, but now he collected another $2,000 from Goldberg.

Harry Goldberg said that in Cleveland Means got drunk—he must have been drunk, because when one of the men at a drinking party in the hotel that night demanded a return of $5,000 that Means had received five or six months before, Gaston pulled a roll from a money belt in which he said there were seventy-two $1,000 bills, and peeled off five $1,000 bills to pay the man.

Two others in the hotel warned Goldberg about giving money to Means. "He's the biggest crook in America," one of the bootleggers said in disgust. Goldberg became frightened and demanded action. Means responded by promising that he was going off to the distillery that very evening, and was just packing. He would come to Goldberg's room before he left on the 6:15 train.

At 5:30 that evening Goldberg's telephone rang, and someone asked if Mr. Means had yet reached the room. Goldberg said no, then called Means's room, where Jarnecke answered and said they were on their way to come and pick him up. They would arrive at any moment.

Ten minutes later, Goldberg went to the hotel desk and asked for Means. The clerk said Gaston had checked out fifteen minutes before. Goldberg went home, and never saw Means again, but he did call Dr. Sacharoff, who took a trip to Washington to try to find Means. Dr. Sacharoff visited the house at 903 Sixteenth Street, but W. R. Patterson would give him no information about Means's activities, and Dr. Sacharoff went home, like so many others—disappointed.[15]

Gaston was pursued by a number of frustrated clients. He decided that something must be done to give him maximum protection against them, so he built a high concrete wall around the back of the house to protect himself from invaders. He barred the windows and the front door, and built a mailbox in front of a window at the ground level. All who came to call were suspiciously conned before they were allowed to enter through the ground floor.

Inside, the house on Sixteenth Street was a complicated ménage, too. Gaston's father-in-law maintained a separate apartment on the fourth floor, with a kitchen of its own, and here Gaston sent friends and acquaintances to dine when he was entertaining others whom he did not wish to mix with his workers. Jarnecke ate upstairs often. So did Rella Lane, who came to work for Means, and

Gaston B. Means

Miss Jacobson, and even Thomas B. Felder when he came to call and found Means occupied.[16]

The ground level of the house was turned over to Gaston's business. He kept a desk there for himself, and one for W. R. Patterson. Jarnecke worked there, and sometimes slept in the office. The other members of the household remained, for the most part, on the three upper floors—especially when Gaston entertained visitors late at night.

February, 1923, was a fateful month for Gaston Means, although on the surface it was impossible to note any differences in his life from the past two years. He continued to visit New York regularly, and to eat roast Long Island duckling and similar delicacies in his hotel suites, where there was no difficulty about consuming wines and liquors.[17] He made promises and important arrangements for shipments of liquor and the "fixing" of Federal cases for those fortunate individuals who sought his assistance. He had become more cautious than in the past. He was quite willing on a trip to Erie, Pennsylvania, to propose the faking of a holdup to take $165,000 away from a man who represented a bootleg syndicate and had come to Erie to meet Means, on promise that Means would deliver 2,000 cases of liquor to him. (The result of that plan is shrouded in the unwritten history of the underworld.) But he was not willing to risk trouble with the authorities. A foreign-language newspaperman from New York had heard that Means could accomplish miracles in appointments, and came to the Sixteenth Street house with a draft for $25,000, which he was eager to give Means if Gaston would only promise to appoint a friend of his as Prohibition Director of New York. Means had said earlier that he could do it for $50,000—but, when faced with the actual cash, Means backed off, for he did not wish to be involved with this man. The man was too well known, and he was a friend of Harry Daugherty's. Means did not want to cause an uproar in the Administration, he said.[18]

But Means was not the only one in control of his destiny in February, 1923. Edward Salomon, the unhappy aspirant to the post of Prohibition Director of Illinois, had given up his attempts at threat and negotiation and blackmail. In February, Salomon called at the Bureau of Internal Revenue in Washington and told his story. A few weeks later, Charles Johnson showed up to tell his story about the bootlegging incident. In April, these matters had gone far. Gaston's connection with wrongdoing was well enough established that Secretary Mellon wrote Attorney General Daugherty an official letter about Means. The question, Mellon said, was who should pursue the investigation? If this man Means *was* an employee of the Department of Justice or was impersonating an agent, perhaps it ought to be investigated by Daugherty's agency. On the other hand, the violations of the law seemed to be concerned with the National Prohibition Act, which ought to be handled by the Treasury.[19]

Daugherty was out of town when Mellon's letter arrived at the Justice Department, but the matter was regarded as so important that he was informed at long distance. He wired back that he had appointed Means only on Burns's request. He had suspended Means, he said, but Burns had pleaded in Means's behalf, since Burns said Means was essential to the investigation of several cases. But because there was already indication that Means was playing fast and loose with the bootleggers, even then Daugherty had ordered that Means be kept away from liquor cases. His orders were disobeyed.[20] So long as Means's didoes had fallen only within the jurisdiction of the Justice Department, Burns, at least, could find reasons for keeping Means out of trouble. There is no question that Burns found Means valuable to him in many ways, and chose to ignore the methods by which Means produced the information and results that Burns wanted. Means had once arrived in Burns's office and thrown $1,000 on the desk, noting that it had come from a Colonel Clifton in New York, a man who was much interested in the liquor situation. Burns ordered Means to return that money, but he had not suspended Means on the spot, or used the attempt at bribery to prefer charges against either Clifton for tendering a bribe or Means for accepting one. It was a strange performance, but one quite in keeping with Burns's estimate of his job.

In May, 1923, Means could be protected no longer. Daugherty replied to Mellon, saying that Assistant Attorney General Crim was making an investigation of the Means matter, and urging Mellon to make his own.[21]

Means was unfortunate in that William J. Burns was not in Washington when the matter came to a head, and Daugherty was brought into it officially. Before Burns could return, the investigation was launched and could then have been stopped only by Daugherty—and not even by him without embarrassment. Slowly, the wheels of the Justice Department began to grind.

It was no longer possible for Gaston to make use of the files and other resources of the Bureau of Investigation, but that difficulty did not keep him from pursuing fortune in Washington. Earlier, in the company of Captain Lloyd of Military Intelligence, Means had begun to work on a plan to collect millions of dollars from the government, from assets of the Germans that had been seized during the war. Means had moved slowly, but he had kept working on this plan all the time he worked in the Bureau of Investigation. One of the visitors who came frequently to Means's downstairs office late at night in the spring of 1923 was Colonel Thomas Miller, Alien Property Custodian of the United States, in whose hands the German assets lay. Miller called the Means house frequently, mostly at night. One time he called at two o'clock in the morning.[22] When he telephoned Means, Colonel Miller used a private line that Means had installed, and the colonel identified himself by saying "the bowling alley is calling."[23]

Gaston's plan to secure some of the millions of dollars in German assets came out of the industrial sabotage committed by German agents in the United States and Canada. The Canadian Car and Foundry Company of Montreal and the Lehigh Valley Railroad had suffered millions of dollars in damages from explosions. By

213

1923, they had made claims before the Mixed Claims Commission, but the companies needed incontrovertible proof that the explosions were actually the result of sabotage. Means employed a Washington lawyer, who approached R. Warren Barrett, general counsel of the Lehigh Valley Railroad, in May, with a proposition to assist in proving the claims. Gaston B. Means, said the lawyer, had valuable evidence. Means was employed by the Germans and when Captain Boy-Ed and Captain von Papen left the United States, they gave Means papers and blueprints that named specific industrial plants destroyed by dynamite under orders from German officials. Means had kept the papers until 1921. Then he turned them over to a pair of men who had been employed by the Germans. That pair of agents had made off for Peru. Gaston could find them again, however, he said, and he could persuade them to bring the papers to Mexico. If the Lehigh Valley Railroad would accept his proposition and pay his expenses, he would go to Mexico.

Mr. Barrett talked this matter over with the lawyer several times. Means wanted $50,000 for the papers and 25 per cent of all the money collected by the railroad from the Mixed Claims Commission.

These conversations continued through the spring and summer. At the same time, in New York, Colonel Miller told an attorney who represented the Canadian Car and Foundry Company that a man named George B. Morris knew something about this destruction. (George B. Morris was a favorite alias of Gaston's. He had often used it in registering at hotels on his hunts for bootleggers.)

That attorney, too, was interested. He asked Colonel Miller to send George B. Morris to see him, and one day Gaston appeared in his office, and made substantially the same offer to the Canadian company that his lawyer had made to the Lehigh Valley Railroad.[24] If either of these propositions worked out, Gaston Means would become a millionaire, as he had always planned.

But other men had other plans for Gaston. By summertime, several of the stories of Means's "shakedowns" and dealings with bootleggers had come to the attention of the newspapers; the Department of Justice investigation was in process; and Colonel Felder, for one, had the wind up, and was trying desperately to cover his tracks. He wrote to Means, expressing astonishment that he, Felder, was reported to be the "New York lawyer" involved with Means in several large liquor transactions. Felder demanded that Means come to his office immediately and deny those reports.[25] Means supplied Felder with an affidavit stating that neither had done wrong. Then Felder wrote indignantly to A. T. Seymour, Assistant to the Attorney General, through whose office the story had been leaked purposely, denying also that he, Felder, had any influence with the Attorney General or had ever pretended to have influence.[26] But the ring continued to close.

In the spring, the lawyers of the Department of Justice decided they had enough evidence to begin an intensive investigation in the hope of bringing Gaston Means to trial. Most of the Glass Casket defendants were thoroughly disillusioned. Felder had committed his own near-fatal error, for in March, harassed by the unhappy Glass Casket defendants, Felder had promised wildly that he was going to make a trip to Washington to see Assistant Attorney General J. W. H. Crim and have the Glass Casket case thrown out of court once and for all. Samuel Safir, to whom he made that statement, asked if Felder would object if one of the defendants went with him. Felder, in an unguarded moment, said he had no objection. Then, because he could not make any such trip without indicting himself as a fraud, Felder disappeared from the lives of the Glass Casket defendants, too. But Samuel Safir remembered the name of J. W. H. Crim, and went to see him in April. As the Treasury looked into Means's affairs, so was Mr. Crim conducting his own research.

In June, the Glass Casket matter was brought to the personal attention of Attorney General Daugherty. It was a ticklish question as far as the professionals of the Department of Justice were concerned, because Daugherty might be involved in this case. He had been associated with Felder in the past. His son, Draper Daugherty, had taken space in Felder's office, and Felder said he had helped Draper establish himself in the insurance business. Felder also said he had helped with the defense activity during the attempt to impeach Attorney General Daugherty in 1922.[27] Felder was using every bit of pressure possible now, to keep his name from being linked with Means and Jarnecke, including a bald attempt to bribe U.S. Attorney William Hayward by offering the support of the Jewish community of New York City to Hayward if he wanted to run for governor.[28]

Hayward could not be bribed. Crim could not be stopped. Assistant Attorney General Seymour could not be intimidated, although Felder, by innuendo, threatened Seymour with a lawsuit. The decision was Daugherty's, but Daugherty had only one possible decision to make. He ordered the investigation to continue, and the various matters to be brought before the Federal Grand Jury in New York City.

Thomas G. Felder was a canny courtroom lawyer, and he was already committed to defend Means and Jarnecke if they were indicted and brought to trial on any charges. Gaston and his "secretary" had become nervous enough in the winter of 1922 to ask Felder that much, at least. Daugherty knew, then, that is was essential that a strong prosecutor be brought in for the government, for to hold a grand jury hearing and lose indictment, or to lose the case, would be worse from Daugherty's point of view than never to have pursued it at all. The Attorney General knew such a man —Hiram C. Todd, who had performed so satisfactorily in the cases of the striking trainmen in the West.

Hiram Todd was a tall, spare upstate New York lawyer, who looked younger than his forty-seven years. He had been practicing law for twenty-three of those years, following his graduation from Union College. Most of that time, except for service in Cuba as a second lieutenant during the Spanish-American war and as a major with the AEF in France, had been spent in his native Saratoga Springs. Early in his legal career Todd's extraordinary abilities as

216

organizer and prosecutor had been noted by his associates. In 1913, he had been one of the counsel for the managers in the impeachment of Governor William Sulzer, a Democratic politician of the old pork-barrel and slush-fund school. In 1921, Todd had been appointed United States Attorney for the Northern District of New York, and had so distinguished himself, by clearing a cluttered legal calendar, that he had been chosen in August, 1922, to prosecute the striking trainmen, when Daugherty wanted a man who could do the job quickly and decisively.

When Daugherty asked him to undertake the Means case, Todd was not eager to do so, but he did promise to study it. When he had done so, he discovered how important the case was, for Means's activities had cast suspicion on two Cabinet departments of the Federal government. Most important to Todd was the effect of the interference of Means and Felder with the processes of justice in the United States. Through the Glass Casket case the reputation of the Department of Justice was threatened, for more than a few attorneys suspected that Federal cases could indeed be "fixed" at the highest levels.

As Todd studied the case he realized that difficulties might lie in the attitude of the Attorney General. Todd spoke to Daugherty frankly, and Daugherty promised him a completely free hand, knowing full well that he and his family might be brought into the affair before it ended. Todd was so distrustful of the Justice Department's Bureau of Investigation that he demanded assignment of one special agent to him alone. That agent would report to Todd and to Daugherty. He would not clear his work through William J. Burns or the usual Bureau hierarchy.[29]

On July 30, it was agreed. Assistant Attorney General Crim added emphasis to the importance with which the honest lawyers in the Justice Department viewed the case. The charges made by Samuel Safir, he said, were first brought to the department by the attorneys for the American Federation of Labor, and later other attorneys had learned of the matter. It was so important in the legal world that no delay could be countenanced, and Daugherty himself said that Means and Jarnecke "ought to be prosecuted in a most vigorous manner." What could be done with Felder was something else—Crim feared that the charges against Felder would bear more investigation, and much more corroboration, because the men who made the charges were themselves under indictment.[30] Todd agreed, and during the summer of 1923, he and Special Agent Lucien Wheeler of the Bureau of Investigation went to work.

Gaston Means was aware of the danger he faced. He responded by doubling his precautions in the house at 903 16 Street. Elmer Jarnecke went home to Chicago. The meetings grew ever more secretive. Means spent much of his time outside the city on automobile trips. He continued his work with the bootleggers, but his supreme effort was now exerted in the search for fortune through the office of the Alien Property Custodian.

In September, Elmer Jarnecke heard that he and Means were being investigated, so he hastened to Washington to talk it over with Means. Gaston calmed him, and invited him to stay at the house for a time. Everything would be all right, he said. Jarnecke should not worry but should leave everything to him.

Jarnecke settled down again at 903 16 Street, but only for a few days. Means announced suddenly that they were going to take a trip to Montreal. Jarnecke did not know why, but he went along, with Gaston, Julie, and the Means boy. They all registered at the Queens Hotel—Means as George B. Morris and Jarnecke as E. W. Jacobs. Means was very busy; he left the others, and he went off to lunch at the Prince George Hotel with officials of the Canadian Car and Foundry Company. At the end of the second day, Means explained something of the plan to his associate. He would have two men in Peru bring the documents to the Mexican border, and the Canadian company would then put in a claim for $30 million. Means would get his fee and his percentage, and they would all be wealthy.[31]

The Canadians were not as firmly impressed as Means thought they ought to be, so he returned to New York City to work on their

Gaston B. Means

New York lawyers, and spent ten days at the Gotham Hotel. Means and Jarnecke were conveniently together in New York City, then, when the Federal Grand Jury that Jarnecke feared brought in its indictments on October 18. On October 22, Means appeared for arraignment, and Jarnecke appeared the following day, both with their counsel, the eminent Colonel Thomas G. Felder.[32] But Means had very little time to spend on such legal trivialities. He was extremely busy with the new plan.

On October 17, Means sent a wire to Colonel Thomas Miller, who had gone to attend the American Legion convention in San Francisco. The wire was addressed to Seton Post, Colonel Miller's temporary roommate at the Palace Hotel, but no one in the Justice Department ever truly identified Seton Post, and the contents were obviously meant for the Alien Property Custodian. Means reported on his trip to Canada. He had proposed a fee of $6,000, plus expenses, to make the trip to the Mexican border and pick up the papers, plus the percentage when the $30 million was collected. Means said he thought the Canadians would make a counter offer, but that he also thought further delay was dangerous in consideration of his and Miller's "interest in the Z-31 matter." Nobody ever figured out what the Z-31 matter was, but it was probably the approach that had been made to the Lehigh Valley Railroad. Means's purpose in sending that telegram was to get Tom Miller to raise some money so he could make the trip to Mexico, and pronto. Gaston was up to his old tricks again, playing one end against the other and all ends against the middle.[33]

Means received an answer to his wire, but it was not preserved. Apparently it was unfavorable, for Gaston did not rush off to the Mexican border, but returned with the quaking Jarnecke to the Washington house to await developments and stir up a few of his own.

While waiting for Colonel Miller to return from San Francisco, Gaston took Jarnecke out one day to look for the money that Grover Cleveland Bergdoll, the wealthy World War I draft-dodger, was supposed to have hidden on Sugarloaf Mountain near Fred-

219

erick, Maryland. Means knew about this money because Colonel Miller had intercepted a letter in the mail sent by Bergdoll to a friend in America, instructing the friend to go up on Sugarloaf Mountain and dig up $125,000 that he had buried there. Means had the exact location, so he made his preparations for the trip. Colonel Miller returned to Washington on November 5, but Means was all ready to go to Sugarloaf Mountain, perhaps there to find the money to take him to Mexico.

The Colonel sent a car to the house. Inside was an older man and a chauffeur. The older man went with them as far as a garage on L Street, then got out.

Means and the chauffeur and Elmer Jarnecke got in to make their trip—but what a new Jarnecke it was! Means had rigged him up in a raincoat and a rain cap, with a huge hood that covered his shoulders and face, so the chauffeur never did see the man he was carrying. Means also instructed Jarnecke to be a German. Jarnecke did not speak very much German, despite the name, but he kept quiet most of the time, and followed instructions.

When they arrived at the bottom of Sugarloaf Mountain, Means and his mysterious friend got out of the car and began to walk. They walked for fully three-quarters of an hour. Jarnecke stumbled once, and when he half turned around, he saw that the chauffeur was following them. This upset Means. When they reached the top of the mountain, Means left Jarnecke on guard while he went out to poke around. He poked for some twenty minutes, then returned.

"All right," said Gaston. "Now we will go to locate a black oak tree here."

Means was carrying a map, and with its help he found a tree he liked.

"Here is the tree," he said. Jarnecke looked and saw a tree that had been blazed with a knife.

They measured off 150 feet from the tree (Jarnecke was not quite sure of the direction). Then they noticed that the ground all around them had been disturbed.

Gaston B. Means

"Apparently someone has been here before," said Gaston, "because everything is dug up. We will simply go back."

Jarnecke was now totally mystified. He had heard the old man who had left them at L Street say to Means that he hoped Means would not be as long this time as last time. So he assumed that Means had been there before and done the digging. But why would Means go through such an act?

On the way home, Jarnecke did nothing but sit in his raincoat and hood, and jabber "*Ja, Ja,*" whenever Means spoke to him. He never did discover what a questioner later ascertained by simple deduction, that the whole act was put on for the benefit of the German-speaking chauffeur, who must have had some relationship to poor Grover Cleveland Bergdoll, who would never see his $125,000.[34]

The mission to Sugarloaf Mountain was an apparent failure (so Jarnecke thought), but it in no way disturbed the growing close relationship of Gaston Means and Colonel Miller. The Colonel's nocturnal visits to the ground floor office of the Washington house became more frequent, and Means and the colonel sat up late in the company of large brown bottles. All autumn and winter the two met in planning sessions. In December, Gaston hired an old acquaintance to assist them in this effort, a man named Edmund Reeves Lee, whom he had known when they were both Burns operatives in 1915.

Lee was down on his luck. His last job had been as night clerk at the Harrington Hotel in Washington, but he had been fired and needed money badly when he ran into Gaston at the cigar stand in the Southern Building one day. Lee spoke to Means, and Gaston looked at him curiously.

"Where have I seen you before?" he asked, picking up the package of cigarettes he had just bought.

Lee said he had worked under Gaston in an investigation or two in 1915—and this reminded Gaston of the current German matter. Means asked Lee where he could be found, and Lee admitted that he spent most of his time hanging around that cigar stand. Means disappeared, noncommittal when Lee asked if he knew of any jobs, but twenty minutes later W. R. Patterson appeared with a note which instructed Lee to go to 903 16 Street.

"Lee, have you got confidence in me?" Means asked.

The unfortunate Lee had confidence in anyone who might offer him a job at that moment. He expressed his admiration, and Means hired him at $45 a week, and gave him $5 in cash on the spot, and told Lee to report for work at the house the next day. When Lee returned, he was given a list of dates which pertained to the "Black Tom" explosions of World War I. Lee was to go to the Library of Congress and inform himself as totally as possible on those explosions. Lee did so, coming back to the house to report. Little by little Means told him more, and finally promised Lee one-third of the profits from his plan. Carefully, however, he put an outside limit of the profits at $100,000. Lee's briefing continued.

Means instructed Lee to gather all the information he could about the Black Tom periods and about the Canadian Car and Foundry Company. Lee might be asked to make some affidavits. He would certainly be pointed out by Means to some men as the man who knew all about the Black Tom affair. Lee would also be sent to Mexico, with the long-suffering W. R. Patterson, to meet the men from Peru and pick up the important documents.

A few weeks later two men called at Means's house—representatives of insurance companies who were intrigued by Means's story of Black Tom, for these insurance companies had been forced to pay heavy claims after the explosions. Means called Lee into the room, where Means and one man were sitting.

"Here is the man," Means said. "He is one of the most famous characters of the underworld and will do anything I want him to do and commit murder if necessary for me."

The lawyer said nothing. Lee went out of the room.[35] Lee did not know it, but Means then characterized him as the man who had blown up Black Tom Island, singlehandedly.[36]

XI

Hiram Todd's presentation before the New York City Federal Grand jury had resulted in the indictment of Gaston Means on three counts and the indictment of Elmer Jarnecke on one count. Todd secured the three-count indictment against Means for his larcenous behavior in the case of Dr. Sacharoff's eighty-eight barrels of whisky and the $7,250 Means had collected from the doctor and from Harry Goldberg. Dr. Sacharoff, after his disappointing trip to Washington to force Means to deliver the goods, had been eager enough to testify against the man who had duped him. Sacharoff and Goldberg, too, were given immunity, in exchange for their evidence against Gaston. It was apparent that Gaston was a prize worth sacrifices. In the end, he was charged with more than one hundred violations of the Volstead Act.

The final indictment against both men involved the affair with Charles Johnson, agent for the two wealthy Pennsylvanians, and the whisky that was to be removed from the distillery and made available to them.[1]

There were several reasons for securing so many indictments.

223

First, of course, was the belief that cases could be made in these matters. Second was the desire to keep so wary a pair of criminals as Gaston Means and Colonel Thomas Felder off balance. It was understood at the Justice Department that the moment the indictments were brought in, Means and Felder would begin covering their tracks and rearranging their histories as completely as possible. By covering many fronts in the Means affair, the government's attorney made life more difficult for Means and Felder. Jarnecke was not seriously considered as a factor, because Jarnecke was recognized to be the tool of Gaston Means. Nor were any indictments brought against Colonel Felder at that moment. Hiram Todd needed more time to prepare a case he hoped would be airtight. But Todd was investigating, and on October 29, less than two weeks after the indictments against Means, he called Colonel Felder to produce evidence about the fee received in the Glass Casket case. Felder had already submitted to an examination in Todd's offices about the case, earlier in the month. This call for further information showed the Colonel how hot the trail had grown.[2]

The Means indictments caused a public stir, because here was the most important case yet in which a government officer was being called to account for actions all the world knew were common enough. Nearly no one in the United States had any faith in the prohibition laws in 1923. Thousands of citizens were rapidly losing faith in the honesty of law-enforcement agencies. The Means indictments were subject, then, for careful appraisal by editorial writers and thoughtful men and women across the land. In an editorial the *New York Times* used the Means case to summarize a growing feeling about prohibition enforcement:

> ... The Sociologist is stirred not so much by the asserted magnitude of the "conspiracy" as by the antecedents and personality of the gentleman from North Carolina charged with being the principal. Mr. Gaston B. Means is a salient character, entirely able to take care of himself. His merits attracted the attention of Mr. Daugherty's Department of Justice, which employed him

as a Special Agent for nearly a year. He came to this town in the summer of 1922 to spy out the working of prohibition in this region. According to his counsel he received "definite instructions to investigate thoroughly the rich, aristocratic people who were engaged in the bootlegging business in and around New York City." Certain "rich aristocratic" bootleggers were sent to the clink as a result. Assistant U.S. Attorney Clark speaks of Mr. Means's "very efficient" work for him "in several important investigations." But now the efficient special investigator is accused of conspiracy to commit more than 100 violations of the Volstead Act, and, apparently, it is the government theory that he began bootlegging about the same time that he began efficiently to investigate bootlegging.

Mr. Means's Counsel darkly intimates that his client got on the track of "high officials" in the Internal Revenue Bureau who had him recalled to Washington to choke off his dangerous inquiries. If this theory looks romantic, at least it may be expected that Gaston Means will make the fur fly. But there is a moral tagged to his story. When Mr. Means came to this town, he brought letters of introduction and recommendation from Mr. Wayne B. Wheeler, general counsel of the Anti-Saloon League. Now it is clear, and the case of Mr. Means may be another proof of it, that be thou as pure as snow thou shalt not escape calumny if thou be a prohibition agent or investigator. A wise man won't recommend anybody for these ticklish posts. "The use by the federal government of political sources in choosing prohibition agents" was lamented by former Governor Allen the other day. The Civil Service League has long lamented it. Mr. Wheeler and other grandees of the Anti-Saloon League, who were willing to invite Congressmen to support the Volstead Act by offering them this prospective patronage, now agree that the prohibition enforcers should be selected by the merit system and not by the recommendation of Congressmen "keeping the boys from having cold feet."

When Congressmen find out that this patronage is dangerous

to themselves, they will give it up. The mere good of the service may not interest them. Their own good does. If every time a Federal prohibition agent is "caught with the goods" the name of his patron is published, Congressmen will soon get sick of having any hand in these sorry spoils.[3]

If Gaston was upset at being held up to the public light as a horrid example of a detestable genus, he gave no public sign. Perhaps he never saw the *Times* editorial, although he was an inveterate newspaper reader, for Means was busy with Colonel Thomas Miller, the Alien Property Custodian, in his schemes to defraud the Mixed Claims Commission. He was not so busy, however, that he forgot his own defense efforts.

Gaston asked Rella Lane to stay at the house, an invitation Julie had made earlier, and put her to work in the evenings "copying his diaries." Gaston also employed two full-time stenographers at this work. What he was doing, of course, was hastily fabricating diaries for the past few years to show himself in various places at various times—and taking care that those places and times not be the one involving his criminal activities. Nearly everyone in the household participated in this effort in the fall and winter of 1923-1924. W. R. Patterson did part of the work. Jarnecke did part of it. Edmund Lee copied some pages and spent hours inserting new typewritten pages into notebooks.[4]

Felder's method of counterattack was much less devious but far more piercing. Failing in the attempt to bribe or intimidate anyone in the Justice Department, Felder, in September, had tried rude blackmail on Attorney General Daugherty. The subject was Daugherty's son Draper. Through Felder, said Felder, Draper had secured a job with the New York Life Insurance Company, as an agent, and within three weeks had written $200,000 in insurance. He had borrowed $4,200 from Felder to repay old debts and Felder was pleased to make the loan because Draper—the son of his old friend—was doing so well. He was behaving himself and staying both out of debt and on the water wagon.

Then Draper fell in with the notorious Arnold Rothstein, and began to deteriorate. He overdrew his bank account. He ran up bills all over New York. Felder finally paid off all the bills to keep Draper free from arrest.

Felder had done all this without thought of reward, he said. He had given Draper letters of introduction to such prominent friends as U.S. Circuit Court Judge Martin Manton. Now Felder was being accused of evil, including the "capitalizing" of the son of the Attorney General.

"I have reached the point in regard to these infamous rumors," Felder wrote, "that, with me, 'patience has almost ceased to be a virtue.'" So saying, Felder enclosed to Daugherty copies of earlier letters to Assistant Attorney General Seymour and to Gaston Means —letters that dealt not with Draper Daugherty but with accusations against Felder.[5]

Felder's letter to Daugherty produced nothing. Daugherty's position at that time was even more difficult than it had been during the spring. President Harding had died in San Francisco in August and Coolidge, "the Puritan in Babylon," could not be expected to take so indulgent a view of government operations for private profit as had his predecessor. In the autumn of 1923, Attorney General Daugherty was skating on thin ice. He could not afford to help or protect anyone.

Felder made a new attempt in November. It was useless.[6]

Felder's letters contained very definite overtones of threat but the Attorney General could not be touched, basically because it was so late that Daugherty could not even help himself. So Felder tried other ways to save himself. In Chicago, the stronghold of the Glass Casket defendants, the Federal authorities asked Alderman Joseph Kostner to make a statement about the splitting of the Glass Casket fee. Kostner agreed to do so, but then backed off, saying it would be unethical. Isadore Padorr, who had told Jarnecke that Means and Felder were crooks, now told Samuel Safir to "stick by the Colonel" because Means would never be convicted and the Colonel had influence in high places.[7]

Hiram Todd decided that his strong case was against Means and Jarnecke in the Johnson liquor deal, because two wealthy and respectable men had been the ultimate victims, and the documentary evidence of crime existed.

Todd moved for trial in December, 1923, but Felder and Means stalled. Felder pleaded ill health and persuaded Todd to put off the case until after the first of the year. Then one postponement followed another. Means and Felder were seeking a way out.[8]

In February, it seemed that Gaston had found the break he wanted. He would help Congress uncover a rotten mess in the Justice Department, and in the screen of confusion it would be impossible for the government to try him, for that would seem to the public to be straight retaliation.

Gaston's opportunity arose by courtesy of Senator Burton K. Wheeler of Montana, a fiery young Democrat who had grown up in Massachusetts. Wheeler had become convinced that Daugherty was crooked. Specifically, he was sure that Daugherty was not prosecuting certain important cases and he suspected that Daugherty or the Ohio Gang were profiting from this laxity. Wheeler began to investigate. Early in 1924 he was steered to Gaston, and Gaston indicated that he could testify and produce documents to prove wrongdoing in the Justice Department. The question of proof settled it for Wheeler. He had found many who would tell him of wrongdoing, but he had found few who had any evidence, or who were willing to testify. Means was one such. Another was Captain H. C. Scaife, who had left the Department of Justice, charging that aircraft cases were being hushed up. Another was Roxie Stinson of Ohio, the divorced wife of the late Jess Smith. Smith had been an intimate of Daugherty's, and had been found dead—with a gun by his side—on the floor of the apartment he shared with Daugherty early in the previous year. Wheeler was sure that Roxie Stinson knew much about the Justice Department, and now Gaston promised to clinch the case with complete diaries he had kept for years.[9]

Gaston's presence as a witness was requested by Wheeler, who wrote Hiram Todd about other witnesses who might be called at the Means trial. Wheeler thought some might help his case. Todd saw immediately that Means would try to wriggle away from trial. He ordered twenty-four-hour surveillance of Means's house in Washington, to see what was going on. He wrote to the Attorney General, warning him that Means and Felder "intend to exhaust every trick known to the slick criminal and cunning lawyer to avoid a trial.

"As a result of my investigation," Todd added, ". . . I am satisfied that he is an unusually cunning crook, and now that he is cornered I believe he is scheming to use the examination before one of the Senate Investigating Committees as a ground for claiming immunity. . . ."[10]

Todd was right, but he underestimated Gaston. Gaston did not just want immunity; he proposed to wreck the Justice Department so that his prosecution would be forgotten. But, to cover himself, on the eve of the hearings Means sent word to Daugherty that he was going to blow the lid off. The implication was clear: if Daugherty would call off his dogs, Means would not testify.

Daugherty refused. He told Means he could go to the devil. Means went to the Committee Investigating the Conduct of the Attorney General of the United States, instead.[11]

On March 14, Gaston began to testify, first waiving immunity with an impatient gesture.[12] Thereupon he sat calmly in the witness chair and with the polish of a movie star began to spin stories about the Department of Justice and his relationships with high officials.

His stories had all the substance of the wisps of cigarette smoke he dragged through his nostrils, but having worked two secretaries, a part-time secretary, and two other assistants for months, Means now had with him two huge accordion cases. He said they were filled with his "diaries" of the government years. When questioned he referred to one big case or the other, and occasionally he dived in to pick out a paper and read from it.

Gaston began with good advance billing. He had been described from the witness stand by his old friend William J. Burns as one of the ablest investigators Burns had ever known.[13]

Gaston began to sketch a gaudy view of the Justice Department and the Harding Administration, which had Jess Smith as a kind of blind genius and Gaston playing the role of "bag man" for the Ohio Gang, a role others attributed to Smith himself.

In brief, Means's story was that he had worked for the Department of Justice faithfully—well, almost faithfully—until August, 1922. Then he had quit to go to work for Jess Smith, and really, for the President of the United States on an extremely confidential assignment. President Harding was much dissatisfied with the enforcement of prohibition. The President had asked Smith to conduct a secret investigation of the Treasury's prohibition efforts. Smith had employed a man named W. T. Underwood, and Gaston. Further, Smith had dictated a letter regarding this investigation, which was then signed by Warren Harding himself. The letter had established all these facts.

The committee wanted to know the identity of W. T. Underwood, and Gaston said he was a man of no fixed address, to whom Means reported when Means or Underwood felt like having a report. Underwood paid Means every month through an agent who was as mysterious as his employer—one Sidney Thompson. Thompson had no address either.

Means had gone to Florida a few days before the hearings began, he said, and had met W. T. Underwood there, along with Sidney Thompson.

What was the point of his investigation for Harding? the Committee members wanted to know.

"They wanted us to investigate Secretary Mellon; the President wanted the information in regard to him—to catch him—and we caught him."[14]

And how had they caught him?

Means had employed Captain Scaife, the vigorous reformer, to investigate the doings of Andrew Mellon. Means had felt perfectly safe in employing Scaife because the captain was a thoroughly honest man, if not a very intelligent one. Means, of course, had earned only his expenses for this patriotic work. Scaife, having left the government, had gone to work as the Secretary of the Women's Clean Government Committee. The Committee had been a great help to Gaston.[15]

(Means had planned to "get Mellon" for at least a year; long before he fabricated the story about W. T. Underwood and Jess Smith, Gaston had told Jarnecke something of his scheme.)[16]

The scheme was a complicated one, but it was only one of half a dozen schemes that Gaston involved himself in at the same time. Gaston shocked committee and public with his revelations before he came to the struggle with Andrew Mellon. He told of the meeting at which he had taken $100,000 from the Japanese gentleman from the Mitsui Company, and linked that payment with the government's failure to prosecute anyone for an alleged $6.5 million overpayment to the Standard Aircraft Company. His statements were calculated to make headlines, and they did. The *New York Times* reporter wrote, "the witness was a complete master of himself. He knew all the members of the committee by name and answered questions, and sometimes asked them as if he and his inquisitors were old friends. He showed no evidence of nervousness or evasion."[17]

Senator Wheeler did most of the questioning of Means, as he did of nearly all the witnesses. (Although the official title of the committee was Select Committee on Investigation of the Attorney General, and Senator Smith Brookhart of Iowa was chairman, it was known popularly as the Wheeler Committee.)

Wheeler asked Means about his birth and background in the very beginning, and gave Gaston an opportunity to show off.

Senator Wheeler: And have you ever been convicted of a felony?
Mr. Means: I have been accused of every crime in the catalogue

but not convicted, so far. I have never been convicted but have been charged with every known crime. Oh, I have been convicted once or twice for minor fights.

Senator Wheeler: How was that?

Mr. Means: I have been in the mayor's court for hitting some fellow or some fellow hitting me, and licking me, perhaps, or otherwise, or something like that but I have never called that anything.

Senator Wheeler: What is your business at the present time?

Mr. Means: Answering indictments.

Those replies were accompanied by mugging for the crowd, dimpled smiles, smoke shot down through the nose or jetted high in the air by the thrust of a mobile lower lip. They certainly did not indicate that Senator Wheeler faced a nervous or reluctant witness.

Perhaps it was an overstatement to say that Means and his inquisitors were old friends, but he and Senator Wheeler were certainly good acquaintances, for during the past two weeks Means had been visiting the Senator almost every day or night, talking over "evidence" he proposed to bring out in the investigation.

Means promised to be most helpful. Gaston advised Wheeler that the Department of Justice had agents watching the Wheeler house (which seemed to be true only at the times that Gaston was there). Gaston offered, in all altruism, to blow the front porch off the Senator's house with dynamite. The resultant headlines, Means predicted, would be most helpful to the cause of the Committee. Shuddering a little, Senator Wheeler rejected Gaston's thoughtful offer.[18]

Gaston brought out several important points—as far as he was concerned. He admitted that he had been involved with the investigation of the investigators who were trying to impeach Daugherty in 1922. He had directed the search of Senator La Follette's office, he said. He talked of the employment of Miss Laura Jacobson to investigate Senator Caraway, too.

Gaston B. Means

Every effort was being made by the Administration to keep him silent, Gaston said. Just the day before, his lawyer had called with a new warning.

"The powers after you are omnipotent and control every situation," Colonel Felder said.[19]

Gaston also said that since he had been subpoenaed to testify before the Committee his telephone had been tapped. (Undoubtedly it was.) A Department of Justice man had warned him that if he testified before the Committee, he would be "put away." This was hardly true. The Department no longer worked that way.

Gaston suggested that Secretary Mellon was behind the attempt to silence him. Later that day, when Secretary Mellon saw the afternoon papers, he characterized the Means testimony as "vicious piffle."[20] The story behind Gaston's story, however, was even more thrilling than the show he put on for the Wheeler Committee. The real story was never told.

What Gaston had done in his attempt to ruin Secretary Mellon was to try to infiltrate the Treasury Department. Late in September, 1922, Gaston hired Captain Scaife, a man already suspicious of the good intentions of government, to help him "investigate" the evils of bootlegging.

Gaston told Scaife he was working in the utmost secrecy, and Scaife would be too, in behalf of President Harding. Gaston showed Scaife credentials from the Department of Justice, the Alien Property Custodian's Office, and the Prohibition Unit of the Treasury. Captain Scaife took to the idea like a six-year-old being asked to play by his elder brother. He asked no questions. He was happy to do just as he was told.

Between September, 1922, and January, 1923, Gaston paid Captain Scaife about $5,000. He took Captain Scaife to New York City with him to show Scaife how rotten the prohibition enforcement was. Of course, to show this, Means had to deal with bootleggers himself. Scaife was in at the kill on the La Montagne case (although Scaife did not know about the blackmail attempt that preceded it).

When they came home from New York, Scaife's eyes were bulging from the terrible evidence he had seen. Means told Scaife the whole sordid story—or a cleaned-up version of his usual "Bootlegger's Sales Story No. 1"—which described the way the money was cut up for benefit of the Republican National Committee and the grafters. He neglected to include himself in this telling of the tale. Scaife was eager to help President Harding, then, to uncover the truth and destroy the cancerous growth that threatened American government.

Means quickly showed Scaife how to help. Gaston drafted a letter for Scaife, the beginning of a long and acrimonious series written by Scaife to Secretary Mellon in all the innocence of the Women's Clean Government Association. The first charge was that some Republicans in the Prohibition Unit were using whisky withdrawals to pay the GOP debt. Mellon took the letter at face value and replied.

From his extensive personal knowledge of bootlegging in America, Means kept feeding Scaife truthful information (that was of no use to Gaston) about prohibition violations. Mellon soon learned that there was something in what Scaife had to report, and, courteously, he carried on the correspondence.

Means was using this correspondence all the time to build Mellon up for purposes of his own.

The next step was to offer to solve the *Gemma* case, which Captain Scaife did, on prompting by Gaston, who gave Scaife all the information needed. The *Gemma* was a steam trawler of British registry that was captured off Montauk Point, Long Island, by the "Dry Navy" boat *Hansen* early in September, 1922. She was carrying a million dollars' worth of liquor in 67,200 bottles.

No one knew who owned the *Gemma,* and, apparently, no one who could find out wanted to do so. The steamer was libeled and sold, but the liquor was taken out to sea mysteriously, under bond, headed for Cuba, and then turned right around, brought back to U.S. shores, and sold to bootleggers.

Gaston B. Means

Means told Scaife confidentially that he knew what had happened and how. He said he did not report it to the Department of Justice because he had left the Department in August. He kept the information for Scaife, in the interest of serving his beloved President Harding by throwing Mellon to the dogs. Scaife, on Means's instructions, had written to Mellon, offering to solve the case if Mellon would let him put his own men in the Treasury Department to do the job.

The object of Gaston Means now becomes clear. All Gaston was trying to do from the beginning of this correspondence in behalf of truth and justice was to put four men of his choosing, with the Women's Clean Government Association label on their collars, inside the Prohibition Unit. Had he succeeded, what a field day Gaston and the bootleggers would have had. There might not have been a barrel of whisky left in a distillery on the eastern seaboard after six months of such management. Mellon, of course, rejected such conditions.[21]

On March 17, Hiram Todd wrote Senator Brookhart a letter, signed "respectfully," with contents that were more than a little frigid, for Todd regarded the Senate investigation as a political gesture against Daugherty. More important, he wanted to try the Means case, and the Wheeler Committee was holding his principal defendant under subpoena. Todd described in detail the delays that Means had accomplished, first by Felder's complaint of illness, then by Means's complaints of illness (in which the letters for physicians to sign were written on one of the typewriters in the Means office[22]). Todd requested that the Committee regulate Means's appearances so there would be no further interference with the trial, which was scheduled again for March 31.[23]

The Senate Committee was in no mood to be ordered around by the Department of Justice. Senator Wheeler felt that he had been harassed enough by Daugherty's agents. Just before the opening of the hearings Wheeler had gone to Washington Courthouse, Ohio, where Miss Roxie Stinson lived, to persuade her to testify.

He had planned to stay overnight in Columbus, before going on to Chicago the next day where he was scheduled to make a speech. But at the hotel a young woman had stopped him in the lobby, to ask his advice on opening a beauty parlor in Washington. Shortly afterward, Senator Wheeler was tipped off by someone that the young woman was a plant. If he stayed in the hotel that night, she would appear in his room, and then the authorities would break in and find them together.[24] On receiving this information, Senator Wheeler left posthaste for Chicago, but that and other suspicious incidents gave him no love for Mr. Daugherty, his agents, and his friends.

Brookhart replied tersely to Todd that the Committee would hold Means until finished with him. Todd asked Brookhart if he intended to obstruct justice. Brookhart wired back that Means was being held. Matters went from bad to worse—and on March 31, when Means and Jarnecke did not show up for trial, the Justice issued a bench warrant for them and called their bail forfeit.[25]

But matters were to take a turn for the better, immediately. The whole purpose of the Daugherty Investigation was served and ended on March 28, when Attorney General Daugherty resigned at the request of Calvin Coolidge. The President made the request almost entirely because of the public pressure brought by the Senate hearings, and the charges of the witnesses about wrongdoing in the Justice Department. Daugherty protested that he should have a chance to clear himself; Coolidge was reminded that Daugherty refused to testify. Coolidge took the position that whether Daugherty was tarnished or guiltless, his effectiveness as Attorney General had been mortally impaired.

Acting Attorney General James Beck was able to smooth the ruffled feathers of the Senate Committee, and the equally ruffled Hiram C. Todd. The bench warrants were vacated, the bail was restored to good standing, and the trial was delayed. The trial was to be delayed again too, in an almost Puckish gesture by Senator Brookhart, who noted that the Committee would have been finished with Means before the first of May, had not indictments been brought against Senator Wheeler in Montana, which delayed the proceedings for a month.[26] (Those indictments were made ridiculous in a trial.)

On April 16, Means took the stand again to testify to more corruption in the Administration. He talked of taking a quarter of a million dollars in behalf of Jess Smith. With his records, he was prepared to testify to much other wrongdoing in the past three years, too, he said.[27]

The Committee had heard a great deal about those records, and they had been exposed to view in the two accordion cases that Means brought to the witness stand. Gaston continued to dive into those cases from time to time, to pull out papers and read from them. Would it not be sensible to have those records brought into the hands of the Committee staff, so they could be examined in an orderly fashion? The Committee members were beginning to believe so, since Means was their star witness, once Roxie Stinson had left the stand, and so much depended on his records.[28]

Late in April, Gaston Means dropped a bomb in what had threatened to become a dreary recital of Administration wrongdoing. Three weeks before, on March 31, he charged, his records of five years had disappeared. Two men, showing badges that said they were assistant sergeants-at-arms of the Senate, came to his house at 903 16 Street bearing a letter from Senator Brookhart.

"Dear Sir," said the letter. "You are hereby commanded to deliver to the Select Committee on Investigation of the Department of Justice all of your records, files, diaries, reports and copies of reports, and all papers in your possession in connection with the Department of Justice, to be impounded." It was signed by Smith W. Brookhart, chairman of the committee.

Naturally, Means had hastened to comply with the demand, and the two officials had walked out of his house and gotten into a truck, carrying three large suitcases and one trunk full of Gaston's precious files.

The Committee first learned of the disappearance of the papers a few hours before it was made public. Roy Rankin, of the Committee staff, asked Gaston to bring his records to the office of the Committee for examination and safekeeping. Gaston telephoned Rankin to tell him that he did not have his records and diaries any longer. Rankin expressed disbelief, and accused Gaston of destroying them, if they ever existed. Means replied that he had delivered them. The conversation ended acrimoniously.

A few minutes later, Means burst into Senator Brookhart's office and accused one of the secretaries of giving the letter to a sergeant-at-arms. The secretary said Senator Brookhart had signed no such letter. Means insisted that Brookhart had signed it, and said he had the letter.

Rankin told Means to produce it.

Gaston began a long harangue, claiming that all his diaries had been lost or stolen, and he would not give $40,000 for them. Rankin cut him off, insisting that he see the letter. Gaston went home to get it. An hour later he returned to the Senate Office Building with the letter. It took Rankin only a few minutes to see that the letter was a forgery. First of all, he noticed that it was typed on stationery that Brookhart no longer used, since the committee lists at the top had been changed.[29]

The course of the investigation was changed, then, to discover what had happened to Gaston's all-important papers. William and Jessie Duckstein were called before the Committee on May 21. William was confidential secretary to Ned McLean, publisher of the Washington *Post* and a prominent socialite. Mrs. Duckstein was confidential secretary to the Bureau of Investigation and was listed as "special agent." Both said that the operatives who had taken the papers from Means's house were directed by Hiram C. Todd.[30]

Hiram Todd was riding the subway toward his Park Avenue apartment from his downtown law office in New York when he read that statement in a newspaper account of the Daugherty investigation. He leaped off the subway car at the next stop, and at the street level hurried to a Western Union office to send a telegram to Senator Brookhart demanding that he be allowed to testify before the Committee.[31]

One reason that Hiram Todd insisted on testifying was that for once he was sure the Department of Justice had caught Gaston in a flat lie and could prove it. Gaston had known during March that he was under surveillance. Once in a while, crossing the street, he would stop and embarrass one of the agents by talking to him or going up to shake hands. But by the end of March, Gaston had grown careless. The Department of Justice had grown more careful. March 31 was the important day on which Means had been ordered to appear in court in New York, and so the Bureau of Investigation men were watching his actions closely.

They reported that at 9:15 in the morning Means had gone to the Senate Office Building, where he remained until 5:30 P.M., then drove home, arriving at 5:45. No one entered or left, from front or rear, between that time and 8:50 P.M., except a newspaperman named Pierce Miller, who had no bundles with him. At 8:50, Means went out, got in his car, and drove to Senator Wheeler's house, where he stayed until 10:30. Means then went home and no one else came or left the house that night.[32]

On May 24, Special Assistant to the Attorney General Hiram C. Todd went to Washington to testify before the Committee. He faced a most unfriendly group, with Gaston Means sitting behind the Committee, smoking cigarettes, and acting as though he were the prosecutor and Hiram C. Todd the defendant in the case.

Prosecutor Todd and Senator Wheeler clashed from the outset because each believed he was being misused by the other. Wheeler suggested that one of Todd's law partners was a close friend of Harry M. Daugherty. Wheeler then came to the matter of Means, indicating by his questions that Means was indicted on evidence provided by known bootleggers. Todd bridled at the implications. Wheeler asked if Assistant U.S. Attorney Clark had not found

Means's work "very efficient" and said so publicly. Todd said he
had talked to Clark at various times, "and he had told me that he
would not believe him [Means] under oath."

So it went. Wheeler wanted to show that Means was hired by
the Department of Justice because he was useful in dealing with
crooks. Todd did not like the question. He began to say that he
understood. . . . Then Senator Ashurst got into the discussion.

> *Senator Ashurst (interposing):* No; not what you understand.
> You are a lawyer, and you know Mr. Daugherty employed Mr.
> Burns, do you not? And you also know that Mr. Daugherty knew
> that Mr. Burns employed Mr. Means? Now don't be dodging and
> twisting. Just tell right out.
> *Mr. Todd:* I am not trying to dodge and twist, and don't in-
> sinuate that I am.
> *Senator Ashurst:* I am not insinuating. I am charging. I do
> no insinuate; I charge.

The heat and sarcasm grew greater as the questioning continued.
Senator Wheeler wanted to show that Means had done exactly as
he was told to do. Prosecutor Todd had come to Washington to
refute the statement that he had directed the pirating of Means's
files, but question after question was asked that had nothing to do
with those files. Wheeler also wanted to try the government's case
against Means right there, and Means sat at a front table, cheering
him on and making notes.

> *Senator Wheeler:* Let me ask you this: Does your evidence
> show that Means ever got a quart of whisky out of any of these
> places? That he, Means, got any whisky?
> *Mr. Todd:* Senator, I don't think it would be proper for me
> at this time to disclose evidence given before the Grand Jury. I
> think that is an improper question, and you appreciate it your-
> self.

Gaston B. Means

Senator Wheeler: Wait a minute. You made the statement that he was conspiring with these people.

Mr. Todd: That is a conclusion which the Grand Jury has found and I am justified in making that statement.

Senator Wheeler: And you also called him a crook.

Mr. Todd: He is a crook.

The Committee took violent exception to that remark, and charged that Prosecutor Todd was trying to railroad Means, when he should be concerned only with "getting the facts." Todd noted that he was prosecuting Means and that the Committee was investigating *him* as if they were trying to protect Means. Senator Ashurst replied that Todd had shown the most bitter malice against poor Gaston Means; and Gaston sat and grinned, his dimples showing, as the representatives of two arms of government fought about him.

Wheeler wanted to know the names of the witnesses Todd had subpoenaed for the Means trial, whereupon Todd grew very angry.

Mr. Todd: I refuse to state that.

Senator Wheeler: You said you had brought them on from a distance. From what points?

Mr. Todd: I do not care to state that.

Senator Wheeler: They were under subpoena, and it was a public record.

Mr. Todd: Very well; you can get it from the record, but I do not intend to give any information here which can be used by Gaston B. Means, who sits right behind you, in trying to reach those witnesses.

For an hour, Todd tried to get to his point, but the Senators wanted no part of his point. Chairman Brookhart charged that Todd was angry because Means had appeared before the Committee. Not at all, said Todd, but he did feel that the United States

241

Court had suffered an indignity from the Committee, because the Committee had refused to release Means for trial.

> *The Chairman:* I want to say to you that this Committee has suffered some indignity at the hands of some of these officers of the law.
>
> *Mr. Todd:* I wrote a letter to this Committee on March 17, to you, Senator Brookhart, as Chairman of this Committee—
>
> *The Chairman:* Yes, I remember.
>
> *Mr. Todd:* —In which I very courteously requested you to co-operate with the United States government to the end that—
>
> *The Chairman:* I do not remember that as a courteous letter—

The squabbling went on, with no more evidence of maturity than Gaston and his friends had shown in the days when Joe Fisher had slugged him with a ball bat on Judge Montgomery's lawn in Concord. Senator Ashurst lectured Todd on the responsibilities of a public prosecutor; Senator Brookhart complained that the Department of Justice delayed hundreds of cases for years, but wanted to rush this one to trial; Senator Wheeler remarked that former Attorney General Daugherty was to become a member of Todd's law firm. (Todd denied that flatly.)

Senator Brookhart, angry, shouted that Todd was unfit for the job as prosecutor, and the most violent argument of the day began.

> *Mr. Todd:* I had anticipated that the reason I was asked to come here as a witness was that you might endeavor to create a situation upon which you might apply to the Attorney General that I be removed as special assistant in the prosecution of Means. I anticipated that.
>
> *Senator Ashurst:* Why did you anticipate that?
>
> *Mr. Todd:* Because I think the actions of this Committee here are in behalf of this man Means.
>
> *Senator Ashurst:* As one member of this Committee, I crave permission now to answer that. I never saw—

Gaston B. Means

Senator Jones of Washington: I hope the Committee won't get into a controversy with this man.

Senator Ashurst: I do not intend to.

Senator Wheeler: But you cannot let a contemptible statement like that go unchallenged.

Senator Jones of Washington: But you may have called it out.

Senator Ashurst: I did not call it out.

Senator Jones of Washington: I was not referring to you, Senator Ashurst.

The Chairman: I was not saying he was in contempt of the Committee.

Senator Ashurst: This Committee cannot possibly have any interest in Means. I never saw him before he took the witness stand. I care as little about what happens to Gaston B. Means as I care about what happens to one Hiram C. Todd. They are both citizens of the United States, entitled to a square and fair deal. But Means has his enemies and I believe it is fair to assume that you have your enemies. So between Gaston B. Means and Hiram C. Todd it seems to me it would be difficult to make a choice, judging by their conduct on the witness stand.

(Means squirmed in pleasure at that last remark, but the members of the Committee seemed to realize that they were approaching dangerous ground, in which the Committee might be forced to charge Todd with contempt, or admit his point, unless the tenor of questioning changed; nor were they remaining even close to the point in their exhibition of antagonism.)

Finally, after nearly two hours on the witness stand, Todd began to hope that he might be able to make his point. Senator Wheeler asked if Todd had not assigned detectives to watch the Means house, and Todd began to tell why he had asked that detectives of the Bureau of Investigation watch Means—to try to anticipate the tactics of Means and Felder in delaying the trial. They talked about Means's illness, which had been caused by the extraction of three teeth and removal of part of Means's jawbone, but Todd mentioned only the teeth.

Senator Wheeler: Did he tell you that part of his jawbone was extracted?

Mr. Todd: He did.

Senator Wheeler: Why do you say that he only had three teeth pulled? Why do you make that statement?

Mr. Todd: Because it has been my experience that a part of your jaw was pulled out when you had a tooth pulled; it felt that way.

Senator Ashurst: Well, you have not had your own jawbone extracted; I will say that.

That last riposte seemed to clear the air. Todd said he was only trying to do his best against five of them, and Senator Ashurst replied that Todd was doing very well. They did then allow Todd to testify that at 6:25 P.M. on March 31, when Means said that two men were lugging away his documents, Bureau of Investigation agents were outside that house and saw nothing at all. The Committee could not close on that note. Senator Wheeler tried to show that Todd was the "hatchet man" of the Justice Department, who was assigned to a case when Daugherty wanted to be as sure as possible of a conviction, and that the Department had also sought the services of one particular judge. But Todd replied evenly. He had made his point, and he was ready to call it quits.[33]

The end of the session left the Committee, press, and public puzzled. What had happened to Means's files? Senator Brookhart had examined the signature on the letter in Means's possession, and found it to be a forgery. Who had forged his name to the document? None other than Gaston Bullock Means.

Gaston had not intended to make his files disappear; otherwise he would never have gone to so much trouble to prepare them in the autumn of 1923. His hand was forced by two events. Roy Rankin of the Committee staff had been asking Means from the beginning for the files, and it became apparent toward the end of March that Rankin's patience was wearing thin, as Gaston gave one excuse after another for not turning them over. Also, a newspaper writer named Travis Hoke had come to Washington from New York, representing the Hearst Sunday magazines. He was engaged in writing the life story of Gaston Bullock Means. Even as Means was testifying before the Committee, Gaston was spending part of nearly every evening in the company of Hoke. The newspaperman was also eager to see the celebrated files, since they would provide the most sensational part of his articles, according to Gaston's advance billing, and Means had promised to let Hoke use those files on the day they disappeared.[34]

Arranging for the disappearance took a considerable degree of skill and planning, too. Gaston was quite aware of the difficulty of his position. His entire story, to Senator Wheeler and the Committee staff, depended on his mysterious documents for verification. The original copy of the letter signed by President Harding, which accounted for Means's consort with criminals since August, 1922—that was "in the records." The facts about Gaston's financial transactions with Jess Smith—they were also "in the records." The names of the bootleggers who paid off the Republican National Committee, the "evidence" against Secretary Mellon for wrongdoing, and hundreds of other tidbits of information, all reposed in Gaston's impressive filing cases. Or—all this *was supposed* to be in those cases. If the case had been turned over, and the material had not been found in them, Gaston would have been in even more serious trouble.

During his many hours in the offices of the Committee, Gaston had acquired several sheets of the Committee's stationery and some of its envelopes, which he kept in a bureau drawer in the ground floor offices of 903 16 Street.

When it became apparent that the records must disappear, Means wrote out in longhand the letter demanding the records, then asked Rella Lane to type it. She typed two copies, each on Senate Committee letterhead stationery, and gave them to Gaston.

"These letters will keep me out of the penitentiary," he said.[35]

Following the testimony of Hiram Todd, the Senate Committee brought its work to an end very quickly. The Senators had begun to doubt the truthfulness of their star witness. One reason for their doubts was the story told by Todd about the records; another was a series of affidavits secured by enterprising Committee personnel from prisoners in Federal penitentiaries. The Committee workers went to Atlanta penitentiary to see if they could find convicts who had information that might reflect on Daugherty. What they found was a number of convicts who had information that Gaston Bullock Means was the greatest swindler they had ever known. This was unpleasant information, and Senator Wheeler and the others began to distrust all that Gaston said. Besides, their work was done. They had shown, incontrovertibly, the laxness in the Department of Justice, and had indicated a degree of criminal activity that was to be followed up by other arms of government, and that was later to bring Attorney General Daugherty, Colonel Thomas Miller, and others to trial. William J. Burns, director of the Bureau of Investigation, had resigned his post on May 9, as the Committee continued in session, and if this resignation came about because Harlan F. Stone, the new Attorney General, did not like the way Burns ran his department, at the same time the Committee had put a useful spotlight on that department. The youthful J. Edgar Hoover, new Director of the Bureau, had come before the Committee to give statistical information, and he gave the information in such a manner that no one doubted his efficiency or his ability to clean out the musty corners of the government's major detective bureau.

The Committee hearings came to an end on May 23, having accomplished that amount of housecleaning, but the results were greeted publicly with less applause than they deserved because of the bad manners that had been shown on all sides, and because the newspapers were extremely leery of the testimony of Gaston Bullock Means.

Senator Ashurst referred to Hiram Todd as a "shyster"; Todd

called Means a "crook"; Paul Howland, one of Daugherty's lawyers, called Senator Wheeler a liar; and Senator Wheeler accused Howland of employing Means to search the offices of Congressmen and Senators when Daugherty was under investigation for impeachment.

"I would not hire him to clean cuspidors," Howland shouted in anguish.

Means took exception to that remark—more than to anything else said about him during the hearings—and after the Committee adjourned, Means met Howland in the corridor of the Capitol and wanted to argue. What he really wanted to do was fight, but Howland refused to talk to him, and a Capitol guard sent Gaston about his business.[36]

In the beginning of the hearings, Senator Ashurst had complimented Gaston, after Gaston finished his first day of testimony.

"Mr. Means, you may be under indictment, but you have today rendered the cause of truth and justice a valiant service. It is the first time I have ever seen the end justify the means."

At the end of the hearings, the humor of that pun was lost on the nation's newspapers. The *New York Times* editorialist said of the disappearance of the Means papers that "his two deceivers may have escaped by a subterranean passage or by the chimney and adjoining roofs,"[37] lugging a trunk and three suitcases, of course. The Atlanta *Constitution* called Means's testimony "disgraceful," and particularly castigated the Committee's acceptance of attacks on Andrew Mellon.[38]

Mellon characterized Gaston's testimony succinctly in a letter to Senator Brookhart.

"It is difficult," he said, "to reply concisely to statements which are either partial, misleading, or misstatements, and which depend for their entire effectiveness on innuendo and not on facts. . . ."

There had never been a better description of Gaston's method of operations.

XII

For all the money that Gaston Means had taken from trusting bootleggers and criminals under indictment, in June, 1924, he was short
of cash. He borrowed $2,000 from Rella Lane that month, promis-
ing to pay it back in two months. Colonel Tom Miller, his new
associate, was going to Europe, "after some of their money," he
said. When Alien Property Custodian Miller returned, Gaston
would pay. He was worth a quarter of a million dollars, Gaston told
Miss Lane. He just happened to be short of cash, and he did not
like to borrow from banks.[1]

Miss Lane was not gulled quite as easily as Gaston might have
expected, but she did lend him the money, for she was deeply indebted to the Means family in other ways. When she had fallen
ill, Julie had helped her and nursed her. Julie had insisted that Miss
Lane come to live with them in her convalescence. It was not easy
to refuse a loan to the husband of her friend.

The trial of the liquor conspiracy charge was set for the middle
of June. Hiram Todd and his assistant prosecutor, Clifford H.
Byrnes, were taking no chances that Gaston might join Colonel

Miller in Europe. Twelve agents of the Bureau of Investigation, with three automobiles at their disposal, were assigned to twenty-four-hour surveillance of the house at 903 16 Street, N. W.[2] William J. Burns had told Clifford Byrnes, confidentially, that Gaston intended to stall or somehow to escape trial.

But Gaston did not find it easy to stall or escape. He and Elmer Jarnecke took the train to New York on June 1. The moment they left Washington, J. Edgar Hoover sent a wire to alert Hiram Todd. Todd then asked the FBI agent in charge in New York City to keep an eye on Means. The agent threw up his hands. It was possible, he said, to keep someone under surveillance in New York if he did not know he was being shadowed. But in the case of a professional like Means, who knew all the tricks, it was not possible. The agent suggested that Todd's only assurance that Means would not escape was to have him placed in the custody of a United States Marshal.[3]

Todd and Byrnes thought this over. They decided it was troublesome, and might react against the government case to take so strong a step. They eliminated "shadowing" from their plan, but they insisted that regular checks be made on Means. So that became the course of action.[4]

Gaston was not idle as his trial date approached. He traveled often between New York and Washington, searching for a way out of the maze. He wrote a letter to Attorney General Stone, asking that Todd be removed from the case. Todd had shown prejudice against him during the Daugherty hearings, Gaston said.[5] The new Attorney General did not think so. "I have yet to learn that zeal for the cause of the government disqualified a prosecuting attorney, or that courts of the Southern District of New York are not fully capable of safeguarding the rights of the defendant," Stone said in a wire to Todd,[6] when the matter was first raised.

After ten postponements, then, the trial of Jarnecke and Gaston began on June 17, before Federal Judge C. E. Wolverton of Oregon, who was assisting New York judges in an effort to clear an overcrowded docket. One of the major problems of Prosecutor Todd—of which he was well aware—was the shady nature of many of the state's witnesses. He opened with a frank statement that many of the witnesses had prison records, and said he hoped that the jury would not disregard their stories because of this. Even the chief witness, C. W. Johnson, had a conviction outstanding against him. The government's case was based on the Johnson transaction, on the $15,097.60 he had given Means to remove liquor "legally," and on the promises of paying Means $200 a barrel once the liquor was removed.

Colonel Felder immediately tried to impugn the state's witnesses. It was a logical move. But Felder went too far. He tried to connect the bootlegging transactions to Andrew Mellon, Secretary of the Treasury of the United States. Todd knew what line the defense would follow—to try to bombard the jury with so much indication of wrongdoing in high places that Means and Jarnecke would appear to be innocent babes in the wood. Todd tried to forestall the defense case by objecting, time after time, to the attempts of the canny Colonel Felder to lead the case into irrelevancies.[7]

As the prosecution presented its case, new and astounding bits of information came to light, revealing how busy Gaston had been during the past three years. Among other attempts, he had met the Secretary of the United Brewers Association of Illinois, and had tried to shake down the entire brewery industry of that state for protection. He had promised New York City bootleggers that he would "fix" the whole New York City Police Department. And, of course, he claimed to have the entire judiciary of the Federal government stowed in his hip pocket.

The government completed its case in less than a week—a simple, strong case. Its weakness was in the character of the witnesses, for even the two rich Pennsylvanians involved were admittedly engaged in illegal activity when they dealt with Means through Johnson. The strength of the case lay in the documentary evidence: letters from Jarnecke, which indicated the general activities of Means and Jarnecke; and the damning receipt that Jarnecke had signed.

On June 22, a Sunday, Means and Jarnecke spent the day conferring with Attorney Thomas B. Felder. The next day, the defense began to present its case.

Todd tried to close all loopholes. He asked J. Edgar Hoover and other enforcement officers for more information about Means and his activities. He wanted to know where Means was on the day Jess Smith died. Former Attorney General Daugherty provided a clue. Warren Martin, special assistant to the Attorney General, had spent the day with Smith, so Smith could not have been with Means, as Means had said. But Martin had to confess that he had not spent *all* that day with Smith—so the loophole, seemingly closed, was open again. Daugherty suggested that if Means tried to claim he was paid by Harding (which he did), the records would show that the President had no contingency fund, so Means could not have been paid.

But Means and Felder were too clever to fall into such traps. Their attempt was concentrated on trying to prove that so many distinguished men were engaged in violation of the prohibition laws that to single out Gaston Means was infamous, and it had been done only because Means threatened the safety of men in high office.

In the hub of the defense lay the real importance of this case. If Means could get off, the cause of prohibition would suffer a mortal blow, and the Justice Department would be a long time in recovering the respect of bar and public.

Means made an impressive witness, as always. He charged that he was ready to expose the Ohio Gang, and that was why Jess Smith had died.

"On May 29, 1923, Jess Smith committed suicide," Gaston said. "It was the day after I told him I intended to go before Congress and tell all about the transactions. Smith was worried about threatened indictments. Certain people wanted back a total of $21,000.

Smith asked me and Jarnecke to return the money. I refused and Jarnecke refused and I told Smith I would tell Congress everything. The next day he killed himself."[8]

The story made headlines across America. Gaston implicated President Harding, Secretary Mellon, and Attorney General Daugherty in wrongdoing. He testified that in his dealings with bootleggers—such as Mannie Kessler—he had been offered huge sums, which he spurned. (Mannie Kessler, an inmate of Atlanta Penitentiary, sent Hiram Todd a wire when he read this. Kessler said he had never offered Means a penny, but that Gaston had offered to steal the evidence in his case from the Department of Justice files if Kessler would pay him $100,000.)[9]

When Hiram Todd rose to cross-examine, Gaston was self-assured and seemed to welcome the fray. Todd began by calling attention to that fact—to what he had termed Gaston's cockiness. Todd drove home the point that Means had been a witness many times before, in courts and committee rooms.

Gaston committed what a later generation might regard as a "Freudian slip" when Todd asked him about his experience as an investigator:

A.: Quite an expensive—extensive experience.
Q.: You started to say expensive. Did you mean that?
A.: It may have been expensive, too.

And expensive it certainly had been. Earlier in the year, when J. W. H. Crim had leaked the information to the press about Gaston's business with bootleggers, Crim had used a figure of $300,000 to total Gaston's "take." Now it appeared that Crim's figure was extremely conservative.

Where had his money come from? Todd asked.

It had come from W. T. Underwood, by way of Sidney Thompson, said Means.

Todd sneered openly at the concept of a man who worked so

253

secretly that he had no known address, who never stayed twice in the same place, whose name never appeared on a hotel register, who had no records, no friends, who left no trace at all of his existence.

Called upon to describe Underwood, Gaston said he was a man of about 225 pounds in weight, six feet one inch in height, around fifty years old, with hair, no mustache, beard, or identifying marks, and a voice that had no mark of accent.

Gaston had so remarkable an ability as a witness that he managed to make this implausible story sound plausible. It was the high point of his case. If the jury could be convinced that Underwood existed, there was a chance that the jury could be convinced that Gaston had, indeed, been working for President Harding personally, as he claimed.

But under the triphammer cross-examination of Hiram Todd, the story began to develop leaks. The only man who could say he had ever seen Underwood was a newspaperman, a friend of Gaston's, who had met a man in Miami whom Gaston introduced as W. T. Underwood.

Former Attorney General Harry Daugherty had offered to come and testify for the prosecution, but Hiram Todd did not want him. Andrew Mellon did come and testify, subpoenaed as a witness for the defense. The object of Felder and Means was to show that Mellon was implicated in distillery ownership and bootlegging. But Mellon's forthright manner, and his facts, hurt their case. He noted that he had divested himself of his Old Overholt distillery stock long before, and that the Pittsburgh banks with which he was connected had not accepted liquor permits as collateral since 1915. Means had testified that one reason he was indicted was that he had gathered evidence against a man named Fatkin, a superintendent of the bottling department of the Old Overholt distillery. Felder questioned Mellon about Fatkin. Mellon said he had never heard of the man. Mellon also told his side of the attempt to put H. L. Scaife's Clean Government Committee men on the Federal payroll in Gaston's behalf.[10]

Gaston B. Means

During the second week of trial, Thomas Felder began to plead illness, and repeatedly called on the Judge to recess the court as close to four o'clock as possible. Felder *was* ill. He was suffering from an advanced case of syphilis, which had begun to affect his central nervous system. He did not tell the court this fact, of course, but pleaded "tonsillitis." His illness grew worse, and as the trial ended its second week, he could not go on. An associate counsel was called to present the rest of the case.

The weekend recess did not help Attorney Felder enough, so on Monday, the associate again appeared. That day, June 30, the case against the two men was completed. Gaston was supremely confident, as always, that he would be acquitted. Each day during the trial he had returned to his hotel and telephoned Julie in Washington. The message was always the same: everything was going well. He would be home soon.

Gaston had so much information about the Department of Justice that he thought it a joke, at first, when he was indicted. Even at this date, he was certain that acquittal was in the air.[11]

The next day, Attorney Fred J. Coxe, who was appearing for Means and Jarnecke in Felder's behalf, made his closing argument. Means and Jarnecke were victims of a conspiracy of confessed criminals, who had been brought together by a government that was bent on persecuting the two men.

Hiram Todd's summation was one loud hoot at the defense contentions. W. T. Underwood, the mysterious paymaster, and Sidney Thompson, the mysterious courier, had been dragged into the trial by the defense. Who were they? They were Means and Jarnecke, none others, said Todd.

"The world is losing a great fictionalist by keeping Means so busy with investigations," he said. "Let him have some leisure so he may write. As his first great work we suggest a book entitled *The Adventures of Gaston B. Means Among the Bootleggers, or, Conspiracy with the Rumrunners by The Old Man Himself—Means.*"

The summations finished, Judge Wolverton charged the jury, then sent the jurors out to deliberate at 4:30 in the afternoon.

Julie Means, who had come up from Washington with their son, arrived in the courtroom just as the jury filed in to make its report. The jurors had been out only fifty-five minutes.

And how did the jury find? asked the clerk of the court. Had they agreed on a verdict?

"Yes, sir," said the foreman.

"How say you?" asked the clerk.

"Guilty as charged," said the foreman.

"Both defendants?" asked the clerk.

"Yes, sir," said the foreman decisively.

Elmer Jarnecke's face fell, and he showed the strain of the weeks as he sagged in his chair. But not Gaston. He looked around the room, smiling, caught the eye of the grief-stricken Julie, and smiled more broadly, encouragingly.

Then the deputy marshals took Gaston and Jarnecke by the elbows and escorted them to the gray dankness of the Tombs, New York's ancient jail, to await the day of sentence. It was a pleasant, cool evening, especially for July in New York City. The temperature stood in the high sixties, which meant that the Tombs would not be unbearable. That was the consolation of Gaston Bullock Means on the night of his first conviction for a crime. He was ten days short of his forty-fifth birthday.

That night, congratulatory telegrams began pouring in for Hiram C. Todd from Attorney General Stone, from Harry Daugherty, and from lawyers and citizens around the country. It was nearly a year since Todd had begun assembling the facts in the case. Now it was almost over.

The next day, Judge Wolverton called Means and Jarnecke for sentencing. Handcuffed and guarded by three deputy marshals, Gaston and his assistant were brought up from the Tombs to stand in the dock. Hiram Todd recommended leniency in the case of Elmer Jarnecke. It was apparent, Todd said, that Jarnecke had been a tool for Means. Although Jarnecke's past was spotty, he had no real criminal record before he encountered Gaston.

Gaston had no criminal record either, for his acquittal in the

256

murder trial in 1917 had wiped out those charges, but there was no suggestion that he be treated with leniency. Judge Wolverton imposed the maximum sentence on Gaston—two years in Federal prison and a fine of $10,000. Jarnecke was also sentenced to serve two years in prison, but was fined only $5,000.[12]

The next day, Gaston was out of jail on $25,000 bail, pending an appeal. Poor Elmer Jarnecke could not raise bail money, so he was confined in a dingy cell in the Tombs, to sweat out the summer in loneliness and unpleasant anticipation.

The *New York Times* greeted the conviction of Gaston with an attitude that seemed odd: ". . . There is a feeling among our best Gastonians," said the *Times*, "that only a change of venue to Concord, North Carolina, could give Mr. Means the full protection to which his innocence is entitled . . ."[13] So much emotion was emanating from a staid and responsible newspaper because, to the public, Gaston was a symbol of the wrongdoing of government men under the Harding Administration. As the facts were uncovered in the Daugherty Investigation and the Teapot Dome Investigation by Congress, responsible citizens were stirred. Following up his telegram, Attorney General Stone wrote Hiram Todd that "hardly any recent judicial determination will have a more profound and more favorable effect on the public mind than Means's conviction and sentence."[14] In the election campaigns that began that summer, Gaston became a symbol of all that was wrong with the Republican conduct of high office. John W. Davis, the Democratic candidate for President, mentioned Means as he attacked former Attorney General Daugherty. In a letter to Davis, Daugherty protested. The test was not to be found in the past, he said, but "are we real Americans and are we against those who seek the overthrow of their government under leaders fresh from a baptism of Bolshevism in lurid and suffering Russia?"[15]

That was a straight jab at Senator Robert La Follette and Senator Burton K. Wheeler, who were running for President and Vice President on the Progressive party ticket that year. Wheeler, who had been to Russia, was a favorite target.

But Davis was not to be drawn to the side of Harry Daugherty. Speaking in Welch, West Virginia, Davis said, "Any Attorney General who put Gaston B. Means on the payroll ought to have been dismissed the next morning," and for this remark he drew a hearty round of applause.[16]

In the development of wholesale corruption as a political issue, Gaston saw hope of squirming out of his difficulties. He returned to Washington. He visited Senator Wheeler and tried to persuade the Senator to reopen the Daugherty Investigation, promising sensational new disclosures and "documentary evidence" to back them up. Senator Wheeler listened, but he did not accept Gaston's offer. Gaston then was in touch with Blair Coan, an investigator hired by the Republican National Committee to work on the campaign. Means wanted to see Harry Daugherty. Daugherty was cautious but also most eager that Gaston be persuaded to repudiate his testimony before the Senate Committee. Daugherty asked Todd if he should see Means. Todd said he saw no objection.[17]

Apparently, in the course of discussions, someone indicated to Means that if he would deny his words, Daugherty would try to help him. At least, Gaston grew to hope so. Gaston returned to see Wheeler again. He was undecided as to which political faction offered him the best chance of escape from prison. Senator Wheeler told Gaston to follow his conscience—which was no help at all to Gaston.[18]

But perhaps Gaston did follow his conscience, after all. On September 21, Harry Daugherty announced that he had a statement from Gaston in which Gaston repudiated all his charges against Daugherty and declared that he had perjured himself in testimony before the Senate Committee, prompted by Senator Wheeler. Pressed by newspapermen, Gaston first denied that he had made any such statement, then grew vague, and denied that he had signed an affidavit. Finally he denied nothing, but said he wanted to see the statement of Senator Wheeler on the matter before saying more.[19]

Gaston B. Means

Attorney Thomas B. Felder said that Means had given the statement voluntarily. Gaston had a change of heart, the lawyer told the press, and decided the time had come "to consider his own moral and spiritual welfare."

Senator Wheeler was deceptively benign. He was in Chicago when he learned of the Means change of heart. Gaston had told him earlier that he was under great pressure to repudiate his testimony, said the Senator. The public should not now judge Gaston too harshly for his words, for Means was under threat of imprisonment. It proved all the more need for housecleaning in Washington if the Administration could force repudiation by threats, said the Progressive party candidate for Vice-President of the United States.

Gaston, it seemed, had gotten himself into more trouble than ever. Blair Coan denied discussing Means with Daugherty or with the Republican National Committee. The Democratic National Committee released copies of correspondence on this matter that purported to be letters exchanged between Attorney Felder and Daugherty. Senator Smith Brookhart announced that he was ready to reopen the Daugherty inquiry if Daugherty would promise to testify. Roxie Stinson, whose testimony Gaston had also repudiated (as an afterthought), said that Gaston was "ridiculous." The newspapers said they expected Gaston to repudiate his repudiation at any moment.[20] Gaston took cover from the press and fled home to Concord.

Means's decision to go home while he awaited the results of his appeal was not entirely directed by the storm he had created. He had run out of money. In Washington he tried unsuccessfully to borrow $300 from Sidney Bieber.[21] He could not pay Rella Lane the $2,000 he owed her, or even pay the rent on the house on Sixteenth Street. In the middle of August he had sent Julie and his son to Concord, their belongings packed in nine pieces of luggage.[22] On the day before Julie left, she and Gaston had tried to persuade Rella Lane to take over the Washington house. Means said he would keep his office in the basement, and would live there. He would pay off his share of the rent by finding people to pay "big rent" for the rest of the house, and he would see that liquor was furnished to them, as an additional inducement.

Miss Lane was not interested in running an apartment house.

Gaston tried to persuade Miss Lane's sister to open a roadhouse, where he and his family would live and take care of the place, or to open a "beauty parlor" on F Street, which would in fact be a bootlegging establishment.[23] Two months before, Gaston had been talking about his wealth to Miss Lane. Now he was willing to turn his hand to work as a bootlegger.

As Gaston retreated to Concord, two judgments were filed against him in New York by a Chicago attorney, for old services. They came to $8,500. The Bureau of Internal Revenue filed a lien against him for $267,614.40 for unpaid income taxes and penalties for the years 1921-23. The Bureau based this claim on the testimony of Gaston and other witnesses in his trial. Hiram Todd thoughtfully furnished the Bureau with a record, which showed the following sources and moneys:

Dr. Sacharoff	$5,250
J. T. Houston and Mr. Morrison	8,000
I. D. Padorr	8,000
Herman Weise	10,000
Japanese man from Mitsui	100,000
"Various Sources," from 1921-23, according to Means Testimony	300,000
W .T. Underwood payment for Means defense	2,000
Harry Steinfeld	5,000
C. W. Johnson	15,000
W. T. Underwood, three years' pay at $150 weekly	23,400
W. T. Underwood, expenses three years at $1000 monthly	36,000
Various Items not specified, according to Means testimony[24]	21,000

Even Gaston must stagger under such a blow. On September 29 he said he was bankrupt. He applied for a three months' extension of the time necessary to file a record of the trial in the appeal. He had paid $300 to the stenographers, he said, but he could not pay the rest.[25]

Had the money been rolling in as in past years, perhaps Gaston would have avoided his most serious error in judgment. The error was to allow Elmer Jarnecke to sit and think in loneliness in the Tombs that summer. Admittedly, Jarnecke was not a rapid-fire thinker, but he had much time. Two months after their conviction, Jarnecke had thought about his own situation very seriously. The canny Hiram Todd let him sit there for nearly two months without bail, and never went near him. Then Todd began to make overtures which shed new light into Jarnecke's prison cell. First, an Internal Revenue agent went to see Jarnecke to talk about his income tax. The revenue man softened Jarnecke up. Then, one of the U. S. Attorney's men went to see Jarnecke, and was followed by a second lawyer. Finally, Jarnecke was persuaded that if he told the truth, his affairs might take a turn for the better. No promises were made, but the implication was clear. Jarnecke felt that Means had abandoned him, and that he could not be worse off than he was.[26] Jarnecke was correct. It was not totally a question of money with Gaston. Jarnecke's letters to Samuel Schmidt, and Jarnecke's signature on the damning receipt given to C. W. Johnson, had carried great weight with the jury. Worse, when Jarnecke took the stand, his performance was miserable. Means told several acquaintances that he had the case won until Jarnecke wrecked everything.[27]

In the beginning of their talks, Todd was disappointed because Jarnecke apparently had little to offer. But before the interrogations ended, the prosecutor discovered that Jarnecke had been a key figure in the negotiations to "fix" the Glass Casket case. Jarnecke, then, could be a key government witness in the case Todd now wanted to try against Means and Felder.[28]

It was agreed that Jarnecke would be released from jail if he would testify. But then, Todd asked, what would Jarnecke do to provide food and shelter for himself until the second Means trial? Jarnecke said that he had been offered a large sum of money by a newspaper if he would tell his story to a reporter. Todd winced and hastened to persuade the Justice Department to put Jarnecke on the Federal payroll as an informer, lest his new case be tried in the newspapers first.[29]

The Department of Justice was ready to try the case against Means and Felder in October. Felder stalled. Hiram Todd suspected that the attorney was again playing for time. For once this was not entirely true. Felder was very sick. Todd ordered examination of Felder by a New York City neurologist, who reported that while Felder should be well enough to stand trial about the middle of November, he had been undergoing "heroic intensive medical treatment."[30]

Still there were delays and confusion. Todd was surprised and upset to discover that the U.S. Attorney in Pittsburgh was preparing to try the Glass Casket defendants on charges arising from their fraudulent stock sale there, after he had asked that the cases be suspended so the Glass Casket defendants could help make the case against Means and Felder. Those defendants had already been convicted in New York Federal Court. Sentence had been stayed because they were assisting the government. The attorneys for the defendants protested, and Todd spent nearly a month unraveling red tape that threatened to deprive him of his key witnesses.[31]

Without the testimony of the Glass Casket defendants, there was no case, for they had been mulcted of $65,000 by Means, Jarnecke, and Colonel Felder. Todd was equally concerned lest the apparent breach of faith by the Federal authorities persuade those defendants that it was useless to help the government. Finally, however, he had the matter straightened out.

Another complication was interjected by Thomas B. Felder, who wanted to use character witnesses—mostly judges from the South. Todd said hastily that he would be satisfied with depositions as to Felder's sterling character, but these had to be obtained from the witnesses by overworked U.S. Attorneys around the country. It took time.

Felder then tried to secure a separate trial on the grounds that Gaston's previous conviction and Gaston's notoriety would prejudice Felder's case.

All these complexities caused adjournment of the case until January 5, 1925. While the lawyers fenced, Gaston remained in Concord for the most part, less active than at any time in ten years. He traveled occasionally to Washington and New York, but he never stayed long. Harry Daugherty was afraid that Gaston would jump bond. "He will swim out to sea," the former Attorney General predicted.[32] But Daugherty did not know that so reduced were Gaston's circumstances that he had been forced to exchange his cash bond for a personal bond, and the signers who backed that were his brother-in-law and two friends who were prominent in business in Concord. Further, the bond was secured by the signatures of Gaston's mother and sisters, and the house on Union Street was their stake.

On December 12, Gaston left Concord for New York City to confer with Felder. Means had no attorney at this point, for Felder could not represent him properly, and Gaston had no money to hire another. He remained in New York until two days before Christmas, and arrived in Concord again on Christmas Eve, to spend the holiday season at home.

It must have been a miserable Christmas for all the Means family in 1924. Gaston was already convicted and faced a prison term. He had failed in his bid for freedom through appeal to the politicians at election time. Now that the Republican Administration was to continue, he could expect no major changes in the Justice Department. He must have come close to losing hope, for he had no money or any way to earn money. He and Julie and their son had only one refuge—the house on North Union Street. Here Julie would remain while Gaston went North again to fight for his freedom.

But not before Gaston had made one vigorous last stand.

The trial at the U.S. District Court in New York City's Foley Square was to begin on the morning of January 5, before Judge Walter C. Lindley. When the case was called, Elmer Jarnecke appeared and changed his plea from one of not guilty to one of guilty. He had no funds to hire an attorney, Jarnecke said, so the court appointed one to represent him. Prosecutor Todd made it clear to the Judge that Jarnecke presented no problem.

Thomas B. Felder was ready, with counsel.

Gaston B. Means was not ready, or even in the courtroom. Felder produced a telegram stating that Means was sick in Concord and faced an immediate operation for removal of gallstones.

Hiram Todd snorted. He said it was a patent attempt to stall the case, as Means had stalled his first trial for months. Todd demanded that the court issue a bench warrant for Means's arrest and immediate transportation under guard to New York City. Judge Lindley adjourned the case temporarily until the true condition of Means could be ascertained. Special Assistant Attorney General Clifford Byrnes went to Charlotte to demand Means's appearance before a Federal judge there. Deputy U.S. Marshal M. C. Coin of Charlotte was ordered to go to Concord with an impartial physician, to determine Means's condition. The Justice Department was not willing to take the word of the Means family doctor.

In Concord on January 5, Gaston consented to see a reporter from the local *Daily Tribune* who wanted an interview.

"From his sick bed at the home of his mother here, Mrs. G. W. [sic] Means, where he has been visiting for the past several weeks, Gaston B. Means Monday offered his body as evidence that he is suffering keenly from gallstones, which disease he declared kept him from appearing in Federal Court in New York City that day." So wrote the *Tribune's* man. The article continued:

" 'Anyone who looked upon my wasted body could see that I have been wracked with pain,' Means said. He was far more concerned with his ailment than with the warrant. He had lost 55

264

pounds during the last six or seven weeks, Means declared, and he was unable even to discuss the matter intelligently because his pain was so severe."[33]

Todd did not believe a word of it, yet it was true that Gaston was ill and had been suffering from gallstone attacks for several years, recurrently. His physician had recommended an operation, but Means had always been extremely reluctant to undergo an operation.

The next day, the Assistant U.S. Attorney and two deputy marshals appeared in Concord with a doctor from Charlotte. The marshals and the doctor went to the Means house. When no one answered their knock they opened the door and went upstairs, to be shooed back down again by Julie, who told them to wait until her husband was ready to see them. The doctor examined Gaston and found that he did, indeed, suffer from gallstones, but the doctor believed he was well enough to travel to New York and stand trial.

Gaston was arrested and taken from the house to Charlotte by automobile. When he arrived, he was hustled to the office of the U.S. Attorney, where he immediately demanded to see a lawyer— Jake F. Newell, one of his counsel in the King murder case. Newell came to the U.S. Attorney's office prepared to fight against extradition, but Federal Judge Webb signed an order that Gaston be taken that night to New York City by train, in a drawing room, accompanied by a trained nurse.

On January 7, Gaston appeared in the New York Courtroom on Foley Square, looking thin and ill. He said he had no attorney and no funds, so the court appointed Abraham I. Menin to defend him. The jury was selected and the trial began.[34]

Samuel Rosenblatt, one of the Glass Casket defendants, said that Means had pretended that Attorney General Daugherty and Secretary Mellon were his intimate friends, who would help Means in any enterprise. Rosenblatt corroborated the important part of the story—which was the existence of a conspiracy by Means, Felder, and Jarnecke to convince the Glass Casket defendants that they could use influence in Washington to keep the defendants out of jail. It did not make any difference (as a point of law) whether or not the proposition was preposterous. The point at issue was whether or not Means and Felder had pretended to such influence, and having proclaimed it, used it to obstruct justice. It was a fine point, and one that it might be difficult to explain convincingly to a jury.

Former Attorney General Daugherty wanted desperately to testify in this case, not because he could add any information that would help convict Felder and Means, but because Daugherty hoped to use the trial as a podium from which he could get his own story across to the newspapers. The defense wanted Daugherty to testify. Hiram Todd was not at all eager to have Daugherty testify, but, out of courtesy to the man who had appointed him, he could not refuse to let him come. Daugherty came, however, as a witness called by the defense.[35]

Daugherty testified that he had known Felder for fifteen years, and that none of the defendants had ever spoken to him about the Glass Casket case. His most shocking disclosure, or it should have been his most shocking disclosure to those who believed Gaston's statements about his own high position in government, was that Harry Daugherty had actually talked to Gaston Means only once in his life, and that he had encountered Gaston only once in the Department of Justice halls, and that on that occasion Means had apparently not even known his ultimate superior by sight.

Daugherty said he wanted to talk about conditions in Washington when "certain people were Hellbound and on the other side spellbound. It is time that the truth about some things ought to be told," he said. Judge Lindley regretfully told Daugherty that his courtroom was not the place to tell those things.

That was all Daugherty was allowed to say. Hiram Todd objected to all the questions that tried to lead Daugherty to say that he had not been bribed. The attorneys for Means and Felder objected to all the questions from Todd that tried to lead Daugherty to say that he had ordered the investigation and prosecution of Means. The judge sustained nearly all the objections from both sides, and it became apparent that the former Attorney General had nothing to contribute to the case at hand. He was dismissed without getting the chance he longed for to make a case for his own conduct in office.

Gaston testified. So did Felder. Both protested their innocence and it seemed that they hardly knew one another, the way their stories went. William J. Burns testified, too, and the defense tried to show that Burns had never met with Means and Daugherty at the Waldorf-Astoria Hotel, although Gaston had missed a meeting with the Glass Casket defendants because he said he was going to attend such a high-level conference.

Keats Speed, managing editor of the New York *Sun*, testified to the general good character of Thomas B. Felder. U.S. Circuit Court Judge Martin Manton did the same. No one came to testify to the good character of Gaston Bullock Means. Even Burns did not try to build Means up, nor was Burns asked to do so. But the issue was not good or bad character, or whether or not Burns had been bribed, or even that an attempt had been made to bribe him. The Glass Casket defendants had been told that was what was happening, and that is why they paid over their $65,000.

Hiram Todd made that point for the jury in one simple way. Every time the defense tried to prove that Means and Felder had not really bribed anyone, Todd objected, and the court sustained the objection, explaining the point several times. Any jury would eventually get the idea. In the nearly three weeks of trial, this jury got it.

The story of the "missing papers of Gaston B. Means" was revealed, or at least one version was revealed, when Gaston testified that the papers which he had charged were taken away by two deputy sergeants-at-arms of the Senate, were actually taken away by the Ducksteins. This was puzzling testimony because the Ducksteins had been Gaston's main supporters in the tale he told the Senate Committee about the theft of the papers. The Ducksteins, *persona non grata* in Washington after the Senate investigation, had moved to Chicago. There Jessie Duckstein read of Gaston's testimony and indignantly wired Hiram Todd that she had been duped by Means into believing that she saw two men remove the papers.[36]

But Means had already admitted the truth, as part of his "confession" of September 20, about the testimony he had given before the Senate Committee. He had decided that the papers ought to disappear, so they disappeared. And where did they actually disappear to? This was not to be known publicly, but they went to Sidney Bieber's office, for Gaston had asked Bieber to keep some things for him for a time, and then had carted his telescope cases up to the back room, and had left them there for six weeks in April and May, 1924.[37]

The unraveling of old mysteries and the creation of new ones interested the newspaper audiences, but these were not germane to the case. Conspiracy cases are notoriously difficult for the prosecution, but, in this affair, Hiram Todd was aided immeasurably by the testimony of Elmer Jarnecke. If Means believed that Jarnecke's testimony had "done him in" during the first trial, he certainly must have been convinced that Jarnecke finished him off in the second one. Jarnecke was there during Means's talks with the defendants. Jarnecke saw. Jarnecke took money. Jarnecke knew the Glass Casket men, and they knew him. The state's case dovetailed in every way, and the testimony of most of the witnesses had that inimitable ring of truth to it.

On the evening of January 29, the jury reached a verdict after five hours and forty minutes of debate. The next day the jury announced that both men were guilty—the long debate had been involved with the question of the *degree* of Felder's guilt. The jury recommended clemency for Felder, perhaps not realizing that conviction was all the punishment he need be given—for automatically, conviction disbarred him and took away his livelihood.[38]

Means was not shocked, or he did not seem to be, by the outcome of his second trial. He had looked on apprehensively as the jury went out. He seemed to know that his luck had run out. Felder, jaunty as the jurors filed from the room, was brutally shocked by the verdict, although the sentence he received was light enough: he was fined $10,000.

Gaston's sentence was as stern as the Judge could devise under the law. He was given two more years in the Federal penitentiary and another fine of $10,000. Worse, the second prison term was to be served after the first had expired, which meant that Gaston could look forward to some three years in the penitentiary, with time off for good behavior, and then he must pay the $20,000 in fines.

This blow, coming on the heels of all the others he had suffered in the past twelve months, was enough to make a strong man wince. And if it was not enough, just two months later the Federal authorities indicted Gaston once again—this time for forgery in signing the name of Senator Smith Brookhart at the bottom of his spurious order to turn over the Means files to the Senate Committee. It appeared that Gaston had been quite wrong when he told Rella Lane that the letter she typed would keep him out of the penitentiary.

XIII

The initial conviction of Gaston Means had brought praise for Prosecutor Todd, but the second conviction brought far more. Attorney General Stone expressed pleasurable surprise at the outcome of the case. Assistant Attorney General William J. Donovan called it a "most healthy advance in the administration of justice." J. Edgar Hoover said he knew of no public official who had performed a greater service to the public than Todd.[1]

Did Gaston realize how he had become the symbol of the dishonesties in law-enforcement agencies under the Harding Administration? Gaston was not concerned with such matters. His interest lay in devising a method to keep out of prison. He realized, in the Republican victory of 1924, that he had backed the wrong horse when he testified before the Senate Committee that was investigating Attorney General Daugherty. Less than three weeks after his conviction, Gaston wrote to Daugherty, imploring the former Attorney General to grant a personal interview. Gaston said he wanted to discuss ways in which he might make some amends for the wrongs he had done Daugherty. He hinted darkly at some obscure purposes of the Wheeler-Brookhart Committee. Daugherty, Gaston said, and the public, did not know the real story behind the investigation.

In February, 1925, Harry Daugherty ought to have known better, but Gaston had struck Daugherty in his most vulnerable spot—his vanity. Daugherty was eager to find any evidence, even Gaston's kind, to show that the motives of the Committee that had caused his resignation were less than noble.

Daugherty asked Hiram Todd for advice. He wrote that he wanted to see Means. Todd advised him to see Means in the presence of Daugherty's lawyer, Howland, and at least one other person. "If I were conducting such an interview I would prefer to have both Senator Chamberlain and Mr. Howland present, as Means is such an infernal liar it is well to have plenty of witnesses on hand when he talks—particularly when he carries on an interview which he has solicited."[2]

Thus encouraged, Harry Daugherty wrote to Gaston,[3] who was in Concord. He consented to the interview, but he promised nothing. They met in New York, and Gaston dictated a long, rambling statement—an attempt to create an apologia for his life since the fall of 1921. The only wrongdoing to which Gaston confessed was injuring Attorney General Daugherty, and this, said Gaston, was all the fault of Senator Burton K. Wheeler.

Senator Wheeler's plan, said Gaston, was to "frame" Daugherty and thus create a political issue on which Senator La Follette could rise to become the Democratic nominee for President in 1924. If this could not be done, said Wheeler—according to Means—La Follette would become a presidential candidate on an independent ticket.

Since Senator La Follette had become an independent candidate, and Senator Wheeler had become his running mate, the story sounded promising to a man who wanted to believe it anyhow. Gaston had used one of his standard devices. He had twisted recent history to play on the emotions of his intended victim.

Gaston B. Means

Senator Wheeler had consulted Gaston about bringing Roxie Stinson to Washington (said Means). Wheeler had suggested taking her out to the Wheeler house to protect her from Daugherty's spies, but Gaston had advised him that Miss Stinson was not the kind of woman Mrs. Wheeler would want in the house. (Daugherty, betrayed by Miss Stinson, appreciated those words, surely.)

Gaston said, too, that Miss Stinson's testimony, like Gaston's, was all planned in advance. Not a word of it was true. The plan was to smear the entire Harding Administration, to launch "an attack on the entire Judiciary system of the United States, from the Supreme Court down . . . ," to attack President Coolidge for speculation in oil stocks. In other words, Senator Brookhart and Senator Wheeler had set out "to destroy, if possible, the government."[4]

Harry Daugherty grew enthusiastic, even though Gaston refused to sign his name to the statement. Daugherty tried to persuade Hiram Todd that it was in the interest of the Justice Department to make the Means trial for forgery of Senator Brookhart's name into an exposure of the Brookhart-Wheeler Committee, and, of course, a defense of Harry Daugherty.[5]

Todd was sympathetic but wary and restrained in his replies. He was also investigating some of the transactions of Mal Daugherty, Harry's banker brother, and the Alien Property Custodian's conduct of his office during the Harding Administration. Part of the evidence that this was worth looking into had come from the Means investigations and from Elmer Jarnecke, who told Prosecutor Todd about the intimate relations between Gaston and Colonel Thomas Miller, the custodian.

On May 5, the United States Court of Appeals affirmed the conviction of Gaston and Elmer Jarnecke in the bootlegging conspiracy case, and, since Gaston had no money to pursue the matter to the Supreme Court, it was time for him to go to prison and begin serving his sentence. He and Julie were now living in a furnished room in Washington.[6]

Gaston went to see Clifford Byrnes at the Department of Justice, hoping to secure a nominal bond in the forgery case, but Byrnes refused to make any recommendations. Byrnes was interested in Means's tale about the motivations of the Brookhart-Wheeler Committee, but also wary.

Gaston saw in this a ray of hope. He was eager that the case be tried, partly because it would again stall off the fatal day on which he must surrender and go to Atlanta to begin serving his sentence. Gaston was the eternal optimist. As long as he was free, he felt that he had a chance to escape, if only he could discover the correct formula.

Officials of the Department of Justice were of differing minds about the wisdom of reopening the Daugherty Investigation in any way, and the trial of Gaston Means would certainly do so. Gaston had now made two separate "confessions." First, he had said that "it was decided" that his papers should disappear. The implication was clear: the decision had been made by Gaston and Senator Wheeler. Second, Gaston had come forward with a fantastic story of a "plot" by Senators La Follette and Wheeler. The implication here was that Wheeler and La Follette were a pair of Bolsheviks who were trying to bring revolution to America.

The Department of Justice had enjoyed about all of Gaston Means that its officials wanted for a time. Prosecutor Hiram Todd did not want to try this case. He was eager to return to private practice, and so he did his best to shuck the case off on Clifford Byrnes, who was serving in Washington.[7]

Toward the end of May, it was decided within the Department that it would be unwise to raise issues that might reflect on the Administration at that point. No other conclusion can be drawn from the rapidity with which enthusiasm for the third trial of Gaston Means diminished.

It was becoming apparent that there would be grounds for a trial of other officials of the Harding Administration on criminal charges. The Veterans Administration had already fallen, and Charles R. Forbes had been convicted of accepting bribes. The investigation of Colonel Miller was under way. Investigations were shaping up against former Attorney General Daugherty, and against Albert B. Fall, Harding's Secretary of the Interior. It seemed an excellent time to let Senator Burton K. Wheeler alone.

On May 19, it was decided that there was to be no third trial, and, on May 20, Gaston was ready to go to prison. Deputy Marshal Costanzo Cerimele was ordered to escort Gaston to the penitentiary. The next day they set out, Gaston wearing a well-fitting dark suit, his usual butterfly bow tie, carrying a pocket full of documents, and sporting the dimpled grin that never seemed to desert him, even in the worst of times.

Julie was distraught. How would she earn a living for her son and herself with Gaston in prison? The Means family again came to the rescue. Belle and Kate Means were teachers in the Concord school system, and they helped Julie find a job as a teacher, too. The post paid very little, but Julie lived in the house on Union Street, and she could survive.[8]

And what of Gaston's associates in crime? Elmer Jarnecke remained on the Federal payroll as an informer for the Department of Justice as long as his usefulness continued. He returned then to Chicago, and went to work for the prohibition enforcement authorities, all the while protected by stays of sentence, so he would not have to join Gaston in the Atlanta penitentiary. In October, 1925, Jarnecke was pardoned by President Coolidge.

Thomas B. Felder fought a hard battle to persuade the Circuit Court, and then the United States Supreme Court, to reverse his conviction. But it was a losing battle. When the case came before the U.S. Circuit Court of Appeals, Judge Martin Manton was sitting on the bench with two other jurists. He made no move to disqualify himself, although he had testified in Felder's behalf as a character witness. Prosecutor Todd stepped forward resolutely that day and asked the Judge to disqualify himself, since he was a friend of the convicted man. Judge Manton did so then, embarrassed, and with reluctance. (A few years later, Judge Manton was convicted of taking bribes and was disbarred.)

In the end, less than two years after his conviction, Felder went home to Georgia. Despite warnings from his doctors, he went on a spree. One might almost say that the unfortunate Georgian sought release, for, as the doctors had warned, the spree killed him.[9]

The Glass Casket defendants, or at least the ones who had helped the government convict Means and Felder, spent months in the toils of government red tape. The Justice Department tried first to obtain suspended sentences against Safir, Sideman, and Rosenblatt, but Judge Learned Hand, before the case came, refused to review it on that basis. It was up to the President to ameliorate sentences, he said. Eventually, the defendants were granted conditional pardons, and finally their civil rights were restored to them.[10]

Gaston, in prison, fared very well as those things go, and soon seemed to be enjoying his stay in Atlanta. Warden John Snook was a very understanding man. Earl Carroll, the Follies king, was serving time in Atlanta for income tax fraud. Carroll served his sentence while living in the warden's house and eating the warden's food. Gaston was not quite on Carroll's level, but he soon had many privileges. In the summer of 1925, L. C. White, the Superintendent of Prisons, took an interest in Gaston's welfare. He wanted to know when Gaston had arrived, how he was employed, and how was his conduct. Warden Snook replied that Means had arrived on May 22, that he was employed in the record office, and that his conduct was perfect. Apparently that was so. Gaston was soon occupying a private room in the prison hospital.[11]

It is always valuable for a warden to have the confidence of a few inmates of a prison. He thus hears all the gossip and rumors and can protect himself against breakouts and other unpleasant incidents. Gaston saw this quickly. He kept the warden informed and the warden gave Gaston extra privileges. He went to work in the prison library. For a man of Gaston's temperament, if he had to be in prison at all, there was no better place to serve out his time.

Gaston's prison sentence was punctuated by brief respites of freedom from the walls of Atlanta, for he was called several times to testify before grand juries that were investigating other shady affairs of the Harding years. On October 27, 1925, Gaston testified before a New York City grand jury that was investigating the assets of the American Metals Corporation. This was the beginning of the legal case brought by the government against Gaston's friend Thomas Miller.[12]

The longest of these periods of freedom came in January and February, 1926. Gaston was brought to New York for nearly a month, most of which he spent in waiting rooms, waiting to testify. While Means was in New York City, Senator Edward Edwards of New Jersey and Senator Brookhart debated publicly on the subject, "Prohibition—Success or Failure?" Senator Brookhart said prohibition was successful. Senator Edwards said prohibition was a miserable failure, and he cited case after case of bootlegging and other law violation.[13]

The reports of this debate seem to have stimulated Gaston's imagination. In late spring he wrote to William J. Burns, his old friend, suggesting that he had information of great value to the government in connection with bootlegging. Burns had returned to his private detective agency in New York City, but he sent the letter on to the Attorney General, suggesting that the Bureau of Investigation look into Means's offering. J. Edgar Hoover sent an agent to see Means in the Atlanta penitentiary, and the agent returned with a long report of conversations with Gaston. Hoover was impressed enough to turn over the matter to an Assistant Attorney General. There was not much the Department of Justice could do, because it had no appropriation for investigation of prohibition matters. All that work had been returned to the Treasury. The Department found enough of interest in Gaston's statements, however, that Gaston was sounded out to see if he would co-operate with Treasury agents if they were sent to Atlanta.[14]

Gaston would co-operate with the devil if it would help him get out of jail. He faced some serious problems in that regard, however.

He had been sentenced to a total of four years and to fines of $20,000. His sentences began on May 22, 1925, and would expire in full term on May 21, 1929. If he received full credit for good behavior, nearly a year would be dropped from the sentences, and he could be released on June 19, 1928. But he could be paroled after September 21, 1926, under the Federal parole regulation then in force.

Under those parole regulations, however, no action could be taken as long as other indictments were pending against a convict. Several indictments were outstanding against Gaston, especially that one for forgery in the Senate investigation of Attorney General Daugherty.

Gaston had not been very fond of Prosecutor Hiram Todd in the period in which Todd was concerned with his affairs. In fact, Gaston had bragged before the Daugherty Investigation Committee that he "could whip him and still smile."

"Todd was a flagrant liar," Gaston told the Committee, "and under the rules of the bar association he could be disbarred."

Gaston had also told the Committee that while he had not yet called Hiram Todd a crook, he would before he was through, and he would prove that Todd was a crook.[15]

Nor was that all. At the end of the first trial, when Gaston had been convicted, in his shock he spoke to Prosecutor Todd as Todd passed by him on the way out of the courtroom.

"You son of a bitch," Gaston had hissed at the Special Assistant Attorney General. "I'll get you for this."[16]

Well, Gaston was through, for the moment at least. He had not "gotten" Todd. He had not called him a crook, publicly at least, and he had not even tried to pursue these matters, being busy with others more important to him. But, consequent to these statements, there was little reason for Hiram C. Todd to have any love for Gaston B. Means. As was customary, shortly after Gaston's conviction, sentence, and incarceration, the Federal parole authorities requested a routine statement of opinion from the prosecutor in

278

the case. Todd said then that he did not find Means eligible for consideration for parole.[17]

Yet Hiram Todd was not a vindictive man. Despite the record of personal conflict, when Gaston began to hope for parole, just before the beginning of spring in 1927, he turned to Hiram Todd for help. He wrote to Todd, pleading in behalf of his "wife and little boy and seventy-year-old mother." If the forgery indictment and the others were *"nolle prossed"*—if the government decided not to prosecute Means—then he could be eligible for parole. Means said, and it was true, that his gall bladder had been acting up again, and that he needed an operation. He intended to have it, but he wanted to have it at home.

"In sending me here with the maximum sentences, I do not be lieve you intended that I should be debarred from parole eligibility if I conducted myself properly," he wrote.

"I have certainly learned my lesson. My only hope and wish now is that I be allowed to return to my old home at Concord, North Carolina, where my wife and little boy and my mother are living. I am sure and positive that the authorities will never again be caused any trouble by any act of mine."[18]

Hiram Todd *had* intended that Means be barred from parole, but it seemed less important to him two years after the conviction. Todd bore no personal grudge against Means. From a political standpoint there was absolutely no sense in reopening the Daugherty Investigation conducted by Senator Wheeler. The former Attorney General had now been brought to trial himself on charges of conspiracy, in connection with violations of the federal laws and failure to prosecute law violations in the Veterans Bureau. He had won a hung jury and acquittal. But in the spring of 1927 there was nothing to be gained by anyone in bringing Harry Daugherty into the limelight again.

Todd was bombarded with letters by Julie Means, Gaston, and by Gaston's mother, who said she could not understand why so many calamities had befallen her son. Julie wrote that she was supporting herself and her son on the $88 per month she received as a schoolteacher. She said she was certain that Gaston would not break the law again.

Gaston also wrote to Mabel Walker Willebrandt, asking that she use her influence, and promising that if paroled he would remain in Concord. Women seem to have longer memories than men in such matters. Mrs. Willebrandt had been personally embarrassed, too, because she had once said publicly that Gaston was a fine investigator. She wrote back bluntly, "Under the circumstances I do not feel that I can consistently recommend that the pending indictments be *nolle prossed*."[19]

Todd and Clifford Byrnes shared the view that, while Means would not reform, it was no service to the government to seek conviction of a twice-convicted man on charges that were five years old in some cases, and three years old in others. They recommended that all the indictments be dropped, and the indictments were dropped that year, although not in time for Gaston to be considered for parole in the spring.

In the autumn of 1927, Gaston brought forth all the pressure and influence he could muster in his behalf—a considerable showing in view of his recent history. The Chairman of the Republican County Committee of Cabarrus County signed a petition for Gaston's parole. So did the Chairman of the Democratic Committee. So did the Presidents of the Rotary Club of Concord, the Women's Club, the Kiwanis Club, the Secretary of the YMCA, and an editor of the Concord *Observer*.[20]

Warden Snook favored the parole. So did the parole board, and so did Gaston's prosecutors. Mrs. Willebrandt won, however, because the parole was granted on October 14, 1927, but was never actually awarded to Gaston. The parole regulations stated that no man could be freed on parole unless he had satisfied all his obligations to the government, and Gaston had no money to pay the $20,000 in fines assessed against him.

So Gaston served his full term, with time off for good behavior, but with an extra thirty days of time added to his sentence. He appeared before a United States Commissioner and took a pauper's oath, which relieved him of the $20,000 in fines after he had served the last thirty days. On July 19, 1928, Gaston was a free man once again. With the old insouciance, Gaston stopped in the Commissioner's office and invited newspaper reporters there to "fire away" with questions about his life and plans.[21]

Gaston had already given a clue about the changes prison had made in him to a reporter from the Raleigh *News and Observer* earlier that year, when the reporter had visited Atlanta.

"Hello, Gaston," said the reporter.

"Hello, boy," Gaston had replied. "I'm glad to see you."

"How are they treating you here, Gaston?"

"Oh, bully," he said. "I have three good meals a day and a good bed to sleep in, a good library, movie shows once a week, a gymnasium, frequent concerts, religious services, and a big Sunday school on Sunday. And the beauty of it is it doesn't cost anything."

If that statement seemed a little too long for one mouthful, and the reporter had taken liberties in his role as amanuensis, at least there seemed to be no doubt that the reporter had grasped Gaston's philosophy. The same cherubic grin appeared on Gaston's face, the newspaper man said, and the dimples were wreathed in that same attractive smile.[22]

Gaston smiled more on July 19, as he left the Commissioner's office with Julie and his son and walked to the automobile that would start them on the trip home to Concord. It *was* the same old Gaston, as Mrs. Willebrandt apparently had suspected it would be, and as Hiram Todd and Clifford Byrnes were sure it would be.

What was he going to do in the future? a reporter asked.

"Anybody I can," Gaston said. And, laughing, he entered the car and was driven away.[23]

The next day, dressed in his usual blue suit, white shirt, and polka dot bow tie, Gaston arrived with his family on the Southern Railroad's Train No. 36 in Concord.

This was a different Gaston entirely, the home-town boy breathing the clear country air.

"Gee, but it's great to be home again," he said as he pulled up a chair on the broad front porch of the house on North Union Street. He had never felt better, Gaston told a visiting newspaperman from the local paper. Warden Snook was one of the finest men he had ever met. (The warden was later removed after a tenure in which he exhibited excessive kindness to prisoners.) Prison, Gaston said, was a sort of "educational institution. There you meet all kinds of people and have all kinds of experiences," he added.

How did Gaston feel about his misfortunes? the newspaperman asked.

"Well, what's the use of crying?" Gaston said cheerfully.

The next question was a measure of Gaston's position in his home town. Who would be elected President in that autumn of 1928?

"I'm no prophet," Gaston replied.

Did he believe in prohibition, asked the reporter, sturdily pressing for a story.

"I don't know. I've never seen it tried," said Gaston.[24]

Homecoming was pleasant, for others treated Gaston with the same respect the reporter had shown, but friendliness did not solve Gaston's problems of making a living. If he ever really meant to settle down in Concord to nurse his gallstones and behave himself, Gaston had quite forgotten that resolution by the summer of 1928. Less than a week after arrival at the house on North Union Street, Gaston was off again.[25]

During his prison years, Gaston had met Mrs. May Dixon Thacker, the wife of a prominent southern evangelist. She was also a writer for *True Confessions* and similar publications. When the Thackers visited the Atlanta penitentiary, Gaston told Mrs. Thacker imaginative tales of his experiences, and she decided his story would make an interesting book. When she learned that he had been released from prison, Mrs. Thacker wrote to Gaston, telling him that when he was ready to tell his story to the world, she would be willing to help him. Gaston responded to the invitation by taking a train for New York, to see Mrs. Thacker. He borrowed a few hundred dollars from her on his prospects and on July 27 he brought Julie and their son to the city. The family took rooms at the Herald Square Hotel, where he planned to remain for a time. Then Gaston set out to find a publisher for his book.

His first approach was to Nan Britton, who had set herself up in publishing after the huge success of her book, *The President's Daughter*, which bared her illicit romance with Warren G. Harding. Miss Britton had an office in midtown New York. On January 4, 1929, Gaston telephoned Miss Britton's office, seeking an appointment. She was not inclined to see him, and asked him to write a letter stating his business. He did so on January 5, noting that he had been an "undercover investigator" for the Department of Justice, and that in his work he had come to know General Sawyer, the White House physician.

"This situation enabled me on occasions, through Gen. Sawyer, to obtain history-making documentary evidence of great importance to you then and of tremendous financial importance to you now in connection with your literary work. . . ."

Nan Britton was not interested in whatever Gaston Means might have to say, but she did agree to see him and heard him propose that together they write the story of his investigation of *her* in 1921 and 1922, with material to be supplied from his "diaries" plus notes to him from Mrs. Warren G. Harding. Mrs. Harding, said Gaston, had ordered him to investigate Nan Britton in those years.

Gaston was unsuccessful, but in the autumn of that year, Mrs. Thacker again came to see Miss Britton. She was equally unsuccessful in persuading Miss Britton to co-operate. But Mrs. Thacker and Gaston accomplished something with their efforts. They persuaded Maurice Fryefield, who had been Miss Britton's advertising manager, to start a publishing house to issue Gaston's memoirs. It was to be called the Guild Publishing Corporation, and its offices, too, were to be in New York City.[26]

The publishing commitment brought Gaston enough money to begin to live in style once again. In October, the Means family moved to a suite of three rooms and two baths in the Hotel Commodore in Washington. Mrs. Thacker divided her time between her husband's preaching schedule and the Means apartment. When she was in Washington, Gaston dictated to her, day after day. Gaston was interested in the book, obviously, but not entirely in the manner Mrs. Thacker expected. He was much more interested in gaining Mrs. Thacker's confidence so she would introduce him to respectable people, and in the "front" she gave him.[27]

Gaston's affairs seemed to be progressing splendidly. There was only one unhappy note in the fall of 1928—Gaston's mother died in Concord, having barely lived long enough to see her son released from prison. The estate did not amount to very much. There was the house on North Union Street, which went to his sisters. The remainder was divided into seven shares, among the children.

Early in 1929, Gaston met Ralph M. Easley, executive director of the National Civic Federation. The Federation was an eminently respectable organization, dedicated to reform. For a number of years, earlier in the century, the Federation had published a magazine to promote good government and the betterment of relations between capital and labor. In 1906 August Belmont, the capitalist, was President of the Federation, and Samuel Gompers, the labor leader, was First Vice-President. The organization studied the problems of the shorter work day, immigration, child labor, and the Sherman antitrust law. But in 1919 the Federation became seriously immersed in a study of bolshevism, and as communism spread across the world, the wealthy backers of the Federation grew overwhelmingly concerned with that threat.[28] In 1929, when Gaston met Ralph Easley, the major work of the Federation was the study of communism. Some sixteen agents were to be employed to work in the field and report to Ralph Easley on Communist activity.

Gaston persuaded Easley that he was an expert on communism,

although, as Julie Means said, at that time Gaston knew nothing about communism that could not be learned from the newspapers. Easley was convinced when Gaston promised to show him one of the most important members of the Russian Secret Police—the OGPU—and then took the white-haired director to the Library of Congress, where he pointed out a sinister figure who was skulking behind a newspaper.

That was the man, Gaston said. He was one of the most important Russian operatives in the world.

Easley was astounded. On the strength of such persuasive ways, Gaston secured a job as one of Easley's operatives. He was to make a trip around the United States to uncover Communist activity. Easley did not check Gaston's bona fides or his stories. If he had checked, he would have discovered that the "Russian spy" in the Library of Congress was Walter Liggett, an amiable Washington newspaper correspondent, who was sitting quietly under the dome of the Library of Congress that day, minding his own business and doing a bit of research.

The National Civic Federation offered Gaston exactly the employment he had been seeking: good pay, full expenses, unlimited opportunity for travel, and, most of all, no questions asked. Gaston's responsibility was to keep the Federation informed about the secret activities of the Communists in America. Gaston's method of doing this was to buy newspapers from all over the world and sit patiently for hours in his hotel room, culling them for obscure items about Soviet and Communist activity. These items were incorporated in his regular reports to the Federation. They kept the officers of that patriotic organization happy, and kept the money coming in plentiful supply.

Once the basic work on his memoirs was finished, Gaston took the family on a tour of the nation at the National Civic Federation's expense. They went to Chicago, where, between amusements, Gaston curled up in the living room of their suite and prepared his thrilling reports. He predicted strikes and demonstrations and the moves of the men in the Kremlin, by reading the reports of foreign correspondents, commentators, and local reporters. From a handful of facts Gaston could spin a story of intrigue and espionage calculated to raise the hair on the back of Ralph Easley or any other amateur Red-hunter. He and Julie drank the finest of wines and ate the best of foods. They took their son to museums and zoos and other places of public education. They lived the good life.

From Chicago, the Means family traveled to Detroit, where the automotive barons were on watch for Communists, and where, indeed, the Reds were as active as termites in an old New England farmhouse. But what did Gaston see? From the vantage point of his hotel room, not much. Nor did the Communists frequent the dining rooms of the Book-Cadillac Hotel, or spend their afternoons at Belle Isle amusement park.

After Detroit, Gaston headed for Niagara Falls, a well-known hideout for people of furtive behavior, and for Buffalo. He deluged Easley with reports, telephone calls, and telegrams. In particular, he got on the trail of a pair of OGPU agents who, he said, were out to establish sabotage rings in the United States. They were carrying $2 million and countless secret documents in their luggage, said Gaston. The luggage must have been a fearful problem for the agents, since Gaston reported that it consisted of twenty-four trunks and eleven suitcases.[29]

These remarkable foreign agents stayed at none but the best hotels, so naturally Gaston must do the same to keep an eye on them. Gaston trailed them across Canada during the summer season, to stop at Banff and Lake Louise. He went to Vancouver, which Julie adored. The spies were headed south, thank goodness, when fall came, so Gaston took the family motoring down the scenic coastal highway to Los Angeles. There the spies decided to hole up for a time—perhaps sensing that Gaston's son ought to be in school. Gaston rented three suites in an expensive apartment house on Crenshaw Boulevard—one for Julie, one for their son to play in, and one for his office.

Gaston B. Means

February is an excellent month for spy-hunting in Mexico, and that is what Gaston decided to do when it turned a bit chilly. It was the best trip of all, Julie said. Fortunately, while they were visiting Mexico City, President Rubio was shot by an assassin. The assassins—for Gaston knew it was two men—were the Russian agents, of course. Gaston telephoned Ralph Easley and gave him all the details. As always, he was right on the spot when the fur flew.

Gaston smuggled $4,000 in gold out of Mexico, just to keep his agile hand in practice, and he took it into the Carlsbad Caverns. This was an adventure! Suspicious of all around him, Gaston was not content to secrete the gold in his hotel room, so he carried it in the pockets of his trousers. He did not know that when one visits the Carlsbad Caverns, one walks. That day Gaston walked seven miles, sweating profusely, swearing even more profusely. Julie was worried all the way, for her husband's trousers kept slipping lower and lower on his hips. She feared that at any moment he might become unfrocked.

Since their son needed to remain in school, Julie spent the winter of that year in Los Angeles while Gaston went to New York.[30] At least that was where Gaston said he went. But Ralph Easley received a far more exciting story. Means had not lost contact with the OGPU agents for long, he said. One could not have them roaming America at will, unfollowed, carting their trunks full of documents from one city to the next, and ranging into nearby countries to shoot Presidents. Gaston followed them. He followed them without cease, stopping only for cash infusions from the Federation. At one point, he said, he needed $25,000 to get the secret documents.

The Federation, as usual, obliged. Gaston found the men and the documents then, he said. But disaster struck. He was captured by the wily Russians and held in a cabin in the High Sierra while they decided just how they would deal with him. Lord knows what would have happened to Gaston, or to the United States, had not the evil men fallen out one day. One murdered the other and fled, having first thoughtfully burned the twenty-four trunks and eleven suitcases filled with papers. Gaston hastened to civilization to report the crime to Ralph Easley and to swear out a warrant for the arrest of the murderer.[31] (The National Civic Federation was too busy, apparently, to realize what the prohibition blank-burners had learned long ago—that the destruction of papers is so tedious a job that it might take a week or two to burn twenty-four trunks full of documents, in which time Gaston would have died of starvation.)

In the spring of 1930, the result of Gaston's literary efforts was published by the Guild publishers, and it created a sensation. The book jumped to the top of the best-seller list. Perhaps the title had something to do with it: the book was called *The Strange Death of President Harding.* Gaston told of his undercover work for the President's wife in tracing down Nan Britton, and "the President's daughter," who was the result of their affair. Gaston even pictured the White House as a "love nest" for the white-haired President and his youthful inamorata. Gaston explained that his discharge from the Bureau of Investigation had been ordered by Warren Harding himself, from the White House, on the day Harding discovered that Gaston had exposed his guilty secret. All the convictions, all the wrongs that Gaston had suffered, had been the work of the President and his friends. The *pièce de résistance* was Gaston's charge that Mrs. Harding had poisoned her husband in the Palace Hotel in San Francisco, in a moment when she was overcome by a desire for revenge and a fear that Harding's life was ruined anyhow, because of the scandals beginning to break around him.

It was true that Harding's life had been shrouded in mystery, as had his death. After the President's death, Mrs. Harding collected most of his private papers. She wrote to friends and acquaintances, asking them to return to her all copies of letters he had sent them. Then she burned them.

It was not easy for anyone to check a statement about President

Gaston B. Means

Harding's personal life without going to sources where motives might be questionable. The mystery of Harding, coupled with the notoriety of Gaston Means, made a book that appealed to a large American audience.

Of course it was all a pack of lies, from beginning to end. Gaston dictated to Mrs. Thacker in the evenings in Washington; then, after she had gone, he and Julie laughed about the ridiculous things he said. But the intense, serious Mrs. Thacker believed every word; the publisher believed it; and the public loved the book. In fact, some people who were suspicious of the secrecy surrounding Harding's death even believed it. Gaston made a small fortune on this hoax.

Gaston's financial affairs had shown a remarkable recovery by the spring of 1930, but that did not force him to think about old obligations. The lawyers who had defended him in the second trial, in 1925, could not even collect their bill. They began to press for settlement when they heard of his new-found wealth, but Gaston did nothing, so on April 9 the lawyers secured a judgment against him for $3,640.[32] He made no attempt to defend the action, and it did not even slow him down.

Ralph Easley began to grow restive under Gaston's heavy demands for money, so Gaston decided to exhibit another important "Red" for Easley's benefit. He took Easley to Chicago. In front of the Congress Hotel he pointed out a man who was behaving in a most furtive manner. That mysterious fellow was Nils Jorgenson, a powerful figure in the international Communist movement, Means said.

Easley was amazed. The man was well-dressed. He appeared to be a man of culture. He did not look like a Scandinavian. He did not look like a Communist.

That was the secret of it, Gaston said, grinning in his superior way. That was the danger of the Communist movement. Nothing was what it seemed to be.

And who was Nils Jorgenson? He was actually an urbane but

disbarred lawyer of Gaston's acquaintance by the name of Norman T. Whitaker.[33]

Means's bank account grew healthily with the National Civic Federation funds he secured by such coups. Gaston persuaded Mrs. Finley Shepard, the daughter of Jay Gould, to give him $32,000 to protect her from the Communists. Mrs. Shepard was a woman of strong conviction, and she was outspoken in her statements against the Reds. She feared that they were all around her, waiting to strike. Gaston promised to protect Mrs. Shepard, and he did. She was never assassinated!

Gaston suffered an embarrassment that might have slowed a lesser figure in the autumn of 1931, when Mrs. Thacker repudiated *The Strange Death of President Harding* as a hoax. She had discovered, Mrs. Thacker said, that it had been physically impossible for Means to have entered the White House grounds without the knowledge of the guards, and that no record of a Means visit existed. She had also learned of the existence of one of Gaston's many affidavits in which he denied parts of the story he told her. Mrs. Thacker had approached the book in a shower of emotionalism. She backed away from it in the same manner. She had written "in the spirit of righteous exaltation" she said now in an article in *Liberty* magazine. Like so many of the faithful, she had been duped.[34]

Gaston passed off Mrs. Thacker's repudiation cheerily. It was just one more sign of the "omnipotent forces" who were bent on his destruction because he knew too much, he said. He did not even become annoyed with Mrs. Thacker, and when next they met, he was as affable as ever to her.

Gaston was far too busy milking the National Civic Federation to worry about Mrs. Thacker, now that the book had accomplished its purpose. His raids ended shortly after the repudiation of his book, but again he could shrug in careless resignation. He had milked the Federation of $200,000. His bank account stood at more than $100,000. He lived in a house he had taken at 112 Leland Street, Chevy Chase, Maryland, just across the state line from the

Gaston B. Means

District of Columbia. He maintained all the old trappings—four servants and a limousine and chauffeur. He gave Julie $1,000 a month for household expenses. His son attended Georgetown Preparatory School.[35]

It seemed an enviable life, but it had its difficult moments. A neighbor was James Bennett, an official of the Federal Bureau of Prisons. Bennett saw little of Means, but he did note the extraordinary measures that Gaston took to assure himself against invasion. Gaston's grounds were protected by a network of wires and alarms. If an intruder entered, he was almost certain to trip a switch, and the area was then flooded with light.[36]

Nor was Gaston apparently as happy as he once had been. He had begun to drink heavily. His disposition suffered for it. Police were called a number of times to the house in Chevy Chase to break up family arguments. Not long after Mrs. Thacker repudiated the book about Harding, the police were called again. Julie telephoned the Bethesda station hurriedly at nine o'clock on the evening of November 19 and asked for protection. Gaston was at home. They had argued, and he now threatened to kill her.

Two policemen arrived shortly after the call. They had had experience with Gaston. Before, they had been able to calm him, but this time he sulked. Then he struck one of the officers with his fist. It was all right for a man to strike his wife, but if he struck an officer of the law, that was quite a different matter. It could not be countenanced. Gaston was arrested and kept in jail overnight. The next morning, on payment of a $600 bond, he was released and went back home, more sober.[37]

The genial Gaston was not so genial. Julie said that she sometimes feared for his mind, and in their arguments she threatened that she would have him committed to an asylum as insane.

Perhaps Gaston's mind was affected by some injury. His old college friend, Louis Graves, believed that Means had undergone a drastic personality change following the accident in 1912, when he had fallen from the upper berth of the Pullman and alighted on his head. Means had kept in touch with Graves over the years. In

291

this new period of opulence, he had once stopped by the Graves house in Chapel Hill in his chauffeur-driven limousine to chat pleasantly with Graves and his wife for an hour. He had joked about his prison experiences and his past, boldly and unashamedly.[38]

Julie had noted a vital change in Gaston's appearance and attitude when he emerged from prison. He seemed to make a point of calling attention to himself, and seemed to enjoy the raised eyebrows that followed his identification as the notorious Gaston B. Means.[39]

Prosecutor Hiram Todd had taken cognizance of Gaston's railroad accident at the time of the first trial, and had written to Attorney General Harlan F. Stone, suggesting that Means "is probably deranged as a result of a concussion of the brain which he suffered in 1912." But in following up the matter by talking to one of the doctors who had treated Gaston, Todd discovered that if the concussion had damaged Gaston's brain, it had little to do with his criminal tendencies. For, Todd discovered, Means had not only sued the Pullman Company, but he had had the foresight, before the "accident," to take out a number of accident insurance policies with a number of different companies.[40]

What Hiram Todd called Gaston's "criminal perversion and exalted ego" were not so easily explained. Whatever the cause, in 1931 it had become clear that Gaston's inhibitions had decreased over the years, and so had his caution.

In 1923, Assistant Attorney General John W. H. Crim had expressed amazement "that a man like Means would so fool himself into believing that he could lead this sort of life with so many people and expect to get through it without being brought to the final test before a jury."[41]

Nine years later Gaston was to commit a crime so startling that he was to find himself once again an object of speculation—this time by an entire nation.

XIV

On the morning of March 2, 1932, Gaston Bullock Means dashed his morning newspaper to the floor of the comfortable living room of the twelve-room house in Chevy Chase and exploded in indignation.

"This is the most dastardly crime I ever heard of. Whoever did it should be shot," the balding and portly husband and father said to Julie about the kidnaping of baby Charles Augustus Lindbergh, Jr.[1] Then, having expressed himself so virtuously, Gaston sat down to think of a way in which he could profit from this heinous deed. He was not long in developing a plan.

Two days later, Gaston Means sought a meeting with Colonel M. Robert Guggenheim, a prominent Washington figure and a friend of the Lindberghs. Julie Means knew Mrs. Robert F. Fleming, the wife of a Maryland real estate man. Fleming knew Colonel Guggenheim, and Julie went to work to arrange a meeting. Before it came about, Gaston was already off on another tack. He concentrated his attentions on Mrs. Evalyn Walsh McLean, estranged wife of the publisher of the Washington *Post*. Means knew Mrs.

McLean, and he knew a great deal more about her than she suspected, because of his previous association with William O. Duckstein, who had been McLean's private secretary in the early 1920's.[2]

Means knew that Mrs. McLean also was a friend of the Lindberghs, and he suspected that she would be far easier to deal with than Colonel Guggenheim. But, in his careful fashion, Gaston did not cast the Colonel aside, pending the outcome of his plans.

On Friday, March 4, Gaston's diaries showed, he went to the office of Judge Marion DeVries in the Southern Building in Washington, and told Judge DeVries that he could locate the Lindbergh child. Between February 16 and February 26 he had been staying at the Imperial Hotel in New York, Gaston said. He had gone to New York to locate Wellington Henderson, a prominent member of the Communist party, in connection with some of Means's private detective work. In New York he had spoken to Irving Fenton, who also used the name James Feldman, and he had learned from Fenton that Henderson was in New Jersey. Means asked Fenton to locate Henderson, whereupon Fenton told Means about a kidnaping Henderson was planning and invited Gaston to participate as contact man. Gaston had not been interested in the vile plan, said Gaston.

Means came home from that meeting to tell Julie that Judge DeVries had suggested he get in touch with the Lindberghs and obtain authority to work on the case. Julie had already been in touch with Mrs. Fleming. Fleming came to the Means house and then arranged for Gaston to meet Colonel Guggenheim that evening at 11:30.[3]

Meanwhile, Gaston was in touch with Mrs. McLean. (He said she called him, and Julie said she was surprised that Mrs. McLean had called, because Gaston had worked for her earlier, and they had argued over his claim for a fee of $8,000.) After speaking to Mrs. McLean, Gaston went to her town house in Washington, leaving Julie and his sister Kate, who was visiting them. He did not return to the house until after 11:30. This delay conveniently kept Colonel Guggenheim on the hook, in case of need.

Gaston had told Mrs. McLean of his conversation with Fenton, and he said that he had sent a wire to that mysterious character, asking that he call Gaston in Washington. So, Gaston was relatively sure he could regain contact with the kidnapers—for, while Gaston had earlier believed the kidnaping Fenton had mentioned was to be that of a bootlegger, it had suddenly all become clear to Detective Means.

The next day, the Means household erupted in activity. Gaston remained at home until three in the afternoon, waiting for Fenton to call. The mystery man did not call, but Robert Fleming called four times, and Mrs. McLean called five times. Means went to see Fleming and Guggenheim that afternoon. He had no sooner returned than Fenton called, and half an hour later Gaston met him briefly near Mrs. McLean's house on Massachusetts Avenue. So he said.

Then, said Gaston, he went to Mrs. McLean's house to meet Captain Emory Land of the United States Navy and tell him the story. (This was true.) Land talked of rushing to Hopewell, New Jersey, to see his cousin, Charles A. Lindbergh, and secure authority for Means to step in and crack the case. Mrs. McLean urged Land to lose no time. Means then told Land that if Lindbergh agreed, Land was to inform him in code. "The tea is all right," he was to say.

Thus was born Gaston Means's plan to take advantage of the Lindbergh kidnaping. The code was a bit of intrigue developed to impress the friends and relatives of Colonel Lindbergh at these tense hours of supercharged emotion. Means *was* impressive when he talked the argot of the underworld and showed his knowledge of the trappings of espionage and detection. In their urgency, Mrs. McLean and Captain Land were hoodwinked. It is a tribute to the histrionic ability of Gaston Means that with his sorry record as extortionist and liar, he was able to convince the two of them with so little effort, even though he had recently been at outs with Mrs. McLean, and, many years before, was suspected of taking money from Edward B. McLean under false pretenses.

Mrs. McLean wanted action. Gaston gave it to her. He told her she must go out into the Maryland countryside to Farview, her estate, which was tightly locked up for the winter. It was a stormy, cold Sunday, all the better for Gaston. He told Mrs. McLean that the kidnapers would deliver the baby there, but first they wanted a look at her and the lay of the land. So she dutifully bundled up against the blizzardy weather and set out for the enormous house.

No one was there but the caretaker. The furniture was covered, and the valuables had been put away for the winter. Gaston and Mrs. McLean sat in the butler's pantry, and the caretaker brought drinks. Then they waited. Theoretically, according to Gaston, the desperados were clocking their every move.

Gaston told Mrs. McLean what the kidnapers wanted. They demanded $100,000 and a Catholic priest. The money was ransom for the safe return of the Lindbergh baby. The priest was safe-conduct for the kidnapers. They would surrender the child to no other person. Mrs. McLean agreed to supply both. She could get the $100,000, and she persuaded the Rev. J. Francis Hurney, pastor of the Church of the Immaculate Conception, to serve as intermediary.

There was one other thing, Gaston said. He would need $4,000 for expenses. Mrs. McLean agreed to supply that money, too.

One evening Gaston went to the town house of Mrs. McLean and came home with a cardboard box. Julie was in bed when he returned. He put the box on a shelf in their bedroom closet. He warned her that it must never be left unguarded for a moment, for who could attest to the honesty of servants in 1932?

The next day, Gaston began to work. He invented a complicated system of communications. Mrs. McLean was to be known thereafter as Number 11. Gaston was Number 27. Father Hurney was Number 7. Captain Land was Number 9. Max Hassell (supposedly one of the conspirators) was Number 19. But it was not enough just to have numbers. That device might be transparent to the forces that were seeking to interrupt the transaction. The numbers would further be divided for the sake of concealment—Mrs. Mc-Lean could be 56, since five and six added up to eleven. Gaston, then, might also be 8757, if the need arose.

Gaston insisted that this code be used. Mrs. McLean thereafter always identified herself as Number 11 when she called the Means house. Julie Means said she could tell that Mrs. McLean loved every moment of the intrigue.

Once Gaston had obtained the $100,000 for the reward, what was he to do? He could not deliver it to the kidnapers, because he had absolutely no idea who the kidnapers might be. Julie knew that, and tried to persuade her husband to return the money to Mrs. McLean and make a hasty exit from the affair before he landed in trouble again. Gaston's answer to this outrageous request was to pour himself a shot of bourbon and walk out of the room.

On March 9, two of the desperate kidnapers came to Gaston's home, he said, angry and threatening. They wanted to know what Mrs. McLean was up to. She was supposed to have gone to Fairview alone, and there they were going to deliver the baby on payment of the ransom. Instead, Mrs. McLean had arrived with two chauffeurs, a nurse, a maid and "another man" in attendance. The "kidnapers" had been afraid to deliver the baby.

Means told this story to Colonel Guggenheim, complaining that Mrs. McLean had let him down. He suggested that the colonel enter the case. He made arrangements with the colonel to secure an automobile from the Austrian embassy. That was to be the car in which the baby would be picked up.

But Colonel Guggenheim was soon forgotten. He was no longer needed, it seemed. On March 10, Gaston went home to Concord, traveling to Salisbury on the Southern Railroad's Crescent Limited, and then by car to his home town.[4] In Concord, whatever else he did, Gaston discharged an ancient debt of honor. He paid George

H. Richmond, the general storekeeper, the $300 he had owed since the end of the King murder trial.[5]

Gaston had left the cardboard box in care of Julie and his sister at the Chevy Chase house. They were so concerned for its safety that when they went to the movies, they took it with them. But what did the cardboard box contain at this time? Later Gaston was to tell Mrs. McLean that he had buried the money in the yard of his brother's home in Concord.

In his native southland, Means apparently felt more at home than elsewhere. He arranged for Mrs. McLean to come to her house at Aiken, South Carolina. There, he said, the baby would surely be delivered. He also arranged with Norman Whitaker, his associate in the plot to fool Ralph Easley in Chicago, that Whitaker would come to Aiken.

Means went to Aiken. Mrs. McLean went to Aiken. Whitaker went to Aiken and registered at the Commercial Hotel as Neil Williams. Then Whitaker-Williams disappeared. A tough-talking character who identified himself as "The Fox" showed up at the McLean house, snarling and making no commitments, and looking behind the draperies and furniture for wires and secret agents. "The Fox" represented the kidnap gang. He threatened Mrs. McLean and her maid, saying he would "rub them out" with a machine gun if anyone double-crossed him.

On March 22, "Henderson" showed up with the baby in Aiken, said Gaston. Gaston saw the baby and tried to arrange for delivery, but without success. The kidnapers were leery of the arrangements, he told Mrs. McLean. They did not trust her.

Means complained that Mrs. McLean had let him down twice, now, but that he would still try to get the Lindbergh baby back for her. He persuaded her to go with him to El Paso, Texas, where the next appointment would be made, he said. The baby was over the Mexican border in Juarez, safe and sound. To prove it, Means, alone, went across the border, and returned with bad news. The kidnapers wanted another $35,000, he said, but they promised to return in exchange for it $49,500 of the ransom money paid over by "Jafsie" Condon in behalf of Colonel Lindbergh. They were afraid of that money.

The situation had become enormously confused, obviously, with the New Jersey police, the Federal authorities, and anyone who thought he could help offering his services in the real kidnaping —and with Gaston's fake kidnaping going on as a sideshow. But Gaston managed to convince Mrs. McLean that the kidnapers' and his show were one and the same. It was a tribute to his ability to make use of information gleaned from the newspapers.

Mrs. McLean hastened back to Washington from El Paso to try to raise the additional $35,000. She did not have $35,000 readily available. She had gone to her bank the first time. Now she was unwilling to talk to her bankers, lest they become too inquisitive. So she took a diamond necklace and asked Elizabeth Poe, a friend who worked on the Washington *Post*, to pawn it for her. Miss Poe knew Mrs. McLean well enough to become suspicious, and called Mrs. McLean's lawyers. They persuaded Mrs. McLean that she had been the victim of a hoax.

Gaston, meanwhile, had gone to Chicago, leaving Mrs. McLean's nurse to wait for word from the kidnapers. The nurse, Elizabeth Nelson, waited, while Means traveled to Chicago on a new lead. Means was obdurate. He said he would "kidnap the baby from the kidnapers" if that proved necessary. But from Chicago, after telephoning Miss Nelson (Number 29), Means disappeared.

The trouble at this point was that Mrs. McLean wanted her money back, and Gaston could smell trouble. He had promised to return the money, but said he must first go back to Concord to get it, since it was buried there. Gaston did go to Concord, and a few days later appeared once again in Washington.

Mrs. McLean again demanded the return of her money. Gaston expressed surprise. He had been bringing it back, he said, when he was stopped by the kidnapers. When they identified themselves, he turned it over.

Mrs. McLean's lawyers heard the story, then went to see J. Edgar Hoover, director of the Federal Bureau of Investigation. Gaston's adventure was nearly at an end.[6]

J. Edgar Hoover had been spending the past eight years in a determined campaign to make the FBI the finest investigative agency in America. In the beginning, he had been busy cleaning up the debris left by Gaston Means and others like him. Above all, Hoover was determined that the character of the Bureau and its agents must forever after be above reproach. He had never forgiven Gaston Means for dragging the name of the Bureau into the mud.

The emotions aroused in the nation by the Lindbergh kidnaping had already begun moves to make of the FBI a law enforcement agency with real teeth. Until 1932, and even then, FBI agents were not allowed to carry guns. They could not make arrests, even in Federal territory. President Hoover had allowed New Jersey authorities to bring Director Hoover into the Lindbergh case, but only in an advisory capacity. The FBI could assist local officers, and could investigate, but it was seriously hampered by outmoded restrictions.[7]

Director Hoover took an immediate and personal interest when he heard the name of Gaston Means mentioned in connection with the Lindbergh kidnaping. Here was one crime into which the FBI could sink its teeth, because the crime had been committed in the District of Columbia.

Gaston had enjoyed his whirlwind fling to the fullest. His scheme had run a full six weeks before April 17, 1932, when Miss Poe started the chain of events that put an end to it.

Less than three weeks later, the name of Gaston Bullock Means was back on the front pages of the newspapers for the first time since 1925.

Gaston's fall was swift. On May 5, he stepped into his limousine outside the house on Leland Street and directed his chauffeur to drive into downtown Washington. The moment his car crossed the

300

line that divides the state of Maryland from the District of Columbia, Federal men in another auto picked it up and began to follow. When the Means car reached Massachusetts Avenue, the limousine was ordered to the curb.

Gaston knew that the FBI men had no authority to make arrests, so he asked if a U.S. marshal were present. J. Edgar Hoover had not overlooked that bet. There was—Deputy U.S. Marshal J. J. Clarkson. Gaston submitted quietly to arrest. He said he had known that the Department of Justice men were looking for him, but only for twenty-four hours. Otherwise he would have hastened in to Washington to talk to the FBI earlier.

How did he know, the government men asked.

"I was told by someone," Gaston said, smiling his most superior smile.

Means was taken to the office of FBI Director Hoover for questioning. He was arraigned before a U.S. Commissioner and charged with larceny after trust. It was an apt description of his crime against Mrs. McLean.

Gaston pleaded not guilty and posed for photographers, but, for once, he was not saying anything to reporters. His poise was broken, too, when U.S. Attorney Leo A. Rover demanded that bail be fixed at $100,000. Rover said that Gaston's previous record demanded so high a bail. Gaston's attorney argued that the amount was excessive, but no one else in the room believed so. In his failure to raise the bondsman's fee of $5,000 for the $100,000 bond, Gaston was sent to the old red brick District Jail, and put in a cell with John Kendrick, an underworld character charged with assault with intent to kill. Gaston spent most of the time in his cell reading newspaper accounts of his arrest. Devouring them would be a better word, for as Julie had begun to notice in 1928, Gaston had developed a mania for publicity. He was immensely pleased with what he read about himself, and chatted cheerfully with other prisoners.[8]

Gaston, of course, denied that he had done any wrong. Mrs.

301

McLean had come to him, he said, and she had offered him his usual fee as a private detective—$100 a day and expenses. If he had only known that anyone was looking for him, there need not have been all this fuss. He would have come in immediately.[9]

Gaston did not want to talk about the case to reporters. All the information he had was "confidential." But he did want to get out of jail, and, on May 7, he raised the $5,000 and arranged for bail with a bondsman. Prosecutor Rover wanted the court to be firm. He demanded that four bondsmen each take responsibility for the entire $100,000 bond, or, in other words, that the government be given a $400,000 guarantee that Gaston would stand trial.

This amount seemed excessive to some members of the public. No one yet knew what had happened to the Lindbergh baby. Means talked as though the child were in Mexico. A child was found near Galveston by a Mexican couple, and a torrent of speculation was released. Paul Goguloff, the assassin of President Doumer of France, announced across the Atlantic that he had kidnaped the child in behalf of Russian terrorists. The public was thoroughly confused.

If Gaston had taken Mrs. McLean's $100,000, what had he done with it? FBI agents and police checked safety deposit boxes. They ransacked the Means house in Chevy Chase. They questioned Julie Means. They found nothing and they learned little more.

On May 10, Gaston was formally indicted and, on May 11, he was released from jail, on a reduced bond, after six days in a cell.[10] On release, for a moment the old Gaston appeared to come to life. Reporters and the authorities were checking on statements about Gaston's swindling of Mrs. Finley Shepard. But Mrs. Shepard, locked securely in her fortress home at Tarrytown, New York, would not comment. For five years she had lived in fear of reprisals from the Communists because of her pronounced anti-radical views. She would not discuss the matter.

Representative Hamilton Fish told reporters in New York that in 1930 he had been led on a wild-goose chase to Baltimore by

Gaston B. Means

Gaston, who had produced a faked warehouse receipt for twenty trunks of "Soviet documents". (It had been the old Army Intelligence game, dressed up once again.)

But Gaston denied everything flatly—a most unromantic attitude —and the old Gaston flared up only for a brief moment, when he shouted that "Mrs. McLean don't have a leg to stand on," and that he "never took a dollar" from Mrs. Shepard.

Gaston had been in serious trouble before, but, for the first time, Gaston gave evidence of slipping in his command of himself. On May 12, he had an engagement to meet Lee Somers, a reporter for the Washington *Times,* at the Willard Hotel. Somers appeared and waited, but Gaston did not show up for the meeting. Somers then walked across Fourteenth Street to the National Press Building, where he chanced to see Gaston and Julie Means near the entrance to the drugstore. Gaston had been drinking. He invited Somers into the drugstore for a soft drink, then demanded to see the reporter's credentials, suddenly struck by suspicion. Somers was no reporter at all, Means charged, but a Department of Justice man.

In the argument that followed Means began to talk loudly, and he finally struck Somers in the chest. As they scuffled, a policeman arrived, Julie fled, and the officer took the two men to the police station. Somers was charged with disorderly conduct and released on paying a $5 bond. Gaston was charged with being drunk and disorderly, and was held on $65 bond, and until he sobered up.[11]

Following this incident Gaston managed to stay out of jail until the trial, which was called June 8. The case was far simpler than those of 1924 and 1925. Gaston was charged with swindling Mrs. McLean of her $104,000.

Before a jury of eleven men and one woman, Prosecutor Rover began to present the government's case. Mrs. McLean had withdrawn $100,000 from the bank and had given it, in $100 and $50 bills, to Gaston. On his request for "expense money" she had given him an additional $4,000. Witnesses were called to prove these facts. Elizabeth Nelson, the nurse whom Mrs. McLean had hired to take care of the baby once he was found, was called to testify how she had been terrorized by "The Fox" during the badman's brief rampage around the house at Aiken. Robert Fleming, the real estate man, testified that Gaston had warned him to keep his mouth shut about their conversations. If he talked, Fleming said, Means threatened that Fleming might be "bumped off".

Gaston's defense was that he had taken the $100,000 from Mrs. McLean in perfectly good faith, and that in good faith he had delivered the money to men he believed to be the kidnapers of the Lindbergh baby. His case was seriously injured, however, by the news in May that the Lindbergh baby had been found dead. Nor did anyone seem to believe Gaston's story.

"He is a baffling character," said the *New York Times* in an editorial that appeared just before the trial began. "He is incurably romantic, with the unromantic bulk of a rogue elephant. If a true life history of him should or could be written it would not be believable. A Baron Munchausen autobiography would be unconvincing because of too many facts. He belongs to the half-world of fact and fancy, perhaps never knowing himself which is which."[12]

Gaston, somehow, was not his old self at all during this affair, from the time he was arrested inside the District line until he was put on trial. The old verve was lacking. But not always.

He had encountered an acquaintance from North Carolina on Fifteenth Street one day before the trial began.

"Gaston," said the acquaintance, "do you expect to go back to your happy home in Atlanta where board is free?"

"Oh, I don't know yet, but if I do I'll not fret about it," Gaston said. "One thing Uncle Sam does is to treat his prisoners like human beings. I like my old Atlanta home; it's really not like a prison. Many of the poor unemployed I've met lately tell me they would be glad to be sure of a home there until this Depression blows over."

Of course Gaston did not believe that, but in earlier years, another Gaston would have said the same, then would have devoted himself to connivance and struggle to retain his freedom. At least he might have planned to flee—as once he and Julie had talked about fleeing to Germany in the 1920's.[13]

Now, apparently, Gaston had no energy even for flight. In this trial of 1932, Attorney T. Morris Wampler offered the best defense he could muster, but it convinced neither the jury nor the spectators. Gaston did not give the show expected of him. He did not even take the stand in his own defense.

The trial was short. On June 13, both prosecution and defense had completed their cases. In his closing argument, Prosecutor Rover called for conviction of the "picture book detective" for his fantastic scheme to swindle Mrs. McLean. Means, said District Attorney Rover, "dealt in broken hearts and mother's love." Gaston had persuaded Mrs. McLean to go with him to South Carolina and to Texas simply to keep her out of the hands of her lawyers, who might put a crimp in his plans. He had used the code numbers for "the sole purpose" of keeping Mrs. McLean's interest aroused and of appealing to her imagination.[14]

These were unkind words to be applied to an artist. Gaston had done all that Prosecutor Rover said, but there was more to his performance than the cruel government man indicated. Gaston had also swindled Mrs. McLean with the singlemindedness of the born swindler. Pleasure and profit were a part of it, but he had been so excited by the headlines in the Lindbergh case that he could not help himself. He had to get into it.

On June 13, the jurors heard Prosecutor Rover call Gaston the "prince of liars." This was better tribute. Defense Attorney Wampler said that Gaston's story was no more fantastic than Dr. J. F. Condon's tale of tossing $50,000 over a cemetery wall in New York to a man he had never seen. That was better yet. The Lindbergh case was filled with fantastic tales.

Wampler suggested that Gaston did not take the stand because he was afraid of being killed by the kidnapers if he told all. "Means's arrest sealed his lips—put him on the spot," said the defense attorney. "He knew that if he opened his mouth to talk of his negotiations with the kidnaper, his life would be snuffed out—that the dangerous men he dealt with would reply with a sawed-off shotgun."[15]

But no one believed.

The eleven men and one woman deliberated for two hours, then announced that they had found Gaston guilty on two counts of larceny. It was Saturday night, so Gaston was taken to the District Jail to await the pleasure of Judge Proctor on Monday morning. Gaston took the news calmly. There were no grim looks or evil words for Prosecutor Rover. The Judge refused to continue bail, so Gaston went to jail quietly.[16]

On Monday, Gaston was sentenced to serve fifteen years in prison—ten years for taking Mrs. McLean's $100,000 and five years for taking the $4,000 in "expense money." He stood before the court, arms hanging loose, as the Judge announced the sentence.

"The verdict of the jury in this case reveals that the defendant capitalized not only on the sweetest and tenderest emotions of the human heart, but also the basest," said the Judge.[17]

Gaston grinned broadly in the face of this attack, but it was a beaten grin. Still, as he was led away to the District Jail again, Gaston knew that he held in his head two secrets that the government wanted badly. Who was his accomplice—"The Fox"? And what had happened to Mrs. McLean's money?

XV

One of the mysteries shrouding Gaston's last grand venture in crime was solved two weeks after he was convicted of stealing Mrs. McLean's $104,000. The police of New York City arrested Norman T. Whitaker. On June 28, Mrs. McLean went to New York where she identified Whitaker as "The Fox"—Number 19— the "dangerous killer" who had ransacked her house in Aiken.

Gaston had picked the nickname well. Norman Whitaker was chubby and middle-aged, like a middle-aged fox. He wore a small mustache, and had neat brown hair and horn-rimmed glasses. He was well-dressed in a quiet way and well-mannered, as he ought to have been, for "The Fox" held degrees from Georgetown University and the University of Pennsylvania, and was once an Oxford student.

Norman Whitaker looked like an intellectual. He was an intellectual. He played a good game of chess and had achieved some reputation in international competition. He had also been a patent lawyer until 1924, when he was disbarred for exercising a passion for other people's automobiles. He was convicted of transporting a stolen car across a state line, and the disbarment was automatic. Since that time, Norman Whitaker had fallen low. He was arrested in Pleasantvale, New Jersey, for feeding slugs into a pay telephone, and again in Tampa, Florida, on an auto charge, earlier in 1932.[1]

When he was captured at the home of his father-in-law in Brooklyn, "The Fox" showed no emotion. "A mighty cool proposition," one of the detectives called him. Whitaker remained cool, apparently unperturbed, as the flighty Mrs. McLean and her maid, Ingrid Lagerqvist, tremulously identified him as the cold-eyed criminal who had threatened their lives and frightened them half to death in Aiken.

Whitaker had received none of the $100,000, he said, coolly again. Furthermore, the authorities had no case against him, he added.

But the authorities did not agree. They found a case in the efforts of Gaston and Whitaker to obtain the additional $35,000 from Mrs. McLean toward the end of their criminal foray. Conspiracy was the charge. On July 8, Whitaker and Gaston were charged with the crime in the Federal Court of the District of Columbia. They pleaded not guilty, but the foxy Whitaker reserved the right to change his plea in the light of future developments.[2]

This second case against Gaston dragged on for nearly a year before it was brought to trail. Gaston's appeal on the first conviction was rejected in mid-April, 1933. He was kept in the District Jail to await the new trial because the authorities still had not solved the second mystery of his crime—they had never discovered what Gaston had done with Mrs. McLean's $100,000. Some of the Federal men were afraid that if Gaston was released on bail he would produce the money and flee the United States.

The trial began April 29, in Justice Daniel O'Donoghue's courtroom, before a group of spectators that rivaled the crowd Gaston had attracted to Concord nearly sixteen years earlier. Gaston was pale and showed every one of his fifty-three years. He was nearly bald. The old dimples in his pudgy cheeks were dwarfed by hollows of age and worry, and the loss of teeth gave his face a drawn and sunken look that was heightened by his prison pallor and the severe prison haircut. But he still could manage a grin. "He was the perfect picture of a man enjoying the crowd at his own hanging," *Newsweek* reported.[3]

The prosecution's case was an extension of the previous case against Gaston. U.S. Attorney Leo A. Rover had prepared thoroughly, and he took nearly two weeks to make his case, for he went into a great deal more detail than he had the year before. He brought Colonel Charles A. Lindbergh to testify in this trial. The appearance of Lindbergh was enough to weight the evidence, if it had needed weighting, for never had a kidnaping and murder aroused more public outrage than the Lindbergh case. Rover was accused by Gaston's counsel of staging a grandstand play, and it was a grandstand play, but Rover justified it by what he said was the need to prove that the Lindbergh baby was dead, and that the child found in the New Jersey woods was the Lindbergh baby. The defense had made such a case necessary by its constant mention of babies, supposedly the Lindbergh baby, whom Gaston claimed to have seen in Aiken, South Carolina, and in Mexico.

On May 11, the defense began its case. It was all Gaston's show. Norman Whitaker chose not to take the stand, but to rest on an alibi provided by the police of Tampa, Florida. Whitaker was in jail at the time of the Lindbergh kidnaping, although he could not prove he was in jail when "The Fox" appeared at Mrs. McLean's Aiken house.

Gaston was his old self once again, or a reasonable relict of the youthful Means, at least. His story had some of the old ring of true Gastoniana, too.

What had happened to the $100,000? the prosecution wanted to know.

On the way back to Washington from Concord, bringing the money back to Mrs. McLean as she had requested, Gaston met a man who was waving a lantern at a bridge at Alexandria, Virginia.

The man stopped him, and whispered "Number 11?" and straightaway Gaston handed him the $100,000—"still in its original wrappings."

Why, then, was the baby not returned safely?

Two of the kidnapers had told Gaston that they tried to deliver the baby twice—once at Mrs. McLean's estate and the second time at Aiken. At Aiken, Gaston had seen the baby. He was wearing a knitted cap pulled close over his blond head, fastened by a ribbon tied under the chin. The baby wore a buff coat, brown shoes, and white stockings. He had blue eyes and appeared to Gaston to be seventeen or eighteen months old.

Who were the vile conspirators?

One of them, said Gaston, was Wellington Henderson, "head of the Third International in this country." The other was Irving Fenton.

And where had Gaston met these rogues?

He had met Fenton in the Atlanta penitentiary when they were both serving time there during the Twenties. (Here a gasp went up around the courtroom.)

Gaston delivered this testimony on May 10. On May 11, the Communist Party, USA, protested vigorously. "There is no such person as Wellington Henderson in the Communist party," said a spokesman. "This is a silly attempt to shift blame that not even the enemies of the Communist party can believe."

For once, the Communists spoke absolute truth, but that did not prevent Gaston from embroidering the story. The body that Colonel Lindbergh saw and identified was not that of his son, Gaston asserted. "Wellington Henderson told me that the body was a plant they had made up in Jersey, and that later I would see communistic data in regard to it." Henderson had visited him at his home in Chevy Chase on May 17, and had proved that the measurements of the Lindbergh child were not those of the baby discovered dead. The real Lindbergh baby was alive and in Juarez, Means said.

Gaston B. Means

These statements caused the crowd to murmur and the public to talk, but they did not impress law-enforcement officers. Gaston's story surpassed all his others, particularly when he was questioned about the whereabouts of the kidnapers.

Where were Henderson and Fenton?

They were dead.

Who else was involved?

Max Hassel and Max Greenberg.

Where were they?

They were dead, too.

(Max Hassel and Max Greenberg really were dead. They were a pair of racketeers who were killed in a shooting on April 18 that year in Elizabeth, New Jersey. While the FBI and police knew that the pair had nothing to do with the Lindbergh case, the men could not come into court to prove it.)

How had the kidnaping been accomplished?

Hassel and Greenberg had delivered beer to the servants in the Lindbergh house, using "operatives" to do the job. They carried three bottles of beer to the house on the night of the kidnaping and took the baby off without using the celebrated ladder which was to help convict Bruno Hauptmann later.

Gaston related the tiniest details of his trips to El Paso and to Chicago and to Aiken, South Carolina. It was his old way—invent a story and pile up so much detail that it sounds plausible. He capped it with a dramatic statement: the money—the $100,000 ransom—was in a safety deposit box in Elizabethport, New Jersey, under the name of Max Hassell, one of the "conspirators."

But the statement was like so many of Gaston's statements, pure hokum. After Hassell's death, authorities had opened his safety deposit box and found $213,000 inside. Anyone who read the newspapers could have known that—and Gaston had whiled away many hours reading newspapers in the past few months. There was no connection between the $100,000 and Hassell's $213,000. The denominations of the bills did not fit. Nor, as Gaston had claimed, was any part of the Lindberghs' $50,000 found in that box.

Prosecutor Rover scoffed at Gaston's testimony. He called it "a figment of a weird imagination that makes Baron Munchausen look like a piker." Indeed, the tale was so fanciful that it defied serious cross-examination, and it was obvious that Gaston's sole reason for presenting it was in hope that he might be released to assist in the search for the kidnapers.

Gaston gave an address in Detroit where "reports" on Henderson and Fenton might be found—he said. Officers checked the address: 2419 Grand River Avenue. It was a building on the edge of Detroit's downtown district, a sooty area surrounded by small retail stores, and it did house the Worker's Party (Communist). But, as usual, here was a fact readily available to anyone who had spent most of three years on a National Civic Federation expense account in pursuit of Communists.

As the case drew to an end, it was apparent that Gaston had failed to present a convincing story. He made one last, supreme effort to save himself. A month before, he said, he sent a letter to Mrs. McLean's lawyers, informing them that the kidnapers were in Washington and could be apprehended, if only he could get out of jail and help find them. He produced a carbon copy of the letter, and then he produced a carbon copy of another letter, the second one written to Max Hassell in New Jersey, pleading with Hassell to come and testify and tell the truth. It was a bold attempt to persuade the jury that Gaston had not known Hassell was dead when the letter was sent, and if the jury accepted that story, it would accept anything.

When Gaston finished testifying and left the stand, he stopped to speak to J. Edgar Hoover who was in the courtroom.

"How did you like that story?" he asked.

"In all my life I have never heard a wilder yarn," said the Director of the Federal Bureau of Investigation.

"Well, it was a good story, just the same, wasn't it?" Gaston said, grinning.

Gaston B. Means

Good story or not, could anyone be expected to believe this tale of intrigue and mystery, of Communists in league with bootleggers to kidnap a tiny baby? Prosecutor Rover did not think so. He limited his cross-examination to questions designed to show that all the participants Means mentioned were conveniently dead, except the imaginary Wellington Henderson and Irving Fenton. In summing up, Rover posed one question to the jury. Did they believe?

"Can you believe, can anybody believe, can even Gaston B. Means himself believe the web of lies he has told in this case?"

Two hours and twenty minutes after they filed out of the courtroom, the jurors answered Prosecutor Rover's question. The answer was no.

Toward the end of the trial, Julie Means was subjected to the ignominy of a personal search, after she arrived in the courtroom to hope for her husband. Leo Rover had received a letter saying that Julie was carrying part of Mrs. McLean's $100,000 on her person. But when searched by matrons Julie was found to have only about $100 with her, in her purse. She was released, but her husband was not. He was given another two years in the penitentiary, and the bedraggled "Fox" was sentenced to serve a two-year term. Justice O'Donoghue did not specify how Gaston's new sentence was to be served, so it would run concurrently with his other. In fifteen years, less time off for good behavior, Gaston could expect once more to be free to spin his exciting tales for others. Now he must return to prison.[4]

Ordinarily, Gaston Means would have been sent to the Federal reformatory at Lorton, Virginia, but the officers of the Department of Justice were concerned lest he unearth some of the missing $100,000 and use it either to disrupt life at the reformatory or to bribe guards in an attempt to escape. Atlanta Penitentiary wanted no part of him—he knew far too many of the inmates and guards, and his influence during his first imprisonment had been so great that one observer noted "he served his last sentence there about as he pleased." Late in June, Gaston was sent to the Northeastern

313

Penitentiary in Lewisburg, Pennsylvania, where he was put to work as a gardener, grading lawns.[5]

A Federal penitentiary is not a social club, but Gaston was notably unpopular among the inmates at Lewisburg. He kept away from the others, and they kept away from him. He was unpopular with the prison authorities, too, but for a different reason. He caused them constant anxiety, because he was forever scheming to reopen his case, to seek outside assistance in reopening it, and to find any possible loophole through which he could wriggle his way out of prison. Newspapermen took an unhealthy interest in Gaston, too, from the viewpoint of the penal authorities, who had discovered long before that the best medicine for a criminal who loved notoriety was the absence of it. In September, 1934, Lewisburg had enough of Gaston and he was transferred. The Department of Justice told newspapermen that Means was scheduled to go to Alcatraz, where he could be kept more easily under control and away from outside contacts. Had he gone to Alcatraz he would have joined Al Capone, Harvey Bailey, Machine Gun Kelly, and his old friend Norman Whitaker, who was serving out his time on "the rock."[6]

Gaston was not sent to Alcatraz but to the penitentiary at Leavenworth, Kansas. It was not very long before Gaston discovered that Leavenworth was no 1925 Atlanta, and he began to devote himself to an effort to be transferred out of that institution. His method was to unearth a matter long buried.

It was ten years since Gaston had used the 1916 "Black Tom" explosion as a ploy to attract attention. In 1923, when he had introduced Edmund Reeves Lee as the villain who planned and executed the explosions, Gaston was aiming at the millions of dollars he might receive if he were able to persuade the Mixed Claims Commission that the German government had ordered the sabotage. In 1935, when the Black Tom case was reopened by the Mixed Claims Commission, Gaston was aiming even higher. He wanted a share, immunity from prosecution, and immediate transfer to the easier climate of Lorton Reformatory.

Gaston B. Means

Gaston faced a new generation of lawyers, new faces in official Washington, and prison officials at Leavenworth who had never heard of his original maneuverings. Otherwise it is unlikely that the warden at Leavenworth would have allowed Gaston to conduct negotiations with the lawyers for the Commission, because the claim was the same, and only a few details were changed.

Gaston said now that he was personally involved in the Black Tom explosion and the explosion of an ammunition factory at Kingsland, New Jersey, in 1917. He refused to write a statement to that effect, because he said it might incriminate him, but if the Commission would accept his conditions, Gaston would turn over four filing cabinets that he had concealed in two places. As usual, it was Gaston's story that the filing cabinets contained instructions from Captain Boy-Ed, and Rudolph Otto, plus Gaston's daily reports to his German employers in those years so long gone.

The Department of Justice found Gaston's statements unworthy of discussion, but with the millions of dollars involved, the Commission and the Canadian Car and Foundry Company felt that any lead was worth pursuing. In January, 1935, R. W. Hicks, Jr., of the Commission, came to see Means. The next month he returned with William E. Leahy, an attorney for the Canadian company. Means told them he had kept the trunks at his hotel in Washington, when he lived there in 1929. An attorney named Wheeler Bloodgood had taken some of the documents and had not returned them, but most were still extant. Unfortunately, Wheeler Bloodgood could not be reached to verify these statements, because he was dead.

There it was again—the old story, verifiable only by a dead man, depending on trunks full of missing documents. Leahy said that if the claim could be proved, it would be worth $40 million to the company and $1.5 million to Gaston. But the claim must be proved beyond doubt.

Gaston made several long and rambling statements. The documents had been sent to Afton Means in Concord, he said. The really important ones were in a small box about two feet long, six inches wide, and two inches deep, inside another box under the floor of the attic, above his mother's old bedroom in the house on North Union Street. The lawyers listened, and went back to check Gaston's story.

In May, Gaston tried to bribe a guard at Leavenworth. He promised the guard $1,000 if he would tell the warden that a Mr. Anderson of the State Department wanted the warden to co-operate with Gaston Means. Here was a sure sign of Gaston's growing age. How could a guard, even if he were corruptible, and this one was not, persuade a warden that a State Department official would have said such a thing? And who was this Mr. Anderson? There was no such man.[7]

Considering his background and the problems Gaston created for them, the authorities at Leavenworth were remarkably lenient in punishing Means for this offense. He was sentenced to serve three days in solitary confinement. That was all. When he emerged, Gaston returned to scheming.

In June, Lawyer Hicks went to Concord to talk to Belle, Kate, and Afton Means. The three recalled that Gaston had kept several trunks and wooden boxes in the attic of the old house a number of years before. He had sent for them during the Daugherty Investigation, and had never returned them to Concord. They looked in the attic, and saw a number of old trunks, but none of them were Gaston's and none of them contained secret German documents. The Commission and the attorneys were convinced, as the Department of Justice had been from the beginning, that the documents did not exist. When Gaston learned of their attitude, he said that the lawyers had approached Afton in the wrong manner and had frightened him.

As a drowning man flails the water he hates, with uncontrollable vigor, Gaston began writing letters everywhere. He wrote to Julie, proposing that he put together a book about German secret activities in the United States between 1914 and 1918. Julie could arrange it and edit it, and it would sell better than *The Strange Death of President Harding*, he said. He wrote to Belle, to a Catholic priest, to every government official he believed might help him escape from his prison. There was no love in these letters to his relatives, no humanity, no kindness. He was conscious of Julie's reduced circumstances, for she had been forced to find jobs as companion and practical nurse. He expressed concern for the education of his son, and for Julie's welfare, but the expressions had no force to them. Gaston was a man haunted by his past and by a deep need for approval and vindication. Above all he wanted out, and he thrashed and struggled like a drowning man to escape.

In 1936, Gaston wrote to the priest and to Attorney General Homer Cummings, confessing that he, Gaston Means, had kidnaped the Lindbergh baby. He gave a mountain of detail, then declared that he had taken the Lindbergh child to Mexico and left him there unharmed. A copy of Means's letter was sent to Governor Hoffman of New Jersey. Similar information was given to Paul G. Clancy, publisher of *Astrology* magazine. Means even described in detail how he made the kidnap ladder.[8]

When that story did not produce the results he wanted, Gaston changed it. He claimed that he had been hired by relatives of Mrs. Lindbergh to take the child, and that he and the two New Jersey gangsters and a woman accomplice had done so. The child was injured in a fall, so they had murdered him.

The Department of Justice investigated Means's claims and found the essential facts to be truthless. Where Means had the actual facts, they were public information, available to any newspaper reader. The Department of Justice was satisfied that Means had no part in the kidnaping and murder of the Lindbergh baby.

In 1936, it was important that the authorities be sure. Bruno Richard Hauptmann had been convicted of the crime, but a considerable section of the public was not satisfied that Hauptmann had commited the murder, at least not alone.

Sensational newspapers and magazines fed those fires of doubt with any hint of "new information" or even wild rumor that came to them. With an ingenious sense for the tenor of public opinion,

Gaston bombarded Governor Hoffman and the Justice Department with claims of his guilt, and tried to use his confession to secure a stay of execution for Hauptmann, not because he cared for Hauptmann, but because he wanted to focus attention again on Gaston Bullock Means.[9]

The long-suffering officials of the Department of Justice had given Gaston far more leeway than any man deserved, in allowing him to interfere with the due processes of the law. Up to the last moment, Gaston claimed that he had killed the Lindbergh baby. Each time he told the story, it became more sordid and more twisted. The lie first approached the truth, then surrounded it and engulfed it. In a sense this was the worst of all Means's crimes, more damaging to the spirit of those concerned with the Lindbergh case than any other. Gaston had sinned against the Lindberghs when he offered them hope when there was no hope; he had sinned against society when he used a private tragedy to steal from a wealthy woman; he sinned against decency when he tried at the last minute to bring doubt to overshadow the Hauptmann conviction.

After Hauptmann was executed, Gaston subsided for a time. Prison officials grew more careful in examining his contacts with the outside world. May Dixon Thacker tried to see him, but the Department of Justice could see no reason for such a meeting. It was not permitted.

Gaston continued to try to feed information to the outside world, in the hope that somehow he would get out of prison, or at least would be transferred to the easier surroundings of Lorton Reformatory. But he had very little information left that interested anyone. The one important bit of information he never offered, and that concerned the fate of Mrs. McLean's $100,000.[10]

A San Francisco man, disgusted with the reports of Gaston's publicity hunting, suggested that Means be transferred to Alcatraz, where prisoners lost their identity, so he would have no chance to indulge his passion for publicity. The penal authorities apparently considered the move, but decided to leave Gaston where he was.[11]

In the summer of 1936, Gaston applied for parole. He had learned the prison ropes and knew that one modern requirement for parole was the acceptance of responsibility for his crimes. Since Gaston had been so determined and so repetitive a criminal, it would take an unusual set of circumstances to persuade the parole board to release him before the expiration of his sentence. Gaston now invented those circumstances.

He was suffering from "high brain blood pressure," Gaston said. All his troubles dated back to that fateful night in 1912 when he had fallen from the upper berth of the Pullman car. Until that year—and for thirty-five years—he had led an exemplary life. After the accident, his right side had been paralyzed for a time. Thereafter he had developed the "fantastic" imagination which led to his convictions in 1924 and 1925. He had never personally gained anything from his bootlegging and blackmail because he had returned all the money. He knew there was something wrong with him. Julie had been ready to commit him to an insane asylum in 1931. Now he wanted to be sent to St. Elizabeth's Hospital in Washington for a brain operation, and afterward, when it had made him a fit member of society, he wanted to be paroled.

Another prerequisite to parole in the more scientific system of the 1930's was that a convicted man make any possible restitution for his crimes. The $100,000 that belonged to Evalyn Walsh McLean had never been found, and, although Federal officers had spoken to Gaston about it, they had never gotten the truth.

Three years after his conviction, Gaston volunteered the information that he had placed the money in a piece of pipe fixed to grappling hooks and had thrown it in the Potomac River off the old John Clark tobacco wharf. That sounded very much like another bit of Gastoniana, but Federal officers dutifully trooped down to the bank of the Potomac and grappled in the silt of the river. Whatever they found, it was not a piece of pipe with $100,000 inside—

319

but how was anyone to *prove* that Gaston had not used the river as his safety deposit box?

No one could prove it, but no one was forced to believe it. When an ordinary man makes a statement, no matter how fantastic it may sound, usually he has human nature on his side. Strange things do happen. There is a desire by listeners to believe. Only the cynical approach life in a spirit of disbelief. But the unfortunate Gaston had abused his fellow man's sense of belief so many times, and so rudely, in his fifty-six years that he had destroyed the natural receptivity of all who knew him. In 1936, if Gaston told someone to look for a piece of white paper, an acquaintance would begin searching for something black. Had he been drowning in the surf, those who knew him would have watched confidently, certain that he was really riding in on the back of a shark.

Gaston's parole was denied in 1936, and he was left to face prison until the summer of 1943, when he would be released with his time off for good behavior. The disappointment was aggravated by serious illness that summer, for Gaston suffered three serious gallstone attacks in the first half of the year. His general health seemed fair enough, although he was nearly forty pounds overweight. Still, Gaston firmly refused to let the prison doctors operate. He claimed that the gallstone disease was an inheritance from his father and that old W. G. Means had died following an operation to remove the stones. He preferred to suffer the agony of repeated attacks to the uncertainties of surgery.[12]

The gallstone attack brought Gaston another brief flurry of publicity. The Kansas City *Star* and the *Literary Digest* took special note of his illness, and reported that in March he had tried again to smuggle out of prison a letter confessing that he was the mastermind of the Lindbergh kidnaping.

"Those who know Gaston Means firmly believe that no other mind in the nation could have been capable of conceiving and directing the execution of so gigantic a crime," said the *Digest*.[13]

So—someone believed him again at last. But the *Literary*

Gaston B. Means

Digest's reputation as oracle did not survive the year, for the magazine's editors also believed a poll which predicted the election of Alf M. Landon to the Presidency of the United States that November.

Gaston survived. He suffered repeated gallstone attacks. His skin grew yellow. His weight dropped from 230 pounds to 200 pounds, and his cheeks became huge hollows that concealed the dimples. The following summer he was transferred to the United States Hospital for Defective Delinquents in Springfield, Missouri, where he could be assured of proper care.[14]

From time to time, the Department of Justice had sent men to see Gaston to try to persuade him to divulge the hiding place of the $100,000 ransom. The agents were always met with bland silence on that subject. In the fall of 1938, the matter was brought up again, but it came to nothing.

Gaston did not mention the money often in his letters, but he did discuss one scheme after another, all designed to extricate him from prison and assure riches to the family. His letters grew long and rambling and nearly impossible to read, for the sentences were never-ending, the hand was cramped and sloppy at the same time, and the lines were close and ran to the edges of the paper. He wrote in pencil and exerted such great pressure on the paper, writing on both sides, that the texture of the paper was changed. He wrote frequently to Julie and to Belle and kept track of every letter. The habit of making carbon copies of everything never left him. He referred back constantly to old letters, and gave complicated instructions to Belle and Julie to seek out lawyers, talk to various officials, and carry out other missions—all designed to bring Gaston Means out of the penitentiary.

Julie found it difficult to write to him as his mind grew ever more wandering, and she found it increasingly difficult to read or make sense of his letters. Belle tried to cheer Gaston. She discussed the homely affairs of life in their small town. She wrote of having the roof of the house repaired, and she mentioned mutual friends.

She pleaded with Gaston to seek composure and peace, and to try not to think constantly of money, of shortcuts to freedom, or of the old ways. She was totally unsuccessful.

Late in November, 1938, Gaston suffered a serious attack of gallstones and the doctor decided that he must have an operation. Despite his fear, he was too weak to protest. Julie was notified and on December 7 the doctors took out Gaston's gall bladder. There were no complications, and he did not suffer from excessive shock. But two days later Gaston's heart began to fail. Julie was notified again, and set out for Springfield. She arrived at two o'clock on the morning of December 11, and was taken to spend the rest of the night hours at the warden's house. The next day she went to the hospital to see Gaston. He was awake, and they talked. Gaston rambled on, endlessly, about money. He would talk of nothing else. He reminded her of the Catholic priest he had often mentioned in his letters. The priest knew where the money was hidden; all Julie had to do was to piece together the story from fragments of his letters.

Since Gaston's last conviction, Julie had been working hard for her living as a clerk in a department store and as a paid companion. She had worried constantly about providing food and shelter and education for their son. She had struggled alone in a world that had no love for any relative of Gaston Means. And, all the while, she had been reading Gaston's letters, which dealt with nothing but his problems and money. She would not listen to him now.

The talk broke off into fragments, and then Gaston grew delirious.

In the evening, Gaston slept and Julie returned to the warden's house. At 2:30 in the morning he suffered another heart attack. Julie was called, but he died three minutes later, before she could arrive at the bedside.[15]

Gaston left prison then. They took him home to Concord and the house on North Union Street. The Southern Railway station at Concord was surrounded by a curious crowd when Julie came bringing the body of her husband home. Police were on hand to control the gathering, but they were not needed. For no one in Concord wanted to disturb Julie in her grief.

The funeral was held at the house on the afternoon of December 15, in as simple a fashion as it could be done. The rector of All Saints Church conducted the ritual of the Episcopal religion. There was no music, only a recitation of the poem "Now The Laborer's Task Is Done," and that said very softly, for upstairs Afton Means lay in bed, seriously ill from a heart attack. Joe Fisher, who had been the boy with the baseball bat, was one of the pallbearers. Gus Archibald, who had helped count the money at the Express office, was another.

Another memory, for those who had a mind for such things— just twenty-one years ago that day the house had rung with joy and laughter when Gaston was acquitted of the murder of Maude A. King.

Joe Fisher and Gaston's other friends carried the coffin to the family plot in Oakwood Cemetery, and they laid him in a grave beside his mother. The huge tree which had shaded his father's grave was dying, and it gave little comfort now to the bleak hillside.[16]

Gaston was not yet buried when the newspapers asked the last remaining question. What had happened to Mrs. McLean's $100,000?

The money was never found. All Gaston's property had been searched and searched again. Lawns had been turned over. Floors and walls had been rapped and tapped, and broken open. A river had been dragged. Norman Whitaker had bragged in Alcatraz that the money was buried somewhere between Concord and Aiken, South Carolina. May Dixon Thacker said that Gaston had spent it all—every cent.

That speculation was a fitting valedictory, but it was not the only one. There were many, suitable to the life that Gaston had chosen for himself.

"Few men attain so much fame and so little success in so many kinds of crime, and at the same time acquire reputation of a sort in fields unrelated to their strictly criminal activity," said the *Christian Century.*[17]

"He tells lies until he would swear to them as being the truth, the whole truth, and nothing but the truth," said the Washington *Evening Star.* "Such a man does not commit perjury. He gets himself so tangled up that everything he says is both true and false—true as he thinks it, false as others know it to be."[18]

The moralist editors of the *Nation* said, ". . . nor would Mr. Means be worth mention if he were not, somehow, in his complete and buoyant disregard of any possible stigma that might be attached to his way of life, rather typically American. He might, indeed, be set up as a terrible example of what American carelessness of law can lead to."[19]

The gentlest valedictory of all was delivered a quarter of a century later, by a Concord man who had known Gaston from afar, when the man was a youth.

"He was the strongest character who ever came out of this town," he said. "He could have done anything he wanted to do. He could have been anything he wanted to be—Governor, Senator, or president of a corporation."

And how did Gaston fare in his own search for success?

In time, the Federal government sent Julie Means a check that represented Gaston's estate. It came to seventeen dollars and twenty-six cents.

NOTES AND ACKNOWLEDGMENTS

In tracing the career of Gaston B. Means, I am indebted to a number of people who gave freely of their time, and some of whom spoke very frankly to me. Most of all I am indebted to Hiram C. Todd, who prosecuted Gaston Means in 1924 and 1925. Mr. Todd gave me much time and material that proved to be invaluable.

In New York City, Mrs. G. D. Hansen, Mr. Todd's secretary, was very helpful, as were Mrs. Travis Hoke, Joseph Andrews, assistant librarian of the library of the Association of the Bar, and James F. O'Leary, confidential secretary to the District Attorney of the County of New York. I also want to thank the many librarians of the New York Public Library, and Raymond J. Burns of the Burns International Detective Agency. In Washington, former Senator Burton K. Wheeler spoke freely about Means's relationship with the Wheeler investigating committee, and James Bennett, director of the Federal Bureau of Prisons, was very helpful. I am also indebted to J. Edgar Hoover and Special Agent John O'Beirne of the Federal Bureau of Investigation for information about Means's activities and connections with the old Bureau of Investigation. Benjamin McKelway, editor of the Washington *Evening Star* kindly gave me access to the *Star's* library. There Melvin Pettit and the staff went out of their way to locate information.

A number of librarians at the Library of Congress gave me assistance, as did Jack Shulimson, Donald Mosholder, and several other members of the staff of the National Archives' Diplomatic, Legal, and Fiscal Division. Attorney Fred Morrison was helpful in leading me to several sources of information. Washington Correspondent Bulkley Griffin was also generous with his time.

In Chapel Hill, I was steered to several important sources by James W. Patton, director of the Southern Historical Collection of the University of North Carolina Library, and by William S. Powell, librarian of the university library's North Carolina Collection. Mr. and Mrs. Louis Graves and Phillips Russell of that city spoke freely to me of college days and New York days when they had known Means well.

In Concord, John Kennedy, news director of the Concord *Daily Tribune,* was gracious enough to allow me to use the newspaper's files. He was also of more than a little assistance in giving general information about the area. I am also grateful to Dr. Hubert Sapp, Dr. T. N. Spencer, John Sharpe Hartsell, J. M. Baker, George H. Richmond, Robert Haney, and librarians of the Concord Public Library, and clerks of the Cabarrus County Courthouse.

Hayden Clement, who prosecuted Means for the murder of Maude A. King, gave me much information. I am also indebted to librarians of the public library in Salisbury, North Carolina, for research assistance. Mabel Walker Willebrandt of Los Angeles patiently responded to a query by mail about Means.

My wife, Olga Gruhzit Hoyt, assisted me with much research, particularly in Washington and in North Carolina, and undertook the final typing of the manuscript. I am also grateful to Mrs. Joan Downes and Mrs. Edgar Soule for typing assistance.

CHAPTER NOTES

General: Several references were consulted frequently, and I have abbreviated them here in the interest of space and the reader's convenience. A number of references are based on miscellaneous papers in the files of Hiram C. Todd relative to the investigation, trial, and subsequent activities of Gaston Means. They include such matters as trial briefs, memoranda, and miscellaneous notes by Mr. Todd and his assistants. I have abbreviated these to "HCT Files."

Gaston B. Means

In 1924, John T. Dooling, former Assistant District Attorney of New York, gave a copy of a long report he had prepared on the activities of Gaston Means, as disclosed by materials he discovered in the Means apartment in New York City in the autumn of 1917. This reference has been abbreviated to "Statement to HCT by NY DA."

Beginning on September 17, 1939, a series of articles based on the story of Julie Patterson Means appeared in the Washington *Times-Herald.* I have abbreviated references to these articles to *My Life With GBM.*

CHAPTER I

1. *Biographical History of North Carolina from Colonial Times to Present* (Vol. 1), by Samuel A. Ashe, published by Charles L. Van Noppen, Greensboro, N.C.; *A Short History of Cabarrus County and Concord, Yesterday, and Today,* by pupils of the sixth grade, Corbin School, 1932-33; *A New Geography of North Carolina,* by Bill Sharpe, Sharpe Publishing Co., Raleigh, N.C.; *The Natural Bent, the Memoirs of Dr. Paul B. Barringer,* University of North Carolina Press, Chapel Hill, N.C.; Obituary of W. G. Means, Concord *Daily Tribune,* June 1, 1918; Court Records of Cabarrus County, N.C.

2. HCT Files.

3. "Gaston B. Means, Master Bad Man," by May Dixon Thacker, *Liberty* magazine, April 17, 1937.

4. Conversations with acquaintances of Gaston B. Means in Concord, October, 1962. (Several of these acquaintances wished to remain anonymous.)

5. W. G. Means obituary, Concord *Daily Tribune,* June 1, 1918; Concord *Daily Standard,* February-March, 1899.

6. Records of Gaston B. Means, University of North Carolina;

327

The Hellenian, published at the University of North Carolina, 1899; Conversation with Louis Graves, Chapel Hill, N.C., October 1962.

7. Records of Gaston B. Means, University of North Carolina; files of *The Hellenian, The Tar Heel, Yakkety-Yak* (all publications of the University of North Carolina students) 1900-1901; Conversations with Means's acquaintances in Concord.

CHAPTER II

1. *The Tar Heel,* May 9, 1900; GBM testimony before the Special Senate Committee Investigating the Conduct of the Attorney General, March 14, 1924.

2. HCT Files; GBM Statement before the Overman Committee investigating Bolshevism and German propaganda and the liquor interests, 1919.

3. Phillips Russell, Chapel Hill, in conversation, 1962.

4. Phillips Russell and Louis Graves, in conversation, 1962.

5. Letter in files of HCT, June 19, 1924.

6. *Poole vs. Means,* Record in Appeal, U.S. 1st Dept. 990 2248, April 7, 1911.

7. HCT Files; Louis Graves.

8. *New York Times,* September 10, 17, 1917; Louis Graves.

9. *My Life with GBM;* Statement to HCT by NY DA.

10. Statement to HCT by NY DA.

11. *Ibid.; My Life with GBM.*

12. *Ibid.*

13. *Ibid.*

14. *My Life with GBM.*

15. Statement to HCT by NY DA. Statement of Raymond J. Burns to author.

16. GBM Testimony, Overman Committee; *My Life with GBM.*

17. *New York Times,* April 5, 8, 9, 13, 28, 1915; New York

World, April 5, 1928; *My Life with GBM;* Statement to HCT by NY DA.

18. GBM Testimony, Overman Committee, 1919; *Source Records of the Great War,* ed. by Charles F. Horne, The American Legion, Indianapolis, 1930.

19. Statement to HCT by NY DA.

20. *New York Times,* July, 1915.

21. HCT Files.

22. GBM Testimony, Overman Committee, 1919.

CHAPTER III

1. GBM Testimony, Overman Committee, 1919.

2. *My Life with GBM.*

3. Statement to HCT by NY DA; Illinois *Law Review,* April, 1924, "A Local Cause Célèbre—The King Will Case," by Henry K. Urion.

4. *New York Times,* September 10, 1917.

5. *Ibid.;* Statement to HCT by NY DA.

6. *My Life with GBM;* Statement to HCT by NY DA.

7. Statement to HCT by NY DA; *New York Times,* September 16, 1917.

8. Statement to HCT by NY DA.

9. *My Life with GBM;* Statement to HCT by NY DA; *New York Times,* September 18, 1917.

10. Statement to HCT by NY DA; *New York Times,* September 16, 1917.

11. Statement to HCT by NY DA.

12. *New York Times,* September 14, 1917.

13. Statement to HCT by NY DA.

14. Illinois *Law Review,* April, 1924, p. 518; Statement to HCT by NY DA.

15. Statement to HCT by NY DA.
16. *New York Times,* September 13, 1917.
17. Statement to HCT by NY DA.
18. Statement to HCT by NY DA; *My Life with GBM.*
19. *Ibid.*
20. *Ibid.;* Illinois *Law Review,* p. 518.
21. *Ibid.*
22. *New York Times,* September 11, 1917.
23. Statement to HCT by NY DA.
24. *New York Times,* November 29, 1917.
25. Statement to HCT by NY DA.
26. Illinois *Law Review,* April, 1924, pp. 520-521.
27. Statement to HCT by NY DA.
28. *New York Times,* September 7, 1917.
29. *New York Times,* September 19, 1917.
30. *New York Times,* September 12, 14, 19, 1917.

CHAPTER IV

1. *New York Times,* December 12, 1917.
2. Statement to HCT by NY DA.
3. *New York Times,* September 13, 1917.
4. *New York Times,* September 19, 1917.
5. *Ibid.*
6. Statement to HCT by NY DA; *New York Times,* September 14, 1917.
7. Statement to HCT by NY DA.
8. *Ibid.*
9. *New York Times,* September 19, 1917.
10. *New York Times,* September 15, 1917.
11. Dr. Hubert Sapp, Concord, to author, October, 1962.
12. *New York Times,* September 23, 1917.
13. *My Life with GBM.*

Gaston B. Means

14. *New York Times*, September 14, 1917, *My Life with GBM*.
15. Salisbury, North Carolina, *Sunday Post*, April 15, 1956.
16. *New York Times*, September 8, 1917.
17. *My Life with GBM; New York Times*, September 10, 11, 1917.
18. Statement to HCT by NY DA, *New York Times*, September, 1917.

CHAPTER V

1. Statement to HCT by NY DA.
2. *New York Times*, September 20, 1917. Concord *Daily Tribune*, September 20, 1917.
3. *New York Times*, September 23, 1917.
4. *Ibid.;* George H. Richmond, conversation with the author, October, 1962.
5. *New York Times*, September 23, 1917; Concord *Daily Tribune*, September 23, 1917.
6. *New York Times*, September 24, 1917; *My Life with GBM;* Statement to HCT by NY DA.
7. *New York Times*, September 25, 26, 1917; Concord *Daily Tribune*, September 25, 1917.
8. *My Life with GBM*.
9. Concord *Daily Tribune*, October 3, 1917.
10. Salisbury, North Carolina, *Sunday Post*, April 15, 1956.
11. *New York Times*, October and November, 1917; Concord *Daily Tribune*, October and November, 1917; *My Life with GBM;* Hayden Clement to author, October, 1962; *State of North Carolina vs. Gaston B. Means*, No. 33, 1924.
12. *New York Times*, November and December, 1917; Concord *Daily Tribune*, November and December, 1917; *My Life with GBM;* Hayden Clement to Author, *State of North Carolina vs. Gaston B. Means*, No. 33, 1924.

13. *Gaston B. Means Chronology*, Department of Justice records, National Archives, Washington, D.C.

CHAPTER VI

1. George H. Richmond to author, October, 1962.
2. Statement to HCT by NY DA.
3. George H. Richmond to author, October, 1962.
4. *New York Times*, January 6, 1918.
5. Illinois *Law Review*, April 1924, p. 515.
6. State of Illinois, in the matter of the Estate of James C. King, appeal probate B-59605, 1920.
7. *New York Times*, May 2, 1918.
8. Concord *Daily Tribune*, June 1, 1918.
9. *My Life with GBM*.
10. *New York Times*, July 18, 20, 27, 1918.
11. *My Life with GBM*.
12. Illinois *Law Review*, April, 1924, p. 516.
13. Letter of Roy Keehn to Joseph Tumulty, Jr., October 7, 1918; *GBM Chronology*, files of the Department of Justice, National Archives.
14. Statement of GBM, October 3, 1918.
15. Statement of GBM, October 3, 1918; Capt. Charles L. Lloyd to Lt. Col. Nicholas Biddle, undated.
16. Roy Keehn to Joseph Tumulty, Jr., October 3, 1918.
17. John R. Rathom to Col. Nicholas Biddle, October 21, 1918.

CHAPTER VII

1. *New York Times*, October 23, 1918.
2. *Ibid.*
3. GBM Testimony Overman Committee, 1919.

Gaston B. Means

4. *New York Times*, January 10, 1919.
5. Illinois *Law Review*, April, 1924, p. 516.
6. *My Life with GBM*.
7. *New York Times*, June 18, 1919; Chicago *Herald Express*, April 6, 1919.
8. *New York Times*, July 16, 1919.
9. *New York Times*, August 11, 1919.
10. *New York Times*, November 13, 1919, December 11, 1919.
11. *New York Times*, December 14, 1919.
12. *New York Times*, June 23, 1920.
13. *New York Times*, June 30, 1920.
14. *New York Times*, July 1, 1920.
15. *New York Times*, July 2, 8, 9, 13, 15, 16, 18, 20, 24, 28, 1920.
16. *New York Times*, December 11, 1920.
17. *My Life with GBM*.
18. George H. Richmond to author, October, 1962; Statement to HCT by NY DA; *New York Times*, August 3, 7, 1921.

CHAPTER VIII

1. HCT Files.
2. *The Strange Death of President Harding*, pp. 66-67.
3. Statement of Rella Lane, to Department of Justice investigators, November 13, 1925.
4. Affidavit, Gaston B. Means, for Harry M. Daugherty, March, 1925.
5. GBM Testimony before Special Senate Committee Investigating the Attorney General, Vol. 1, pp. 73-124.
6. Affidavit, GBM for HMD, March, 1925.
7. Statement, Sidney Bieber, November 12, 1924.
8. *Ibid.*
9. *Ibid.*
10. *United States vs. Means and Jarnecke*.

11. HCT Files, 1924, 1925.

12. Affidavit George Remus, June 24, 1924.

13. HCT Files, 1924, 1925.

14. Memorandum William J. Burns to Rush Holland; HCT Files.

15. Memorandum, E. J. Swan to H. M. Daugherty; HCT Files.

16. HCT Files; Letter, Colonel Frank Morgan to Department of Justice.

17. Report, June 19, 1923; Investigator Lucien Wheeler to Hiram C. Todd: re Means.

18. Affidavit, GBM for Harry M. Daugherty, March, 1925.

19. Report, Lucien Wheeler to HCT, June 19, 1923.

20. HCT Files, 1923, 1924.

21. Letter, Gaston B. Means to W. J. Burns, March, 1923.

22. Testimony, GBM before Special Senate Committee Investigating the Conduct of the Attorney General, Vol. 1, pp. 74 ff.

23. Report, Investigator Lucien Wheeler to HCT, June 19, 1923.

24. Statement by Howard Jones of Department of Justice on liquor withdrawal requirements for HCT; Files of HCT.

25. Report, Investigator Lucien Wheeler to HCT, June 19, 1923.

26. Affidavit, GBM for HM Daugherty, March, 1925; Statement Major John Holly Clark, Assistant U.S. Attorney for the Southern District of New York, to HCT, undated.

27. Affidavit Rella Lane, November 13, 1924; Letter, Colonel Morgan.

28. Statement, Willie Haar to investigators.

29. Report, Investigator Lucien Wheeler, on Elmer Jarnecke for HCT, HCT Files, 1924.

30. Letter, Elmer Jarnecke to Samuel Schmidt. Offered in evidence, *United States vs. Means and Jarnecke.*

31. Letter, Elmer Jarnecke to Samuel Schmidt. Offered in evidence, *United States vs. Means and Jarnecke.*

32. Letter, Elmer Jarnecke to Samuel Schmidt. Offered in evidence in *United States vs. Means and Jarnecke.*

33. Files of HCT.

Gaston B. Means

34. Statement of Willie Haar.
35. Report on bootlegging activities of La Montagne brothers, files of the Department of Justice, National Archives, Washington, D.C.
36. *United States vs. Means and Jarnecke,* testimony of Jacob Stein.
37. Letter, Jarnecke to Samuel Schmidt. Offered in evidence, *United States vs. Means and Jarnecke.*

CHAPTER IX

1. *My Life with GBM.*
2. *The Inside Story of the Harding Tragedy,* by Harry M. Daugherty, pp. 139-168.
3. Files of HCT.
4. Affidavit of George Remus, June 24, 1924.
5. Letter, Laura B. Jacobson to HCT, May 28, 1924.
6. Statement, Samuel Schmidt to Lucien Wheeler, Investigator for HCT, October 4, 1923.
7. Letter, S. P. Gilbert, Jr., to D. H. Blair, Collector of Internal Revenue, November 9, 1922, National Archives.
8. Letter, Elmer Jarnecke to Samuel Schmidt, September 30, 1922. Offered in evidence, *United States vs. Means and Jarnecke.*
9. Statement, Samuel Schmidt to Lucien Wheeler.
10. Memorandum, Edward M. Salomon to Department of Justice, February 12, 1923, Files of the Department of Justice, National Archives.
11. Statement, Samuel Schmidt to Lucien Wheeler.
12. Statement, I. D. Padorr to Lucien Wheeler, Chicago, May 24, 1923.
13. *Ibid.*
14. Statement, Elmer Jarnecke, September 25, 1924; Statement Harry Goldberg to Lucien Wheeler, July 18, 1923.
15. Memorandum, Edward M. Salomon to Department of Jus-

tice, February 12, 1923, Files of Department of Justice, National Archives.

16. Statement, Elmer W. Jarnecke to Paul Anderson, special agent, Collector of Internal Revenue, April 11, 1923.

17. Statement of Rella Lane.

CHAPTER X

1. U.S. Circuit Court of Appeals, Second District, *Means and Jarnecke vs. United States,* transcript of record, pp. 23-126.

2. Files of HCT; report of Lucien Wheeler to HCT.

3. *Means and Jarnecke vs. United States,* pp. 127-146.

4. Files of HCT.

5. *The Incredible Era,* by Samuel Hopkins Adams, p. 201.

6. HCT Memo of Facts; *United States vs. Means, Jarnecke, and Felder.*

7. Statement of Elmer Jarnecke to HCT, September 24, 1924.

8. *United States vs. Means and Felder,* transcript of record, pp. 553-554.

9. *Op. cit.,* p. 557.

10. Testimony of Elmer Jarnecke, *United States vs. Means and Felder,* p. 564.

11. Letter, Thomas B. Felder to Harry M. Daugherty, September 7, 1923.

12. Statement by Samuel Safir to HCT, August 9, 1923.

13. Statement by Samuel Safir to J. W. H. Crim, April 9, 1923.

14. Statements by Samuel Rosenblatt and H. R. Sideman, Chicago, September, 1923.

15. Statement of Harry Goldberg, New York, July 18, 1923.

16. Statement of Rella Lane, Washington, November 13, 1924.

17. Letter, Edward H. Salomon to Thomas B. Felder, February 10, 1923.

18. Statement of Jacob Stein, June 20, 1923.

19. Letter, Andrew Mellon to Harry M. Daugherty, April 25, 1923, National Archives.
20. Telegram, Harry M. Daugherty to A. T. Seymour of Department of Justice, April 27, 1923.
21. Letter, Harry M. Daugherty to Andrew Mellon, May 4, 1923.
22. Statement of Rella Lane, November 13, 1924.
23. Statement of Elmer Jarnecke, September 25, 1924.
24. Letter, Lucien Wheeler to HCT, October 29, 1924.
25. Letter, Thomas B. Felder to GBM, May 26, 1923.
26. Letter, Thomas B. Felder to Harry M. Daugherty, September 7, 1923.
27. T. B. Felder to A. T. Seymour, Department of Justice, June 6, 1923.
28. T. B. Felder to W. G. Hayward, June 7, 1923.
29. HCT to author, October, 1962.
30. J. W. H. Crim to HCT, July 30, 1923.
31. Statement of Elmer Jarnecke.
32. *United States vs. Means and Jarnecke.*
33. Lucien Wheeler to HCT, October 29, 1924.
34. Statement of Elmer Jarnecke, September 27, 1924.
35. Statement of E. R. Lee, October 25, 1924.
36. Statement of Elmer Jarnecke, September 27, 1924.

CHAPTER XI

1. Indictments filed October 18, 1923, U.S. District Court, Second District of New York.
2. Letter, H. C. T. to Thomas G. Felder, October 29, 1923.
3. *New York Times,* October 24, 1923.
4. Statements of Rella Lane and E. R. Lee.
5. Letter, Thomas G. Felder to Harry M. Daugherty, September 7, 1923.
6. Same, November 9, 1923.

7. Telegram, W. B. Rubin to Wise, Whitney and Parker, November 6, 1923.

8. Letter, Clifford H. Byrnes to HCT, March 8, 1924.

9. Burton K. Wheeler to author, October, 1962.

10. HCT to Harry M. Daugherty, March 11, 1924.

11. *New York Times*, March 15, 1924.

12. Hearings of Committee to Investigate Conduct of the Attorney General, Vol. 1, p. 74.

13. *New York Times*, March 15, 1924.

14. Hearings of Senate Committee to Investigate Attorney General. Vol. 1, pp. 74-86.

15. Hearings of Senate Committee, pp. 638-664.

16. Files of HCT.

17. *New York Times*, March 15, 1924.

18. Burton K. Wheeler to author, October, 1962; Hearings of Senate Committee.

19. Hearings, GBM testimony, pp. 74-124.

20. *New York Times*, March 15, 1924.

21. Hearings, Vol. III, pp. 2195-2253.

22. Statement of Rella Lane.

23. Letter, HCT to Senator Smith Brookhart, March 17, 1924.

24. Burton K. Wheeler to author, October, 1962.

25. Letters, HCT to Sen. Smith Brookhart; Letters, Smith Brookhart to HCT, March 17-24, 1924.

26. *New York Times*, March 29, 1924; Letter, Harlan F. Stone to Smith Brookhart, April 25, 1924.

27. Hearings of Special Senate Committee Investigating Conduct of Attorney General, Vol. III.

28. *New York Times*, April 25, 1924.

29. Letter, Verne Marshall, editor, Cedar Rapids *Gazette*, to Clifford H. Byrnes, April 30, 1925; National Archives.

30. Hearings, Vol. III, pp. 2495-2559.

31. HCT to author, October, 1962.

32. C. H. Byrnes to HCT, April 29, 1924.
33. Hearings, Vol. III, pp. 2601-2662.
34. Hearings, Vol. III, pp. 2670-2672.
35. Statement of Rella Lane.
36. *New York Times*, May 24, 1924.
37. *Ibid.*
38. Atlanta *Constitution*, May 31, 1924.

CHAPTER XII

1. Statement of Rella Lane.
2. Letter, C. H. Byrnes to HCT, May 28, 1924.
3. E. J. Brennan to HCT, June 2, 1924.
4. HCT to C. H. Byrnes, June 4, 1924.
5. New York *Sun*, June 12, 1924.
6. Telegram, H. F. Stone to HCT, June 12, 1924.
7. *New York Times*, June 17, 18, 1924; *United States vs. Means and Jarnecke.*
8. *New York Times*, June 18, 19, 1924.
9. Telegram, Emmanuel Kessler to HCT.
10. *United States vs. Means and Jarnecke.*
11. *New York Times*, July 3, 1924.
12. *Ibid.*
13. Letter, H. F. Stone to HCT, July 2, 1924.
14. *New York Times*, September 23, 1924.
15. *New York Times*, September 27, 1924.
16. *New York Times*, September 22, 1924.
17. Harry M. Daugherty to HCT, July 28, 1924, and September 1, 1924; HCT to Harry M. Daugherty, September 3, 1924.
18. *New York Times*, September 23, 1924.
19. *New York Times*, September 22, 1924.
20. *New York Times*, September 23, 1924.

21. Statement of Sidney Bieber.

22. Report of Lucien Wheeler to HCT.

23. Statement of Rella Lane.

24. *New York Times,* August 12, 1924; HCT files.

25. *New York Times,* September 29, 30, 1924.

26. Files of HCT.

27. Statement of Rella Lane.

28. Statements of Elmer Jarnecke.

29. HCT to Attorney General, October 10, 1924.

30. Dr. W. B. Pritchard, to U.S. District Judge W. P. James, October 22, 1924.

31. HCT files.

32. H. M. Daugherty to HCT.

33. Concord *Daily Tribune,* January 6, 1925.

34. *New York Times,* January 8, 1925.

35. HCT files.

36. *United States vs. Means and Felder;* HCT files.

37. Statement of Sidney Bieber.

38. *New York Times,* January 31, 1925.

CHAPTER XIII

1. Letters in files of HCT from Attorney General Stone, Assistant Attorney General William Donovan, J. Edgar Hoover.

2. Letter, HCT to Harry M. Daugherty, March 3, 1925.

3. Letter, Harry M. Daugherty to GBM, March 7, 1925.

4. Affidavit, GBM, March 7, 1925.

5. Harry M. Daugherty to HCT, April 23, 1925.

6. *My Life with GBM.*

7. HCT Files, March and April, 1925.

8. *My Life with GBM.*

9. *The Incredible Era.*

10. Files of HCT, 1925, 1926.

11. *The Incredible Era;* Files of the Department of Justice in the National Archives.

12. *New York Times,* October 28, 1925.

13. *New York Times,* February 26, 1926.

14. Letter, Assistant Attorney General to Warden John Snook, Atlanta Penitentiary, June 14, 1926 (Files of HCT).

15. Hearings, Vol. III.

16. HCT to author, October, 1962.

17. HCT Files, October, 1925.

18. GBM to HCT, March 7, 1927.

19. Mabel Walker Willebrandt to GBM, March 29, 1927, National Archives.

20. Department of Justice Records, National Archives.

21. *New York Times,* July 20, 1928.

22. Raleigh *News and Observer,* May 9, 1932.

23. *New York Times,* July 20, 1928.

24. Concord *Daily Tribune,* July 20, 1928.

25. Concord *Daily Tribune,* July 27, 1928.

26. *Honesty and Politics,* by Nan Britton, pp. 312-322.

27. *My Life with GBM.*

28. Files of National Civic Federation Review, 1903-1919.

29. J. Edgar Hoover in *American* magazine, December, 1936, "The Amazing Mr. Means."

30. *My Life with GBM.*

31. J. Edgar Hoover, in *American* magazine, December, 1936.

32. *New York Times,* April 10, 1930.

33. *My Life with GBM.*

34. Charlotte *Observer,* October 30, 1931.

35. *My Life with GBM.*

36. Files of HCT.

37. Washington *Evening Star,* November 20, 1931.

38. Louis Graves to author, October, 1962.

39. *My Life with GBM.*
40. HCT trial records, 1924, 1925.
41. J. W. H. Crim to HCT, July 30, 1923.

CHAPTER XIV

1. *My Life with GBM.*
2. *New York Times,* June 9, 1932.
3. *My Life with GBM.*
4. *New York Times,* June 9, 1932; *Kidnap* by George Waller, Dial Press, 1961.
5. George H. Richmond to author, October, 1962.
6. *New York Times,* May, June, 1932.
7. *The Tempering Years,* by Edwin P. Hoyt.
8. *New York Times,* May 7, 1932.
9. *Ibid.*
10. *New York Times,* May 12, 1932.
11. *New York Times,* May 13, 1932.
12. *New York Times,* May 15, 1932.
13. Statement of Rella Lane; Raleigh, N.C., *News and Observer,* August 5, 1932.
14. Washington *Evening Star,* June 13, 1932.
15. Washington *Evening Star,* June 14, 1932.
16. *New York Times,* June 15, 1932.
17. *New York Times,* June 16, 1932.

CHAPTER XV

1. *New York Times,* June 29, 1932.
2. *New York Times,* July 9, 1932.
3. *Newsweek,* May 30, 1933.
4. *New York Times,* May 12, 13, 14, 1933.

Gaston B. Means

5. "Gaston B. Means, Master Bad Man," by May Dixon Thacker, *Liberty* magazine, April 17, 1937.

6. Sunbury (Pa.) *Daily*, September 16, 1934.

7. Washington *Evening Star*, December 12, 1938.

8. *American Mercury*, December, 1936; *Literary Digest*, August 22, 1936.

9. *New York Times*, March 26, March 30, 31, 1936.

10. *New York Times*, December 13, 1938.

11. San Francisco *Chronicle*, March 30, 1936.

12. "GBM, Master Bad Man," by May Dixon Thacker, *Liberty* magazine, April 17, 1937.

13. *Literary Digest*, August 22, 1936.

14. *Ibid.*

15. *New York Times*, Washington *Evening Star*, Concord *Daily Tribune*, December 13, 14, 1938; *Time*, December 19, 1938.

16. Concord *Daily Tribune*, December 15, 1938, Salisbury, N.C. *Sunday Post*, April 15, 1956.

17. *Christian Century*, December 28, 1938.

18. Washington *Evening Star*, December 12, 1938.

19. The *Nation*, June 29, 1932.

Sulzer, William, 217
Swann, Edward, 81, 135, 136-37, 138, 149

Taft, William Howard, 181, 200
Thacker, May Dixon, 282-83, 284, 289, 290, 291, 318, 323
Thompson, Sidney, 230, 253, 255
Todd, Hiram C., 168, 216-17, 218, 223, 224, 228-29, 235-36, 238-44, 246-47, 249-50, 251, 253, 254, 255-58, 261-62, 264-67, 268, 271, 272, 273, 274, 275, 278-79, 280, 281, 292
Tomlinson, J. William, 172, 175
Tumulty, Joseph P., 113, 115, 119, 126-27, 132
Turnage, Commissioner, 172, 173, 175

Underwood, W. T., 230, 231, 253-54, 255, 260
United States Circuit Court of Appeals, 273, 275
United States Department of Justice, 182, 252, 262, 263, 274, 275, 277, 315, 317, 318, 321

Val-Dona Drug Company, 183-84, 185, 186
von Bernstorff, Count, 43, 116
von Papen, Franz, 36, 45, 54, 132, 214

Wadsworth, W. H., 102
Waller International Bankers, 156
Wampler, T. Morris, 305
Washington *Evening Star*, 324
Washington *Post*, 183
Webb (judge), 95, 265
Weddington, L. A., 75, 77, 140
Wheeler, Burton K., 228-29, 231-32, 235-36, 237, 239-41, 242, 243, 244, 246, 247, 257-58, 259, 272-73, 274, 275
Wheeler Committee, 228-46
Wheeler, Wayne B., 186, 225
Whitaker, Norman T., 290, 296, 307-308, 309, 314, 323
White, L. C., 276
Willebrandt, Mabel Walker, 157, 165, 189, 197, 280, 281
Williams, John Sharp, 97, 111
Wilson, Thomas, 36-37, 40
Wilson, Woodrow, 36, 75-76
Wolverton, C. E., 250, 255, 256
Work, Isabella, *see* Means, William (Mrs.)